IN SEARCH *of* NATIONAL ECONOMIC SUCCESS

To my parents

IN
SEARCH *of*
NATIONAL
ECONOMIC
SUCCESS

Balancing Competition
and Cooperation

LANE KENWORTHY

SAGE Publications
International Educational and Professional Publisher
Thousand Oaks   London   New Delhi

For information address:

SAGE Publications, Inc.
2455 Teller Road
Thousand Oaks, California 91320

SAGE Publications Ltd.
6 Bonhill Street
London EC2A 4PU
United Kingdom

SAGE Publications India Pvt. Ltd.
M-32 Market
Greater Kailash I
New Delhi 110 048 India

Printed in the United States of America

Library of Congress Cataloging-in-Publication Data

Kenworthy, Lane.
    In search of national economic success: balancing competition and
cooperation / Lane Kenworthy.
        p.   cm.
    Includes bibliographical references and index.
    ISBN 0-8039-7160-5. (hard cover) —ISBN 0-8039-7161-3 (pbk.)
    1. Free enterprise.   2. Competition.   3. Economic policy.
    4. Comparative economics.   I. Title.
    HB95.K34   1995
    338.9—dc20   95-3259

This book is printed on acid-free paper.

95 96 97 98 99   10 9 8 7 6 5 4 3 2 1

Sage Production Editor: Diana E. Axelsen
Sage Typesetter: Andrea D. Swanson

◐   ◐

Contents

Acknowledgments

This book has been several years in the making. A number of people provided valuable help along the way. John Bowman, Daniel Kleinman, Leon Lindberg, Ann Orloff, Joel Rogers, Marc Schneiberg, Wolfgang Streeck, Erik Wright, and Yuval Yonay read and offered thoughtful comments on part or all of the manuscript. Their advice helped to steer me in profitable directions and avoid wrong turns and dead ends. To Rogers, Streeck, and Wright I owe a special debt. The book might have never gotten off the ground had it not been for my exposure to their wisdom and encouragement during my graduate studies at the University of Wisconsin-Madison. I am grateful to Carrie Mullen at Sage Publications for her support of the project. Most of all, I thank my wife, Kim Backs, for putting up with me through the seemingly endless process of writing and revising, and for never letting me forget that the best moments in life are spent somewhere other than in front of a word processor.

Introduction

One of the most valuable pieces of information social scientists could potentially provide to citizens and policymakers is an explanation of why some countries achieve better economic performance results than others. Yet despite numerous efforts, we lack a convincing theory of comparative economic success.[1] This book attempts to help remedy that failure.

For most of the past two centuries the prevailing view among economists, policy intellectuals, and government authorities has been that economic success is a product of free markets and competition. This *market liberal* view holds that the performance of an economy is impeded by, among other things, nonmarket constraints on freedom of choice, income equality, government intervention, and labor organizations. The book is organized around an assessment of these claims from a comparative perspective. I find them to be largely, although by no means entirely, lacking in empirical support.

In the course of examining market liberalism, we shall encounter a number of criticisms directed at it; a range of theses regarding the effects of free choice, equality, state intervention, and labor organizations on performance outcomes; and various alternative theories of economic success. Although there is much of value in these arguments and the studies on which they are based, I will endeavor to show why some of them are wrong, and why the others are, if not quite wrong, at least not entirely right.

Finally, and most important, I offer my own explanation for why some national economies do better than others. In my view the key factor is the degree to which countries combine competition with various forms of economic cooperation.

Chapter 1 outlines the basic tenets of market liberalism and traces its influence on economic thinking and policy making, with a focus on the United States. Although it has never been uncontested, the market liberal view dominated scholarly and popular thought about capitalist economies during most of the 19th and the early part of the 20th centuries. The Great Depression and World War II ushered in an era in which state intervention and nonmarket institutions such as labor unions were viewed by many as legitimate, even productive, elements of a well-functioning economy. Although it continued to influence policy making throughout much of the industrialized world, market liberalism no longer enjoyed hegemony. In an age of what appeared to be ever-increasing affluence, the notion that there is an inherent trade-off between economic efficiency and social justice and that market impediments severely constrain economic advance seemed mistaken.

Then, with the onset of stagflation after 1973, the tables turned again. Excessively high tax rates, overly generous welfare states, government regulatory meddling, union rigidities, and other inhibitors of the market's invisible hand were effectively portrayed as the chief culprits behind the downturn in economic performance suffered by all of the world's industrialized nations beginning in the mid 1970s. Although its impact on policy has been uneven across countries, market liberalism has once again become the single most influential theory of economic success among scholars and policymakers. And although the 1990s have witnessed a lessening of market liberalism's political influence in the United States and Britain—formerly the homes of its most outspoken proponents in Ronald Reagan and Margaret Thatcher—in a number of other nations its political fortune has been, if anything, on the rise.

Given our limited ability to conduct controlled experiments, social scientists must frequently rely on historical data for empirical evidence.[2] The best uses of historical data are comparative. Comparison helps us to isolate factors that might be relevant causes of whatever phenomenon we seek to understand, by holding other factors constant. Curiously, interest in explaining cross-national variation in economic performance among industrialized capitalist nations was minimal prior to the mid 1970s. In the pre-depression years, this owed to limited data availability and the existence of widespread agreement about the key to economic success. During the post-World War II boom period, the lack of concern stemmed primarily from the similarity of performance results among these countries. All developed economies were relatively healthy and improving rapidly, and it was widely expected that this pattern would continue.

It was the downturn following 1973, coupled with increasing divergence in performance outcomes, that stimulated interest in why some countries achieve better economic results than others. The past two decades have witnessed an outpouring of theorization and research on this question. The most clearly articulated and intellectually and politically influential of the views set forth to explain cross-national performance variation has been that of market liberalism. Any attempt to come to terms with the issue must therefore begin with this theory. Chapters 2 through 5 of the book endeavor to do just that.

Chapter 2 focuses on constraints. Freedom of choice is commonly thought to be capitalism's fundamental attribute and supreme virtue. According to neoclassical economic theory, under conditions of market competition and free choice, actors' attempts to pursue their own selfish interests serve to promote the general interest as well. I argue that the conventional emphasis on freedom of choice is misplaced. The key determinant of efficient economic behavior, even in neoclassical theory, is the constraints economic agents face. But in a number of important instances, nonmarket or extramarket constraints are superior to market incentives at generating such efficient behavior. In a market environment, rational actors with extensive freedom of choice will in some instances be led to make reasonable choices that produce notably suboptimal outcomes. To achieve superior performance, economic actors must sometimes be constrained by non- or extramarket institutions to do what is in their own, and society's, best interest. In elaborating this argument I draw upon the experiences of Germany, Japan, and the United States in the areas of finance, worker training, and purchaser-supplier relations.

Chapters 3, 4, and 5 inquire into the performance consequences of equality, government intervention, and labor organizations, respectively, drawing on a mix of qualitative and quantitative evidence.

The quantitative analysis examines the 17 richest industrialized democracies—Australia, Austria, Belgium, Canada, Denmark, Finland, France, Germany, Italy, Japan, the Netherlands, New Zealand, Norway, Sweden, Switzerland, the United Kingdom, and the United States—over the period 1960 to 1990. Reliable data on economic performance are available for these nations beginning in 1960. The year 1990 provides a useful cutoff point, because (like 1967, 1973, and 1979) it marked a business cycle peak. Developments since 1990 are discussed in Chapter 6.

Economic performance indicators are of two principal types: those, such as growth and inflation, which aim to measure economic efficiency, and those, such as equality or access to health care, which relate more specifically to social welfare. I use only the former here. This is partly to keep the analysis manageable, but in part also because one of the key issues for consideration will be whether social welfare is compatible with efficiency. Instead of focusing on only one or two components of economic efficiency, as is common in comparative analyses, I use a variety of indicators—including productivity growth, output growth, productivity levels, investment, trade balances, inflation, and unemployment.

Readers unfamiliar with statistical methods may panic upon arriving at the first bit of quantitative analysis in Chapter 3. Please don't! I have tried to keep the analysis simple and to render it comprehensible to readers with little or no statistical training. The results can be understood, in any case, simply by following the discussion in the text.

Economic equality is commonly believed to have two nefarious effects: It reduces investment by shifting resources away from those with the strongest proclivity to save and invest, and it dampens work effort. The asserted trade-off between equality and efficiency is perhaps the most widely accepted of the market liberal claims. But is it supported by the comparative record? A heterodox view contends that equality may have beneficial efficiency effects—by augmenting consumer demand, encouraging workers to cooperate in upgrading competitiveness, and enabling society to take full advantage of its human resources. Chapter 3 examines the effects of income equality and equality of opportunity on performance outcomes. Contrary to the market liberal claim, the comparative evidence suggests that greater levels of equality than presently exist in most, if not all, developed countries are compatible with an efficient, successful economy. Indeed, there is strong indication that increasing equality would enhance performance in many nations.

No economic institution has come under more severe attack over the past two decades than government. Government intrusion has been widely blamed for the economic malaise that has stricken much of the industrialized world since the early 1970s. State intervention is accused of producing a variety of adverse consequences. Because governments seldom face a hard budget constraint (that is, they do not face bankruptcy if they act inefficiently) and because politicians can maximize reelection chances by catering to the wishes of rent-seeking special interest groups, state activism is said to be highly susceptible to inefficiency. It is also said to reduce investment and work effort and to fuel inflation. Against this reasoning, proponents of an affirmative state point to an array of potential positive effects. Government spending on transfer programs may help stabilize and increase consumer demand, heighten motivation and workplace cooperation by promoting fairness, and encourage wage moderation. Labor market policies can help increase the skill level of the workforce and reduce friction in the job matching process. Industrial policies can help remedy market failures in the allocation of capital, the supply of research and development, the diffusion of technology, and the frequency of cooperation among firms.

Chapter 4 examines the market liberal view with respect to five types of government intervention: fiscal policy, redistributive policy, labor market policy, industrial policy, and regulation. The only support I find for the free market perspective is a possible, though questionable, deleterious effect of high levels of taxation and government spending on investment and growth. Otherwise, the comparative record tends to support the contrary view. Labor market and industrial policies, in particular, appear to enhance national economic health.

Critics of government also frequently claim that state intervention tends to fail in its direct objective. Redistributive programs fail to reduce the incidence of poverty; policies aimed at reducing unemployment and upgrading labor force skills have no such effect; and so on. I find these charges to be similarly unfounded.

Chapter 5 investigates the market liberal claim that labor organizations adversely affect economic performance by blocking technological innovation, interfering with the market for labor, and raising wages above marginal productivity levels. Here again the comparative record suggests little support for the market liberal view. Unions, works councils, and codetermination arrangements do not generally impede technological change, and they may contribute to better performance by lowering quit rates and facilitating improved communication between workers and managers. Unions also appear to reduce labor-management conflict.

It is in the area of wages that unions are expected to have their most damaging effect. Yet, ironically, it is here that labor size and strength is most clearly beneficial. Encompassing labor movements have proved more willing and able than low-density, fragmented unions to restrain wage demands, and in doing so have contributed to superior macroeconomic performance in the form of lower misery index (inflation plus unemployment) levels. A number of political scientists and economists have advanced this sort of argument over the past decade, but I show that the three currently prevalent versions of this institutional perspective on unions and wages are flawed. I offer an alternative model that, in my view, is more compelling theoretically and more consistent with the comparative evidence.

The final chapter, Chapter 6, is the linchpin of the book. There I attempt to answer the question: If the market liberal view is wrong, what *does* explain cross-national variation in performance outcomes? I argue that the key to national economic success lies in combining competition with cooperation.

Competition has indeed proved an effective spur for economic progress, and markets are certainly the best mechanism with which to coordinate most economic activity. But in a number of critical areas of economic life, the structure of incentives in a market-based economy is such that actions which are optimal for individual actors—workers, managers, firms, unions, government officials, and so on—are suboptimal for the economy as a whole. Locally optimal actions yield globally suboptimal outcomes.

Such perverse incentive structures plague virtually all of the key relationships among economic actors in a market-based economy. Specifically, such problems occur at three levels. At the macro level, they occur in the relations among firms in different industries, among unions, and between government and interest groups. At the meso, or sectoral, level they obtain in the relationships between purchaser and supplier firms, between firms and their investors, and among competing firms. Structural inefficiencies also exist at the micro level—that is, within the firm—in the relationships between labor and management, among workers, and among functional divisions within firms.

In such circumstances economic success requires cooperative behavior, and cooperation in turn depends upon nonmarket or extramarket institutions such as long-term, guaranteed relationships and formal organization. Countries in which such institutions are more prevalent should therefore achieve superior performance results.

The comparative evidence strongly supports a focus on cooperation-inducing institutions. The nations with the best performance records over the past three decades—Japan, Austria, Germany, the small northern European countries, and (northern) Italy—have been those most committed to combining competition with cooperation. Those faring worst—the United States, Britain, Canada, Australia, and New Zealand—rely predominantly on atomistic, individualistic competition. The theory fares well against rival explanations of economic performance outcomes. It provides a more compelling account than perspectives focusing on macro-, meso-, or micro-level institutions alone. And its predictive utility is superior to those theories that can be tested across the full set of developed capitalist nations, including the market liberal thesis.

The Fall and Rise
of Market Liberalism

This book is about variation in economic success among nations. I take as my point of departure a set of ideas that, at least in the United States, have dominated thinking about the economy for most of the past two centuries. Underlying these ideas, which I refer to as *market liberal,*[1] is a belief in free markets, in limited government, and in the prevalence of severe trade-offs between economic efficiency and social justice. Specifically, market liberalism asserts that the performance and competitiveness of an economy are undermined by nonmarket constraints on free choice, by income equality, by government intervention, and by labor organizations. The book is in large measure an assessment of these claims.

Proponents of the trade-off perspective form a loose and informal coalition composed of three groups: conservative[2] intellectuals and policymakers, business leaders, and a share of professional economists. The first group, the policy advocates and policymakers, espouse and implement market liberalism. They are the most visible of its proponents. But the intellectual force of their viewpoint owes much to the fact that it has as its foundation the theoretical structure of the mainstream of the economics profession. Arthur Okun once aptly remarked that "Tradeoffs are the central study of the economist. 'You can't have your cake and eat it too' is a good candidate for the central theorem of economic analysis."[3] In the assumptions and models of orthodox economic theory, conservative policy advocates and politicians have found support for the view that constraints, equality, government, and labor organizations impede economic efficiency. In turn, the political power of market liberalism is largely a result of the fact that its policy recommendations coincide with the perceived interests of a substantial segment of the business community. Business has the money and political influence needed to publicize free market ideas, to bring them to the forefront of public debate, and, not infrequently, to get them institutionalized in government policy.

From 1978 to 1992 the market liberal perspective was the guiding force in American economic policy making. It had not, of course, always been this way. Market liberalism was launched into intellectual prominence by Adam Smith's *The Wealth of Nations* in 1776, and it dominated economic policy thinking in much of the developed world throughout the 1800s and early 1900s. The prevailing wisdom during that period held that economic progress stemmed from unimpeded markets. Radical laissez faire was the prescription for economic success. But following the Great Depression, and particularly in the period after the Second World War, the market liberal perspective lost its hegemonic status. Its core beliefs came to be seen by many as anachronistic, as limited in applicability to the early stages of a nation's economic development. In an age of continuous growth, the classic trade-off between efficiency and justice seemed no longer to apply. The central economic question became how to use prosperity to improve the quality of life of all citizens. Keynesians argued that government had a vital role to play in smoothing out the business cycle. Egalitarians contended that redistribution could be reconciled with economic progress. Public interest groups demanded that government regulate corporate social conduct. And many observers agreed that the adverse effects of unions were minimal and that they could and frequently did play a useful role in workplace governance.

Nineteen seventy-three was a watershed year in the economic history of developed nations. The year of the first OPEC oil price shock marked the end of the long economic boom that had followed World War II and the onset of stagflation and general economic malaise. Nineteen seventy-three also marked the return to intellectual prominence of the market liberal perspective. The turnaround in economic performance opened the door for the return of market liberalism, and its proponents boldly used the opportunity to press their case, setting the stage for the ascendance of their philosophy in the late 1970s and its hegemony throughout the 1980s.

◈ The Affluent Society and the Psychology of Abundance

Prior to the Great Depression, there was virtual consensus among policy elites that government must let the market be. According to the prevailing economic wisdom, self-equilibrating markets would ensure steady growth and material prosperity. Government's task was, as Adam Smith had insisted, merely to enforce the rules of the game—that is, to protect property rights and enforce contracts.[4]

The sustained misery of the Great Depression profoundly altered the views of economic policy advocates and decision makers. The chief policy lesson derived from the experience of the 1930s (a decade of 18 percent average unemployment in the United States) was that government had an important role to play in smoothing out market gyrations and in protecting the common citizen. Fiscal stimulus, in the form of deficit spending and job creation, was seen as critical to pulling the economy out of a downturn, just as fiscal restraint would help prevent prices from rising too rapidly when the economy ran at full steam. Government would help secure peace and cooperation on the shop floor by protecting the right of workers to bargain through unions. It would also provide some monetary support for the jobless (the unemployed, the retired, and poor women with children).

Given the experience of the depression and the uncertainty surrounding the war years, economic developments in the several decades following World War II were nothing less than stunning. The period 1948-1973, commonly referred to as the "long boom" or "golden age" among industrialized capitalist nations, was characterized by striking affluence compared to earlier epochs. In the United States, real per capita growth of gross domestic product (GDP) averaged 2.6 percent per year. Productivity (output per employed person) increased at an annual pace of 2.2 percent. Unemployment during that quarter century averaged 4.7 percent, and inflation ran at a rate of only 2.7 percent per annum.[5]

Perhaps most indicative of the remarkable growth that took place during this period was the change in American living standards. Real median family income grew at a healthy clip of 2.7 percent per year, effectively doubling during those 26 years.[6] The median family, in other words, was twice as well-off in terms of real purchasing power in 1973 as it had been in 1948. Hourly wages rose at an average yearly rate of 2.2 percent; in aggregate terms, they increased 75 percent during the golden age.[7] In 1940, only 44 percent of American families were homeowners. Less than half of all households had a refrigerator, only 40 percent had central heating, and 60 percent had an indoor flush toilet. About a third owned a television, and just more than half had an automobile. By 1970, 64 percent of American families owned their own home. Ninety-nine percent of all households had a refrigerator, 78 percent had central heating, and 96 percent had an indoor flush toilet. Ninety-nine percent of all households had a TV, and four out of five families owned a car.[8]

Other industrialized nations enjoyed equally impressive improvements in economic performance and living standards during the long boom. Between 1960 (the earliest date for which reliable comparative data exist) and 1973 the world's 17 most developed nations averaged annual productivity growth and per capita output growth[9] of 3.8 percent (see Table 1.1 below). Productivity in these countries grew more than twice as fast as it had in the first half of the 20th century.[10] Unemployment averaged only 2.2 percent and inflation 4.5 percent.

Of course, some countries enjoyed better results than others. Japan's record was surely the most astonishing, featuring 8.1 percent average growth in productivity and an unemployment level of only 1.3 percent. Japan transformed itself during this time from a war-devastated nation whose consumer products were a symbol of inferiority, to one of the world's leading exporters, a country on the verge of economic greatness. Germany and Italy likewise rebounded from war devastation to economic success, averaging 4.1 and 5.8 percent annual improvement in productivity, respectively. France, formerly a weak performer among the large developed nations, enjoyed productivity growth of 4.7 percent per year during the boom. The United Kingdom, the world's economic hegemon through the early part of the 20th century, had, along with the United States, perhaps the weakest performance record, averaging 2.9 percent productivity growth. Still, these results were poor only relative to those of other nations. Looked at in comparison with earlier periods, they represented genuine economic success.

By the mid 1960s, the thinking of citizens and policymakers in the industrialized world was oriented by a psychology of abundance. Whereas the prewar years had been dominated by a fear of economic insecurity, the boom period was characterized by an assumption of prosperity. Continuous growth came to be virtually taken for granted. In their 1967 book, *The Year 2000,* Herman Kahn and his associates forecast 4 percent annual productivity growth for the U.S. economy through the end of the century; their most pessimistic scenario called for average increases of 2.5 percent. That same year, *Fortune* magazine predicted that real wages would climb 150 percent by the year 2000.[11]

Views about the economy changed accordingly. As John Kenneth Galbraith perceptively noted in his 1958 book, *The Affluent Society,*

> One would not expect that the preoccupations of a poverty-ridden world would be relevant in one where the ordinary individual has access to amenities—foods, entertainment, personal transportation, and plumbing—in which not even the rich rejoiced a century ago.[12]

In earlier times the foremost question on the minds of the citizenry and the policy establishment had been: How can we secure economic stability? The chief concern of the depression generation was simply making a living. Now that affluence was a given, the challenge facing society was seen as: How can we use economic prosperity to create a more just society? The notion of a trade-off between efficiency and justice was viewed as obsolete. Efficiency had been mastered, and the only relevant policy issues now concerned how best to spread its benefits more equitably throughout society and how to limit growth's adverse consequences. In his 1970 State of the Union address, President Nixon declared:

> As we move into the decade of the Seventies, we have the greatest opportunity for progress at home of any people in world history. Our gross national product will increase by $500 billion in the next ten years. This increase alone is greater than the entire growth of the American economy from 1790 to 1950. The critical question is not whether we will grow, but how we will use that growth.[13]

This shift in thinking is evidenced by the fact that in the United States, some of the most notable economic and political developments of the 1960s and early 1970s focused on justice rather than efficiency. The Civil Rights movement produced legislation outlawing racial discrimination in employment and schooling. Soon thereafter government-sponsored affirmative action was instituted in an attempt to achieve substantive, rather than merely formal, equality of opportunity for black Americans. At the same time, the Kennedy and Johnson administrations launched a War on Poverty. A series of legislative measures established programs to increase educational opportunity, job training, employment, housing, health care, and income support for the poor. To some extent these developments also reflected a change in the thinking of business. Neither the 1964 Civil Rights Act nor the main initiatives of President Johnson's Great Society were opposed by big business. Writing in the *Harvard Business Review* in 1967, Theodore Levitt suggested that

> there is abundant evidence that the American business community has finally and with unexpected suddenness actively embraced the idea of the interventionist state. . . . Important elements of American business have now come to the clear conclusion that the federal government can and probably should be an active agent of social and economic betterment—not just that big government is here to stay, but that government bigness is not automatically badness and that the rising governmentalization of our social and economic affairs can indeed meliorate our lives and improve our society.[14]

A third development was government regulation of business, which aimed to safeguard the interests of consumers and workers and to protect the environment. This began in earnest with passage of the Motor Vehicle Safety Act of 1966, followed soon thereafter by the Fair Packaging and Labeling Act, the Federal Hazardous Substances Act, the Federal Meat Inspection Act, the National Gas Pipeline Safety Act, the Truth in Lending Act, the Flammable Fabrics Act, and the Child Protection Act. The Nixon administration continued the regulatory wave with passage of the Clean Air Act Amendments of 1970 and the creation of new federal regulatory bodies like the Environmental Protection Agency, the Occupational Safety and Health Administration, and the Consumer Products Safety Commission. Finally, in 1969 Congress passed one of the most progressive tax reforms in the nation's history. In addition to providing a modest degree of tax relief for the poor and the middle class, the legislation increased the tax rate on capital gains, eliminated tax credits for investments, limited real estate depreciation schedules, and reduced the depletion allowances for a number of natural substances such as oil and gas.[15]

A similar change in thinking occurred throughout the industrialized world at this time. Indeed, most developed countries went further than the United States in rejecting laissez faire. Although not always formally embraced, Keynesian demand management became the norm. Social welfare expenditures grew steadily, as nations attempted to mitigate the severe distributive imbalance typically rendered by the market. In some countries, most notably Japan and France, government took an active hand in guiding industrial development, selecting certain industries for promotion and channeling finan cial assistance and other supports to achieve that aim. Regulatory measures to protect consumers, workers, and the environment were initiated virtually everywhere. Finally, in a number of countries policymakers encouraged formal or informal pacts between business and labor associations in an effort to reduce labor-management conflict, achieve wage restraint, and obtain agreement by the "social partners" on a variety of public policy matters.

◈ The Age of Malaise and the Market Liberal Backlash

Although isolating a single date as the turning point in any historical development is inevitably arbitrary, by most accounts 1973 marked the end of the long boom. That year brought a rather abrupt halt to the sustained economic success enjoyed by the rich democracies.[16]

Consider the United States first. From 1974 to 1990, U.S. real per capita GDP grew at merely 1.5 percent per year, and productivity increased at an

Table 1.1 Economic Performance Before and After 1973 (Percentages)

	Productivity Growth[a]		Growth[b]		Inflation		Unemployment	
	1960-73	*1974-90*	*1960-73*	*1974-90*	*1960-73*	*1974-90*	*1960-73*	*1974-90*
Australia	2.5	1.0	3.2	1.6	3.4	9.6	1.9	6.6
Austria	5.0	1.6	4.2	2.4	4.1	4.7	1.7	2.7
Belgium	4.3	2.1	4.4	2.1	3.6	6.0	2.2	9.1
Canada	2.6	1.2	3.8	2.2	3.2	7.3	5.1	8.5
Denmark	3.0	1.1	3.6	1.7	6.2	8.0	1.3	7.0
Finland	4.6	2.2	4.4	2.5	5.7	9.2	2.0	4.6
France	4.7	2.1	4.3	1.9	4.5	8.2	2.0	7.4
Germany	4.1	1.9	3.5	2.0	3.4	3.6	0.8	5.5
Italy	5.8	2.2	4.6	2.6	4.6	12.5	5.2	8.8
Japan	8.1	2.9	8.4	3.1	6.2	5.2	1.3	2.3
Netherlands	4.0	1.2	3.6	1.4	4.8	4.5	1.0	7.9
New Zealand	1.7	0.6	2.1	0.4	5.5	12.1	0.2	3.4
Norway	3.4	2.2	3.5	3.0	5.0	8.2	1.3	2.6
Sweden	3.6	1.0	3.4	1.6	4.6	8.7	1.9	2.2
Switzerland	2.9	0.7	3.0	1.1	4.2	3.7	na	na
United Kingdom	2.9	1.5	2.6	1.8	5.0	10.4	1.9	7.4
United States	2.0	0.6	2.7	1.5	3.1	6.6	4.8	6.9
Average	3.8	1.5	3.8	1.9	4.5	7.6	2.2	5.8

NOTE: For data sources see Appendix A. na = not available.
a. Change in real GDP per employed person.
b. Change in real GDP per capita.

annual rate of only 0.6 percent. Unemployment during those years averaged 6.9 percent; inflation, 6.6 percent. Real median family income did not grow at all. In constant (1990) dollars, the income of the median American family fell from $35,474 in 1973 to $31,738 in 1982, before climbing back to $35,353 in 1990.[17] Real hourly earnings, which increased in every year between 1948 and 1973, declined in 11 of the next 17. Between 1973 and 1990 real hourly earnings fell 12 percent.[18] The portrait of economic developments offered by these figures is quite stark, especially when compared to the record of the golden age. By the late 1970s it had become clear that the remarkable economic performance of the long boom was a thing of the past.

A similar turnabout befell most other developed nations. As Table 1.1 shows, every one of the world's richest countries experienced a severe deterioration in economic performance after 1973. The average rate of productivity growth declined from 3.8 percent per year in the period 1960-1973 to 1.5 percent during 1974-1990. Inflation and unemployment both rose dramatically, the former from an average of 4.5 to 7.6 percent and the latter from 2.2 to 5.8 percent.

As a development common to virtually all industrialized countries, the long boom had a number of interrelated causes.[19] To begin with, the golden age was a period of unprecedented investment levels. Combined with extensive technology transfer from the United States, the world's technological leader, massive investment spurred historically high productivity gains. A virtuous circle of high output growth, profit margins, investment rates, and productivity improvement was sustained by stable demand, itself a product of multilateral domestic Keynesianism, the expansion of welfare expenditures, and the postwar business-labor accord. Most governments were committed to something approximating full employment and took necessary fiscal measures to ensure its achievement. The United States aided these efforts by providing massive economic and military support and opening its market to imports from Europe and Japan. The growth of welfare expenditures increased mass demand by raising the consumption base of the poor. At the same time, the fordist mass production regime featured an institutionalized bargain in which wage increases corresponded to the rate of change in productivity. All of these institutional factors were supported by international monetary stability, a result of the Bretton Woods exchange regime created shortly after the war. Finally, inflation during the golden age was moderate, due to wage restraint and a lack of exogenous shocks.

By the mid 1970s, each of these supporting factors had deteriorated in one way or another. Most notable, of course, were the severe oil price shocks of 1973 and 1979. But other changes were no less important. Gains from technology transfer had run their course as Western Europe and Japan more or less caught up with the United States in many fields. Profit margins were eroded by heightened international competition (a result of the rapid expansion of world trade) and a decline in wage restraint beginning in the late 1960s. This in turn caused a reduction in investment levels. Internationalization of product and financial markets also diminished the capacity of national governments to use Keynesian macropolicy measures. Firms became increasingly transnational, so when full employment led to higher wage demands by workers, companies often responded by moving production abroad, which in turn encouraged governments to abandon the commitment to full employment. Capital also was increasingly global, which fostered a deflationary bias on the part of governments; domestic reflation spurs international financial actors to withdraw assets in the fear of inflation, which reduces the value of a nation's currency, in turn leading to pressure on the government to abort the reflationary measures.[20] The ability of the United States to initiate and support multilateral domestic Keynesianism declined as its own economic strength deteriorated. Finally, international monetary stability was upset by speculation against the dollar during the late 1960s and abandonment of the fixed exchange rate regime in the early 1970s.

Whatever its causes, deteriorating economic performance in the developed world opened the door for the return of market liberal orthodoxy. The Keynesian-redistributive consensus was obliterated by the march of events and the rising chorus of voices promoting a return to laissez faire.[21]

Free market ideas had never disappeared, of course. They were merely submerged, due to the prosperity of the boom period. Friedrich Hayek published *The Constitution of Liberty* in 1960, and Milton Friedman's *Capitalism and Freedom* appeared in 1962. These two books were landmark statements of the market liberal perspective on economics and economic policy. But although reasonably widely read by the economic intelligentsia, they were, at the time, also largely ignored—considered more an intellectual curiosity than a statement of principle capable of guiding realistic policy. Barry Goldwater's landslide defeat in the 1964 presidential election offers some measure of the perceived irrelevance of market liberalism in the United States during this period. Goldwater ran as a champion of free markets and limited government, but he was pummeled at the polls by a Democrat who put at the top of his policy agenda the eradication of poverty through extensive government action. "A lot of people may not be ready to be conservative yet," remarked the Republican standard-bearer.[22]

The shift was not long in coming. Sparked by the rise in government spending and regulatory activity along with the growth of labor militancy, American business, together with conservative policy intellectuals and like-minded professional economists, began to marshal an organized counterattack.[23] The economic malaise of the 1970s, and particularly the recession of 1973-1975, encouraged this development and created an audience for its message among policy elites and the citizenry. Wealthy corporate foundations such as Olin, Smith Richardson, and Scaife launched major efforts to influence elite and public opinion. These foundations lavished money on conservative research think tanks, such as the American Enterprise Institute, the Heritage Foundation, the Hoover Institute, and the Institute for Contemporary Studies. They financed neoconservative journals like *The Public Interest* and *Regulation*. They sponsored the publication of popular conservative tracts; two of the period's most influential supply-side books, *The Way the World Works* by Jude Wanniski and *Wealth and Poverty* by George Gilder, were heavily subsidized by the Smith Richardson Foundation. Finally, extensive funds were devoted to lobbying efforts aimed at directly swaying the views of policymakers. This effort was spearheaded by the Business Roundtable, an association of the chief executive officers (CEOs) of America's 200 largest corporations that was formed in the early 1970s, along with the Chamber of Commerce, the National Association of Manufacturers, and the National Federation of Independent Business, representing small business. Between 1971 and 1982 the number of registered business lobbyists in Washington increased from 175 to 2,445, and the number of corporate political action committees (PACs) grew from 139 in 1974 to 1,204 in 1980. By the end of the 1970s, total corporate spending on advocacy advertising and grass-roots lobbying reached $1 billion annually.[24]

The American public was receptive. From 1950 to 1972, an average of only 18 percent of American citizens rated an economic issue as "the most important problem facing the country." Between 1973 and 1979 the percentage skyrocketed to 72 percent.[25] In 1964 only 43 percent of the American public thought the federal government was "too big"; by 1976, 58 percent believed this.[26] In a 1978 poll, 82 percent of the public felt the federal government was "spending too much"; another poll that year found 58 percent agreeing that government had gone too far in regulating business and interfering with the free enterprise system, whereas only 31 percent disagreed.[27] Public approval of labor unions reached a postwar low of 55 percent in 1979, down from a high of 70 percent in 1965.[28]

On the whole, the shift in American public opinion was neither as wide nor as deep as is often portrayed. In fact, judging from public opinion polls, there was little, if any, genuine shift to the right in the views of the American citizenry. Most Americans continued to support extensive government spending programs, regulatory measures, efforts to redistribute income and wealth, and government protection of labor rights. In many cases, the public favored an increase in such activities. What appears to have happened during the past two decades is that popular opinion continued its postwar drift toward greater support for progressive or liberal policies, but the rate of increase in support for such policies slowed markedly after 1973.[29]

Nevertheless, what matters most in determining the course of public policy is the views of economic and political elites, and by 1978 the tide had turned in American elite opinion.[30] In that year Congress rejected a major reform of the nation's labor laws, reduced the tax rate on capital gains and corporate profits, and substantially weakened a bill requiring government to take measures to ensure full employment. During the next two years several major regulatory initiatives were blocked and other already existing statutes, such as OSHA and the Clean Air Act, were diluted. This occurred despite the presence of a Democratic president and a substantial Democratic majority in both houses of Congress.

With the inauguration of the Reagan administration in 1981, market liberalism became firmly institutionalized in American government policy. The

1980s witnessed reductions in taxes and social welfare spending, a turn away from activist government, and an acceleration of the decline in labor union strength. Transfer payments as a share of GDP increased steadily in the United States after World War II, reaching a high of 11.9 percent in 1983. That trend was reversed in the 1980s, and by 1989 transfer payments had fallen to 10.8 percent. The Reagan-Bush years featured an unyielding reluctance to engage in proactive government steering of the economy. With a few exceptions, the only targeted assistance offered by government to civilian industry came in the form of reactive protectionist measures. The growth of government regulation of corporate social conduct slowed considerably in the 1980s. In 1988 the scope of regulation was only marginally greater than it had been when Reagan entered office, although it increased again somewhat during the Bush presidency. After declining steadily during the golden age, pre-tax income inequality has risen since the mid 1970s. Due to the regressive tax reforms of 1981 and 1986 along with cuts in social spending, even after-tax inequality increased during the 1980s. Unions, too, have experienced a dramatic deterioration in strength during the past two decades. The share of employees organized in unions hovered around 30 percent throughout the long boom, but since 1974 it has fallen precipitously, reaching 17 percent in 1990. Although not its fundamental cause, the Reagan and Bush administrations' hostility toward organized labor helped hasten this decline.

In the course of less than a decade, advocates of market liberalism managed to engineer an about-face in elite opinion. The Keynesian-redistributive consensus was replaced by a new orthodoxy similar in many respects to its predecessor of the pre-depression epoch. This perspective idolizes the market and despises government activism, whether in the form of tax and transfer programs, regulation, or industrial policy. It insists that efforts to equalize income only hurt the poor by reducing long-run growth. It maintains that labor unions secure high wages for their members at the expense of the living standards of the rest of society. The Clinton administration has endeavored to reorient U.S. policy away from market liberalism, but its success has been limited—due to opposition in the business community, in Congress, and within the administration itself. Whether the Clinton presidency marks a genuine, sustained shift away from market liberalism or merely a brief interlude in its ascendance remains to be seen.

The United States was not alone in its turn to market liberalism. Developments in Europe have to some degree mirrored those in the United States—although, with the exception of the United Kingdom, no country has so wholeheartedly adopted the prescriptions of economic orthodoxy. Perhaps most remarkably, countries such as Germany, the Netherlands, Denmark,

Belgium, and Britain, which previously strove for very low jobless rates, allowed unemployment to rise to nearly double-digit levels in the 1980s. Monetary and fiscal restraint, along with privatization, were in vogue nearly everywhere. Tax rates and transfer payments were cut in a number of countries. In addition, unionization levels declined in every developed nation except Sweden and Finland.[31]

The trend toward market liberalism, already clearly in evidence by the mid 1980s, appears to have accelerated in the 1990s. This owes in part to the demise of East European state socialism in 1989-1990, which free market advocates effectively protrayed as evidence of the inherent harm caused by impediments to market processes. The return of market liberalism is a result also of persistent high rates of unemployment in Europe, which are increasingly viewed as a product of overly regulated labor markets. A number of European analysts and policymakers have come to believe that the path to labor market success lies in the type of open, flexible employment system that exists in the United States.

Is the key to national economic success to be found in the ideas and prescriptions of market liberalism? If not, what is the key? These are the questions I attempt to answer in what follows.

The Efficiency of Constraint

What from one perspective may appear to be a constraint, may from another turn out an opportunity.

—*Wolfgang Streeck*[1]

Freedom of choice is commonly thought to be capitalism's quintessential attribute. Market coordination of an economy implies a decentralized process of decision making, with actors at liberty to select what to produce, how to finance production, whom to sell to, whom to work for, and so on. The allocation and use of economic resources is determined by the sum of these independent (although plainly interdependent) choices.

Liberal political theory posits freedom of choice as the market's principal advantage over alternative mechanisms of economic coordination, such as planning.[2] In virtue of the fact that humans are innately equal moral beings, and that knowledge of true interests must inevitably be limited, individual sovereignty, in this view, deserves ethical precedence over particular conceptions of the common good or social justice. Restraints on individual freedom are legitimate only when authorized by a majority, and even the majority will is forbidden from impinging upon a certain specified set of individual rights.

Orthodox economic theory views freedom of choice as desirable for instrumental, rather than intrinsic, reasons. Under conditions of free choice, according to the theory, actors' attempts to pursue their own selfish interests serve to promote the general interest as well. Choice permits economic agents to respond effectively to the preferences of other actors. Revealed preferences of customers determine a price schedule that provides producers with information about what consumers want and about how to produce it in the most efficient fashion. If perfect competition prevails, producers will use the available information to choose the least costly methods of producing and distributing the desired goods and services. Decentralized, independent decision making thereby yields a cost-efficient allocation and use of economic resources. Neither ex ante coordination of production decisions nor altruistic motives are necessary. In the classic description of Adam Smith, an individual who "intends only his own gain" is

> led by an invisible hand to promote an end which was no part of his intention. Nor is it always the worse for the society that it was no part of it. By pursuing his own interest he frequently promotes that of the society more effectually than when he really intends to promote it.[3]

Free choice is the mechanism through which the invisible hand is said to work this magic and, as such, is commonly understood to be the key institutional precondition for optimal economic performance. I argue in this chapter that the conventional emphasis on freedom of choice is misplaced. Instead, the key determinant of efficient economic behavior is the constraints economic agents face. And in a number of important instances, nonmarket or extramarket constraints are superior to market incentives at generating such efficient behavior.

Despite its emphasis on choice, neoclassical theory recognizes full well that economic actors must be constrained in certain ways to do what is in their own, and society's, best interest. The reason actors engage in economically beneficial behavior, according to the theory, is not that they have unlimited freedom of choice, but that they must choose within a particular set of constraints—the constraints imposed by market competition. It is competition that encourages actors to attempt to lower costs, improve quality, work hard, and act in other productive ways. There is no physical or legal compulsion involved, but those who do not endeavor to use resources efficiently and make improvements will eventually be driven out of business. It is this constraint, rather than freedom of choice, that is the crucial efficiency-generating mechanism in a capitalist economy.

The distinctive feature of orthodox economic theory, then, is not its emphasis on freedom of choice, but rather its assertion that market competition is the only type of constraint necessary to generate beneficial behavior. The issue is not free choice versus constraints, but what type of constraints promote economically productive activity. In the neoclassical view, market constraints are sufficient; within them actors should indeed be free to choose. I shall argue that this view is profoundly mistaken. In a number of important areas of economic life, market-guided choice on the part of rational, maximizing agents leads to inferior outcomes. Nonmarket or extramarket constraints are needed to promote efficiency.

The general notion that limitations on freedom of choice can produce superior outcomes is not new. The advantages of precommitment, or "binding oneself," have been discussed extensively in the psychological and philosophical literature on individual choice and rationality.[4] But application of the idea to the economic realm outside a neoclassical framework has been limited. Political economists (heterodox economists and political scientists) and economic sociologists have focused their attention instead on other failures of the neoclassical paradigm.[5] I aim to show in this chapter why an understanding of the efficiency of nonmarket constraints should be central to an analysis of economic life.

The first section of the chapter briefly discusses four themes on which critics of orthodox economic theory have tended to focus. The second section introduces the thesis that nonmarket constraints can promote efficient economic activity. The third section discusses two classic applications of this argument, in the work of Max Weber and Karl Polanyi. The next three sections offer some substantive support for the thesis, outlining a set of important instances in which nonmarket constraints prove superior to market incentives at encouraging decisions beneficial to the actors involved and to society as a whole. The issues addressed are financial markets and managerial time horizons, worker training, and purchaser-supplier relations.

◈   Traditional Critiques of Economic Orthodoxy

Political economists and economic sociologists have long been critical of orthodox economic theory. Their criticism has fallen predominantly into four categories. The first challenges standard economic assumptions about human behavior. The neoclassical theory of behavior, expected utility theory, presumes that economic actors are calculative, rational decision makers. Agents are assumed to have a stable set of preferences and accurate information about the costs associated with various strategies for achieving the preferences. Rational behavior, in a neoclassical sense, consists of using this knowledge to select the course of action that will permit attainment of the highest feasible point on the preference scale. The theory further assumes that actors' preferences tend to be selfish; agents aim to maximize their own welfare.[6]

Critics have posed a variety of challenges to these behavioral assumptions. Some contend that instead of aiming to achieve particular outcomes, people and firms often act based on habit, routine, or norms.[7] Others accept that a good deal of economic action is goal-directed, but insist that the degree of rationality in human decision making must be questioned. According to one school, for instance, the limitations of human cognitive capacity are so severe that at best we can assume only "bounded" rationality.[8] Obtaining complete information may also be impossible or excessively costly.[9] For these reasons, actors may rationally choose to "satisfice" rather than attempting to optimize. Experimental psychologists have also found that individuals are prone to inconsistency and error when translating preferences into specific choices.[10] Other critics argue that preferences are not always selfish. Values, such as morality, altruism, and loyalty, may play a prominent role in motivating economic behavior.[11] Few, if any, economists believe that the neoclassical assumptions adequately represent human behavior in full. The assumptions are used primarily because they are viewed as a good first approximation of economic behavior and because they are a useful basis on which to build complex models of economic processes. The critics generally recognize this. Their argument is that reliance on the neoclassical behavioral assumptions leads to faulty models.

The second line of critique focuses on the inability or unwillingness of orthodox economics to recognize that markets themselves are intrinsically social and political in nature, in both their origins and their functioning. Karl Marx long ago emphasized the importance of government force in creating one of the prerequisites of modern capitalism: "free" labor, a segment of society divorced from property so that its members maximize their income by selling their labor power. "Primitive accumulation," the forcible expropriation of peasants from the land, was carried out with extensive state assistance.[12] In a similar vein, Karl Polanyi, in his classic work on the emergence of capitalism, showed how state action played a critical role in engineering the integration of previously isolated local markets.[13] Nor can markets operate without government enforcement of property rights and contracts. Absent some guarantee that the contracts they enter into will be honored, rational self-interested agents would never exchange. Even state enforcement of contractual obligations is typically not sufficient, for governments are not omniscient. As Geoffrey Hodgson has noted:

> In an uncertain world we are forced to rely on institutional rules and standard patterns of contract, with the assumption, which cannot for practical reasons be

confirmed by detailed negotiation, that the other parties will similarly accept the prevailing norms and conventions.

A certain degree of trust, or extracontractual morality, is thus another precondition of a functioning market.[14] Neoinstitutional organizational theorists have noted that firms sometimes aim to maximize legitimacy rather than efficiency; this, too, is a function of the social and political context.[15] A host of other recent studies have explored the ways in which markets and competition are socially constructed.[16]

In a third, related line of criticism, economic sociologists have emphasized that economic interaction in market-based economies is unavoidably embedded in nonmarket social structures, relations, and processes. Among those identified as important are trust, goodwill, social capital, and interpersonal networks.[17] The environment in which economic agents operate, in other words, is never characterized solely by naked, atomistic market competition.

Finally, critics have called attention to the widespread power asymmetries in economic affairs. Contrary to the orthodox assumption of perfect competition in labor, product, and capital markets, power frequently is distributed in a markedly unequal fashion.[18] Labor scholars, for instance, have shown how power inequalities enable employers to implement nonmarket or market-distorting industrial relations practices such as dual labor markets and job segregation by sex.[19] Similarly, an influential school of thought in the sociology of organizations contends that power and control considerations, rather than efficiency concerns, dictate shifts in organizational structure and practice.[20]

◈ Efficient Constraints

Although each of these criticisms has merit, they sidestep what is perhaps a more fundamental flaw in orthodox economic theory. The assumption of individual rationality, although somewhat problematic, is often a reasonable approximation of economic behavior. Indeed, I rely on it throughout this book. And whereas critics of neoclassical orthodoxy have been quite attentive to the importance of nonmarket institutions, little explicit attention has been devoted to the ways in which such institutions constrain economic actors and, more critically, to the resulting impact on economic performance.

My argument begins with the point that in a market-based environment, rational actors will in some instances be led to make reasonable choices that produce suboptimal outcomes. In certain realms of economic life, the structure of market incentives is such that rational decisions by individual agents cannot yield the efficient performance predicted by neoclassical theory. Instead, they produce markedly inferior performance.

Economists have captured this problem to some degree via the notion of *market failure*. But the standard economic treatment of this vital issue is deficient, in two respects. First, market failure—the circumstance in which unassisted markets generate suboptimal performance—is much more widespread than orthodox economists generally admit. Second, because market competitive relationships are believed best left intact, the solution commonly proposed by economists is government intervention. Government is called upon to ensure the supply of goods that markets underproduce.[21] At the same time, however, economists and political scientists using neoclassical behavioral assumptions have argued that governments are by nature incapable of performing this task in an efficient fashion.[22] Government failure, according to this "public choice" view, is made inevitable by two inherent features of democratic politics. First, the state operates under noncompetitive conditions and so does not face a hard budget constraint; its expenditures are limited only by its ability to tax. Second, politicians can maximize their reelection chances by catering to the wishes of "rent-seeking" private groups, often at the expense of the larger collective good. Consequently, government intervention is seen as congenitally inefficient. The logic of the neoclassical paradigm thus creates an unbridgeable impasse. Its assumptions admit of market failure, but those same assumptions render ineffectual the only solution permissible within the confines of the theory.

The public choice view surely underestimates the potential for effective government remedies for market failure,[23] but a solution is available even if its pessimistic conclusion is accepted. A comparative survey of developed capitalist economies suggests that in many instances of market failure, state intervention is not necessarily required. Instead, economies often rely upon institutions generated within civil society to redress market inefficiencies. These nonmarket or extramarket institutions constrain actors in such a way that they are encouraged or forced to "do the right thing." Nonmarket constraints are thus a key contributor to economic success.

The point is not that freedom and efficiency are antithetical. Indeed, as we shall see, constraints can in certain instances increase actors' array of options—thus heightening, in a sense, their freedom of choice. The issue is not free choice versus constraint, but which types of constraints are most effective at generating productive economic behavior. Is the constraint of market competition sufficient, or is efficiency in some instances best achieved via constraints imposed by nonmarket or extramarket institutions? I shall argue the latter.

◆ Revisiting a Classic Theme

The theme of nonmarket constraints contributing to economic efficiency features prominently in the writings of several early economic sociologists, including Max Weber and Karl Polanyi. Weber's famous argument in *The Protestant Ethic and the Spirit of Capitalism* takes precisely this form. Capitalism's essence, Weber observed, is the continuous pursuit of profit via regularized investment of capital. The "spirit of capitalism" is manifested in the accumulation of wealth by capitalists for its own sake, purely as an end in itself. The question Weber sought to explore is: What motivates this behavior?

At the time of his writing, around 1905, capitalism was fairly well-developed in much of Europe and the United States, and for modern capitalism Weber viewed this behavioral query as no puzzle. As economic theory posits, competition encourages capitalists to reinvest profits in order to raise productivity and lower costs. Otherwise, competitors will underbid their prices and push them out of business.

> The capitalistic economy of the present day is an immense cosmos into which the individual is born, and which presents itself to him, at least as an individual, as an unalterable order of things in which he must live. It forces the individual, in so far as he is involved in the system of market relationships, to conform to capitalistic rules of action. The manufacturer who in the long run acts counter to these norms, will . . . inevitably be eliminated from the economic scene.[24]

But what is not altogether clear, and in fact quite mysterious, is why early entrepreneurs, who operated before capitalism was firmly entrenched and thus did not face the compulsion associated with extensive market competition, adopted the capitalist ethic. Why continuously reinvest profits, especially in conditions of considerable uncertainty? As Weber noted, this orientation runs counter to "traditional" rational economic behavior: "A man does not 'by nature' wish to earn more and more money, but simply to live as he is accustomed to live and to earn as much as is necessary for that purpose."[25] Here we have a situation, in other words, in which rational action might well produce suboptimal economic effects—namely, underinvestment and underproduction. Potential efficiency gains of considerable magnitude would go unrealized.

The reason why many early industrialists adopted the capitalist spirit, according to Weber, is that they felt there was no choice in the matter; they believed it their duty to do so. They faced a constraint of an ideological—specifically, a religious—nature. A disproportionate number of these entrepreneurs,

Weber suggested, were Protestant, affiliated with Calvinism or one of several related sects. Calvinist doctrine specified that grace was predetermined, and that election to heaven was revealed by the presence of two behavioral characteristics: performance in one's "calling" and asceticism. The chosen labored intensely in their assigned function and resisted worldly temptations, rejecting the spontaneous enjoyment of life. On the surface, accumulation of capital would seem to conflict with the latter stricture, but in Calvinist theology it was condemned only if used to support a life of idle luxury. Attainment of wealth through hard labor in pursuit of a calling—the calling of entrepreneur—was viewed as a sign of God's blessing.

In conjunction, these two strictures encouraged precisely the type of behavior most conducive to economic growth: the saving of profit and its continuous reinvestment. As Weber wrote:

> When the limitation of consumption is combined with this release of acquisitive activity, the inevitable practical result is obvious: accumulation of capital through ascetic compulsion to save. The restraints which were imposed upon the consumption of wealth naturally served to increase it by making possible the productive investment of capital.[26]

By constraining its followers engaged in commerce to save and invest, Puritan doctrine thus achieved the effect only later assumed by the market itself: it induced industrialists to act as capitalists.[27]

Another defining feature of capitalist economies is the commodification of labor. Free labor—a workforce not compelled to perform services for employers by physical force—distinguishes the capitalist employment relation from its feudal predecessor. In the neoclassical theory of the labor market, workers and capitalists must be free to choose the conditions of employment. Free choice promotes flexibility; it allows labor to be deployed where it is most efficiently used (technically, where its wage equals its marginal product). If employers can productively use additional employees, they will increase the wage they pay for labor, and workers will choose to move to that firm to receive the higher wage. Similarly, when product market conditions deteriorate or productivity declines, employers must be at liberty to lower costs by reducing the wage or the size of their workforce.

Due to the preponderance of government regulations and the influence of unions in contemporary society, employers often yearn for a return to the conditions of early capitalism, when labor markets most closely approximated the neoclassical model of perfect competition and free exchange. But in *The Great Transformation,* Karl Polanyi explained why truly self-regulating labor markets, such as those existing during that period, are not conducive to economic welfare. Because of costs associated with information and with labor relocation, a frictionless labor market can never exist in practice. Workers are not able to switch firms without cost or pain in order to take advantage of the highest available wages. Furthermore, few economies exist without at least some involuntary unemployment. Employee inertia and the availability of a "reserve army" of unemployed labor render the power relationship between workers and capitalists inherently unequal. Employers can, and often do, use their leverage to force down wages and to organize the work process in the manner they favor.

As Polanyi noted, in 18th-century England unregulated labor markets led, for exactly this reason, to a rapid deterioration of the workforce. Abysmally low wages and factory abuses threatened to ruin the productive capacities of the British labor force. In addition, low wages dampened the demand for goods and services, stalling economic growth. Eventually, society chose to regulate the labor market in order to prevent its disintegration. Factory laws were passed and a limited welfare state created in order to sustain the productive capabilities of the labor force and to prevent underconsumption. In Polanyi's words:

> To allow the market mechanism to be sole director of the fate of human beings . . . , even of the amount and use of purchasing power, would result in the demolition of society. For the alleged commodity 'labor power' cannot be shoved about, used indiscriminately, or even left unused, without affecting also the human individual who happens to be the bearer of this peculiar commodity. In disposing of a man's labor power the system would, incidentally, dispose of the physical, psychological, and moral entity 'man' attached to that tag. Robbed of the protective covering of cultural institutions, human beings would perish from the effects of social exposure; they would die as the victims of acute social dislocation through vice, perversion, crime, and starvation. . . . Finally, the market administration of purchasing power would periodically liquidate business enterprise, for shortages and surfeits of money would prove as disastrous to business as floods and droughts in primitive society. Undoubtedly, labor markets are essential to a market economy. But no society could stand the effects of such a system of crude fictions even for the shortest stretch of time unless its human substance as well as its business organization was protected against the ravages of this satanic mill.[28]

The market, in other words, had to be safeguarded from itself. It was necessary to constrain capitalists in order to promote their own, and society's, well-being.

The cases discussed by Weber and Polanyi are not isolated or atypical. They are representative of a broader set of instances in which economies require nonmarket or extramarket constraints on individual actors in order to achieve superior performance outcomes. The remainder of this chapter is devoted to discussion of three elements of successful economic performance that will not be forthcoming unless the choice of economic agents is constrained by nonmarket institutions: long managerial time horizons, worker training, and cooperative purchaser-supplier relations.

◈ Financial Markets and Managerial Time Horizons

Standard economic theory suggests that a very high degree of investor flexibility is a sine qua non of successful capital market performance. The ability of investors freely to sell their ownership shares freely functions as an effective pressure on management to maximize shareholder return. This encourages efficient use of resources. Overlooked by the standard theory, however, is the effect of investor freedom on the time horizons of corporate decision makers. Logic and comparative experience indicate that highly flexible capital markets encourage a short-term focus on the part of firms, whereas investors less able to exit quickly tend to emphasize longer-term results. The latter institutional configuration is more conducive to economic success.

In the conventional economic model of the capital market, most companies are owned by a diffuse mass of investors, and investors tend to allocate their resources across a number of firms. Because the financial stability of a firm is not dependent on the contribution of any single agent and stock shares are a relatively liquid form of investment, owners are free (substantively, not just formally) to sell their shares in a firm if the return is not satisfactory. Assuming they aim to maximize the return on their assets, investors will buy and sell shares based on companies' projected profit success. In this way, stockholders act as an effective arbiter of firms' performance, executing the verdict rendered by the market via the mechanism of exit. Management is induced to maximize efficiency in order to keep shareholders happy. Thus, in principle, decentralized ownership and competitive financial markets ought to foster efficient economic activity.

But overlooked in this sketch is a critical problem that stems from an ambiguity in the notion of profit maximization. The hitch is that there is a time component involved. Actions taken to maximize return in the near term may not be conducive to profit maximization over a longer period, and vice versa. For example, firms often face a choice whether or not to make an expensive investment that might yield a handsome payoff, but only after a number of years. A firm seeking to maximize short-run profits would likely elect not to make the investment, whereas one interested in long-term results would be more inclined to do so.

Firms in a decentralized, equity-based financial system face strong pressures to focus on near-term performance. This stems from the lack of incentives for disengaged investors to commit to any particular firm, the quality of information they must rely on to evaluate company prospects, and their lack of capacity to directly influence managerial behavior.

Disengaged investors have no incentive to hold onto their shares in a company that is not currently performing at a satisfactory standard. Their interest in a firm is confined solely to its ability to yield a high return. There is no other attachment or tie linking the investor to the company. Selling the stock has only a negligible effect on the firm in any case, because each individual investor owns an inconsequential share of the company.

Disengaged investors must rely chiefly on the market for information about firms' performance and prospects. This, too, encourages a focus on the short run, because the quality of information the market uses to value companies is inadequate. Ken Froot, Andre Perold, and Jeremy Stein summarize the problem of "information asymmetries" as follows:

> Suppose a company's board approves a $100-million expenditure that it believes will produce $300 million in added revenues, leaving $200 million as profit. (For simplicity, ignore the time value of money in this example.) If management is able to communicate the strategic and economic merits of the project to the market—and the shareholders listen—then when the project is announced the value of the company's stock should rise by $200 million. This is the paradigm of market behavior that academics and investors generally espouse. However, if management fails to communicate the benefits of the capital investment to the marketplace—because it does not want to publicly disclose its competitive strategy, because shareholders ignore the press release, or because investors have lost faith in management's projections—then the market will not incorporate the full value of the project into the stock price.
>
> In the early stages of the project, the shareholders note a decrease of $100 million in the company's cash flow. Not knowing otherwise, they construe this as a decline in the company's business prospects and adjust their valuation of the stock downward. Not until the profits from the capital investment show up in reported earnings would the market fully incorporate the merits of the capital expenditure into the value of the stock. The market is behaving rationally, given available information, but from the perspective of corporate managers, investors are behaving myopically.[29]

A near-term focus is further induced by the difficulty small shareholders face in implementing desired changes in management strategy. Stockholder meetings are typically held only once each year, and in order to influence managerial decision making, small shareholders must form coalitions, the collective action costs of which are, understandably, often viewed as prohibitive. For these reasons, the tendency of dissatisfied minor shareholders is to simply sell their stock. As Albert Hirschman noted in his classic treatise on exit and voice, difficulty in exercising voice as a response to ineffective managerial performance encourages resort to exit.[30]

In sum, where they are relatively free to shift assets from firm to firm, investors seeking to maximize the return on their assets tend to buy and sell frequently. To please such investors, to keep them loyal, corporate managers must strive to maximize the short-run profits of the firm. Failure to do so brings a severe penalty. As investors exit, the company's stock price drops, precipitating further exit. It now costs the firm a good deal more to raise new funds, because it must sell a greater number of shares than before in order to raise whatever amount it needs. And a low stock price opens the door for corporate raiders to buy the company and replace its management.

Empirical evidence suggests that where firms focusing on short-term performance compete against those able to take a more long-term perspective, the latter have a competitive advantage. A comparison of U.S.-based manufacturing firms with their German and Japanese competitors bears this out. Japanese and German firms tend to place greater weight on long-term growth in market share than do U.S. companies. Japan's success in industries such as steel, automobiles, consumer electronics, machine tools, semiconductors, and computers owes to a large extent to the ability of Japanese companies to sell their products at very low prices in foreign markets for a considerable period of time. Short-run profits are sacrificed in favor of market share. This tactic enables them to gain a foothold in these markets and to lower costs by moving down the learning curve and achieving scale economies.[31] A good illustration of the ability of Japanese firms to prioritize long-term performance occurred in the latter half of the 1980s, when the yen appreciated dramatically relative to the dollar. Many Japanese companies chose to cut back on profits by holding export prices constant, in an effort to retain market share.[32] Consequently, the massive U.S. trade deficit with Japan has not subsided in recent years, despite a substantial decline in the dollar's value. German firms, which tend to produce specialized goods for the high end of the product market (e.g., in industries such as autos and machine tools), have demonstrated a similar tendency to sacrifice near-term profits in favor of gaining or holding market share.[33]

U.S. firms, by contrast, tend to focus predominantly on the short run. That this is the case, and that it has contributed to declining U.S. market share and profits in a variety of important industries, is little disputed.[34] Investment in property, plant, and equipment, as well as research and development, is lower among American firms in a wide array of industries than among their Japanese and German counterparts.[35] U.S.-based companies have often proved unwilling to make investments or contest particular product markets because of an aversion to low near-term profit margins.[36]

These differing time horizons, and the consequent divergences in economic performance, stem to a considerable extent from the different incentives firms in these countries face in obtaining capital.[37] The German financial system is centered around banks.[38] Many German banks have substantial equity holdings in firms. The large universal banks own significant portions of virtually all of Germany's biggest industrial corporations.[39] Their investment is so substantial that it is effectively much less liquid than that of a small investor. Banks also tend to function as the principal lenders to firms in which they are part-owners. Consequently, the primary interest of the bank is not maximization of short-term profit, but continued lending activity and a stable stream of dividends. The bank's principal concern therefore lies in the long-run performance of the firm.

Its large equity stake typically permits a bank one or several seats on the company's board of directors. And because banks also engage in securities activities, institutional and individual shareholders frequently give the banks proxy rights to vote their shares; banks sometimes vote up to 90 percent of a company's stock.[40] Banks thus have access to detailed information about corporate performance and prospects, along with substantial input into company decision making. Given this structure of incentives, information, and capacities, German banks are both less willing and less able to use exit to convey their judgment about firm performance. Their institutional position instead encourages them to rely on the mechanism of voice, and to use this voice to direct management's focus toward long-term performance.

In Japan a similar effect is achieved via two institutional arrangements: cross-ownership among firms and the "main bank" system of financing.[41] Many Japanese firms are part of an industrial group, or *keiretsu*. These groups consist of companies in a variety of industries, in many cases linked together as suppliers and customers, along with one or several banks. Firms within a keiretsu are generally connected through extensive cross-ownership. Japanese law prohibits companies from owning more than 5 percent of another firm's equity, but as much as 25 percent of a Japanese firm's stock is typically owned by other members of its keiretsu. Moreover, an even larger portion of its shares may be owned by firms outside the keiretsu to which it is vertically linked. In total, some 75 percent of the stock of the typical large Japanese corporation is locked up by firms that have ongoing business relationships with the company.[42] Ownership is thus formally diffuse, but in effect highly concentrated.

Because their supplier-customer relationship places them in a situation of tight interdependence, the primary concern of keiretsu members and other stable shareholders is that firms of which they are part-owners achieve long-term growth and stability, not large short-run profits. When a firm suffers a setback, these owners do not unload their shareholdings. Instead, they work together to find a solution to the problem in order to get the troubled firm back on the right track. The lead bank in the keiretsu, known as the main bank, may temporarily suspend loan payments owed by the firm and even lend new money to stabilize the firm's financial situation, in exchange for the company making changes the bank and other keiretsu members believe necessary. Like the German universal banks, these important financial institutions are interested first and foremost in the firm's long-term health, rather than its short-run payout.

The U.S. financial system, by contrast, is perhaps the world's closest approximation to the textbook model of a decentralized capital market. Ownership of firms is seldom concentrated in the hands of large investors who might prioritize long-term success and stability. Instead, companies are dependent on a multitude of owners with small shareholdings, who tend to focus on near-term returns.[43] More than 50 percent of all U.S. corporate stock is owned by institutional investors (pension funds, insurance companies, and so on), whose holdings are diversified across hundreds of firms and traded frequently. Stock turnover (the volume of traded shares as a percentage of total listed shares) on the New York Stock Exchange amounts to nearly two-thirds during the course of a year, and the average holding period of stocks has declined from more than seven years in 1960 to two years today.[44] Facing the specter of stockholder exit on a quarterly basis, American firms often fail to invest sufficiently or ignore new productivity-enhancing innovations or product markets. They choose instead to use their resources to make slight adaptations to existing technology, shift production abroad, diversify into other lines of business, lobby for protection, engage in financial speculation, or simply advertise massively. The 1980s wave of hostile takeovers may have further accentuated this tendency, although it has abated somewhat in recent years.

This discussion of the logic of financial markets and their empirical manifestations in Germany, Japan, and the United States suggests that market-based incentives for investors are not conducive to superior economic performance, and may in fact seriously impair the international competitiveness of firms. Instead, firms and nations may benefit substantially where investors are encouraged to use voice rather than exit to convey dissatisfaction with company performance. Where investors, because of the nature and size of their equity holdings, have as their primary interest the long-term performance of the firm, management is encouraged to make investments with long-run payoffs, thereby enhancing competitiveness and growth. By contrast, where investors are at liberty to exit the relationship with little friction, management faces strong shareholder pressure to maximize near-term profit. As the behavior of U.S. firms consistently demonstrates, managerial preoccupation with the consequences of poor quarterly returns does not lend itself to an orientation toward the long run. Evidence suggests that differing time horizons have been a key contributing factor in the divergent performance of Japanese and German versus U.S. firms in a variety of industries during the past two decades.[45]

◈ Worker Training

Next, consider investment in human capital. The quality of a nation's workforce is without question one of the key determinants of its competitiveness and economic welfare. A crucial component in the skill formation process is job training. Standard economic theory assumes that firms and employees will make sufficient investments in human capital. This supposition, however, lacks logical and empirical support. Market incentives tend to be such that neither companies nor individuals will choose to invest in an appropriate level of skill training. Only under conditions of extramarket or nonmarket constraint do these actors find it in their interest to make such investments.

Employee skills have certain properties that make it irrational for firms unilaterally to provide sufficient training for their workers.[46] First, there is a substantial amount of uncertainty involved. The returns to training are very difficult to estimate, much less to predict in advance. Second, there are disincentives associated with the public goods nature of skills. Because workers are generally free to move from one firm to another, companies risk not being able to capture the full benefits of investments they make in training. Workers can simply take their skills and move to another firm.

To some, these disincentives present no cause for alarm. According to human capital theory, workers themselves have an incentive to invest in skills training because it will yield higher income over the course of one's lifetime.[47]

The onus for skill development is thus taken off firms. But human capital theory unrealistically assumes that individuals have perfect information about the skills they need and the future payoffs these skills will generate. In most cases people don't have this sort of information; uncertainty about the payoffs from human capital investment is no less severe for individuals than for firms. Furthermore, because skills (unlike a house or a business) cannot be used as collateral, individuals may have trouble financing such investments. Consequently, worker investment in skill formation will tend to be inadequate. In short, absent some sort of extramarket incentive, rational individuals and firms will underinvest in training.

One solution to the provision of skills is to have government fill the void. As noted earlier, this is the standard neoclassical remedy for a public goods problem. In addition to providing basic education through schooling, government can assist the process of skill formation via vocational training and retraining services. Vocational training programs in Sweden and Denmark have been crucial contributors to the development of those nations' highly skilled workforces.[48] Sweden, for instance, allocates 2 to 3 percent of its gross national product (GNP), a relatively large amount, to its public training programs. Sweden also has a model system for retraining current and displaced workers. Similarly, the U.S. government has assisted the skill formation process through a series of public training programs—the 1962 Manpower Development and Training Act, the 1973 Comprehensive Employment and Training Act, and the 1982 Job Training Partnership Act. Public vocational-technical schools and community colleges also contribute to the preparation of the American workforce.

Helpful though it is, there are limits to the effectiveness of skills training in schools. As Wolfgang Streeck has observed: "Learning requires doing. Work skills can be ultimately acquired only at work."[49] A recent report by the congressional Office of Technology Assessment reaches the same conclusion: "Recent research as well as anecdotal evidence from companies indicate that knowledge gained outside of the normal job context (such as in a classroom) is difficult to transfer back to the worksite."[50] A substantial share of the burden for effective training, therefore, must rest on the shoulders of firms.

Under what conditions will firms provide a sufficient level of training for their workforce? There appear to be two such conditions, each revolving around an extramarket mechanism that constrains employers. The first obtains in Japan.[51] For historical reasons associated with labor-management struggles following World War II, industrial relations in large Japanese firms are characterized by a set of peculiar institutional arrangements. These arrangements feature lifetime employment for the worker, payment based largely on seniority, extensive employee participation in shop-floor decision making, and company unions. With regard to training, it is chiefly the first two characteristics that are relevant. Because workers are guaranteed (barring exceptionally poor performance) lifetime employment with their firm, they can have reasonable confidence that skill training they undertake will be put to use and, to an extent, compensated. More important, because employee pay is based largely on length of tenure with the firm, companies can be fairly certain that employees will not switch to another firm after receiving training.[52] The fear of "poaching" by other companies is practically eliminated. Furthermore, lifetime employment makes labor more or less a fixed cost for the firm. Lacking the freedom to discard workers, firms find it in their interest to raise the skill level of their workforce so that they can compete based largely on product quality rather than price. In sum, both employers and employees have a strong interest in skill development. It is not surprising, then, that company training of workers is extensive in Japan.

Japan is rather unique in its labor relations institutions, but not entirely so. Large automobile producers in Sweden and Germany and U.S. electronics firms such as Motorola and Xerox also provide sustained, well-funded training programs for their employees.[53] A characteristic shared by these firms, which helps account for their willingness to engage in systematic training, is a strong commitment to job security for their employees. With employment flexibility effectively curtailed, these firms, like their Japanese counterparts, find it in their interest to invest in the development of a solidly trained, high-quality workforce.

What about in conditions of open labor markets? Can firms in these circumstances be persuaded or constrained to train their workforce adequately? There is indeed a solution here—one best exemplified by German industry. In Germany, training for more than 400 occupations is centered around a highly effective apprenticeship system based within the firm.[54] The programs, in which all firms in relevant industries must participate, last two to three years and consist of extensive on-the-job training along with one day per week spent in the classroom. Given the incentives for companies to underinvest in training, how can such an apprenticeship system be sustained? The key lies in cooperation between and within organizations representing employers and workers. The apprenticeship system is monitored and enforced by strong employer and labor associations, with relatively limited state assistance. In effect, these associations protect firms' investments in training by making sure other firms make similar investments. Poaching is not entirely eliminated, but because each company is required to train its own workforce in any case, the threat is greatly reduced.

Neither of these solutions to the market failure in training prevails in the United States. It should come as no surprise, then, that worker training in the United States is widely judged to be grossly inadequate. Training within American firms is sporadic, informal, and unstructured. Workers often learn their skills simply by "following Joe around." Investment in formal training by U.S. employers amounts to between $30 billion and $44 billion annually, or 1 to 2 percent of private sector employee compensation. The problem lies less in the aggregate amount of expenditure than in its composition. Almost all of this spending is accounted for by 15,000 companies, or a mere 0.5 percent of all American employers, and only 100 to 200 firms spend more than 2 percent of their payroll on formal training. Only 12 percent of the workforce receives any formal training on the job, and nearly two-thirds of these recipients are managers or professionals. Furthermore, whereas a majority of German workers complete apprenticeship programs, only 300,000 U.S. employees (0.25 percent of the civilian workforce) have done so; and more than half of those are in construction.[55] The overall assessment of a recent, very thorough government survey on the skill level of the U.S. workforce is that "When measured by international standards, most American workers are not well trained."[56]

Here again, then, market incentives are not conducive to superior economic performance. Instead, it is under conditions in which employers are constrained by extra- or nonmarket institutions—either lifetime employment and tenure-based payment for workers or pressure from interest group associations—that they are most likely to make the investments in skill formation necessary to sustain a high level of competitiveness.

◈ Purchaser-Supplier Relations

"Good purchasing strategy, from a structural standpoint, involves the avoidance of switching costs. . . . Avoiding switching costs means resisting the temptation to become too dependent on a supplier."[57] This advice from management strategy expert Michael Porter epitomizes the traditional economic view regarding the approach firms should take toward their suppliers of materials, parts, and equipment. As Susan Helper has observed, the strategy is exit-based.[58] Its underlying rationale is a belief that purchaser freedom is the key to efficiency. The primary danger facing a customer is thought to be too much dependence on a particular supplier, because dependence heightens the costs associated with switching to an alternative source of supply. If the supplier's prices increase or its quality declines, the customer firm will find itself forced to bear either the extra cost of sticking with the supplier or that of changing to a new one. Purchasing flexibility is therefore held to be the secret to efficient supplier relations.

The purchasing strategy followed by the three U.S. automobile manufacturers exemplifies the orthodox approach. These firms' standard relationship with suppliers is short-term, arm's length, adversarial, and based first and foremost on price considerations.[59] The designs for each vehicle part are performed by the engineering staff of the automaker, with drawings then distributed to a group of potential supplier firms. Each supplier is asked to submit a bid based on a given number of parts and a quality specification. The bidders offering the lowest price for the part are awarded the job. The contract applies for one year and specifies that the purchaser is free to cancel at any time if volume or specification needs change or if supplier performance is considered unsatisfactory. Instances of suppliers being dumped in favor of lower-cost competitors, after only a year or even less, are legion. The system is designed to elicit intense cost competition between supplier firms, and to allow the purchaser maximum flexibility in order to most effectively reap the benefits of this competition—the bottom line being to minimize supply costs.

Yet the traditional U.S. automotive supply relationship illustrates a fundamental flaw in the exit-based purchasing strategy. As we observed for capital markets, the problem here stems from the distinction between short-term and long-term performance and between exit and voice as mechanisms for eliciting performance. The price-centered strategy may be effective at minimizing supply costs in the short run, but the incentives it creates are such as to inhibit the pursuit of a variety of practices necessary for long-term cost minimization. In striving to achieve a high degree of flexibility, U.S. auto manufacturers have structured their relations with suppliers in a manner that makes actions conducive to long-run efficiency seem irrational.[60]

Perhaps most important, the exit-based strategy discourages communication between purchasers and suppliers, thereby blocking the transfer of information. Parts and components are designed in-house by the manufacturer, with suppliers instructed to simply follow the blueprint. In this way the automaker avoids becoming too dependent on the specialized skill or capability of a particular supplier. But at the same time, the manufacturer sacrifices potential benefits that might arise from the supplier's extensive knowledge of its specialty. Supplier firms are given precious little information about the other parts of the vehicle, and thus have little basis for making suggestions about possible design enhancements. Moreover, suppliers have no incentive to provide any such suggestions, because the purchaser can simply take the new design idea and then give the order to a lower-cost supplier.

Communication between suppliers is similarly discouraged by the prevailing arrangement. The search for the lowest cost effectively creates a zero-sum competitive game among supplier firms, in which a gain by one can come only at another's expense. Supplier companies are thus discouraged from sharing information about improved organization and process techniques. By playing suppliers off against one another, the auto manufacturers thereby foreclose a wealth of potential efficiency gains, particularly because technology transfer is a critical source of productivity enhancement among small and midsize firms.

Finally, the exit-based system discourages suppliers from making large-scale investments unless they will produce an immediate reduction in costs. This is especially true of asset-specific investments—that is, investments in equipment or knowledge that are useful only for a supply product needed by a particular manufacturer. Given the uncertain future of the relationship, suppliers take a considerable risk in making such investments. Investment decisions are made knowing that the manufacturer might sever the relationship at any moment, leaving the supplier with substantial excess capacity. Suppliers are thus encouraged to lower costs by making short-term adjustments—for example, shedding labor, seeking wage reductions, or sacrificing quality—which tend to be detrimental to long-term productivity.

As the U.S. automakers have recently been discovering, an alternative mode of structuring the purchaser-supplier relationship can, by creating a different set of incentives, yield striking dividends in performance. In contrast to the exit-centered arrangement, the basis of this strategy is a commitment by the purchaser to work with suppliers over the long term, to elicit performance improvement by exercising voice rather than by threatening to withdraw. This commitment may be expressed formally through the use of multiyear contracts, or it may be informal. What matters is that both parties believe it to be genuine. Commitment to a long-term, cooperative, voice-based relationship is the backbone of the highly successful supplier system used by Japanese auto manufacturers.[61] The commitment is such that Japanese automakers consider their suppliers, like their employees, to be largely fixed costs. In making such a commitment, these automakers force themselves to take an interest in the long-term health and productivity of their suppliers, with the result that they find it in their interest to engage in practices that optimize their own long-term payoff.

Japanese automakers work intensively with their suppliers on the design of parts and components and encourage suppliers to work closely with each other, in order to maximize synergy effects. The assemblers likewise insist on effective and timely transfer of information on process techniques among the participants in the supply chain. Supplier firms readily comply, knowing that sharing this information poses little genuine threat to their own success. The auto manufacturers also require that suppliers steadily reduce costs by a set amount, established through mutual discussion between supplier and assembler. Any cost savings beyond the agreed-upon level accrue exclusively to the supplier. Supported by the assurance of a long-term relationship, this requirement stimulates suppliers to seek continuous and rapid improvement in productivity. Evidence suggests that these practices pay off. The superior efficiency of Japanese auto manufacturers at least through the 1980s is virtually unquestioned, and their supplier relationships are widely acknowledged to be a key factor contributing to that superiority.[62]

An alternative mechanism for remedying the information and motivation problems involved in manufacturer-supplier relations is to bring the production of supplies in-house through vertical integration.[63] Indeed, the U.S. automakers have relied extensively on this strategy throughout the post-World War II period.[64] But there are important disadvantages to internal sourcing. It is difficult for a single company to stay at the technological forefront in a wide array of areas. This is particularly true of an industry such as automobiles; a typical car has around 10,000 distinct parts and components. Perhaps more important, reliance chiefly or entirely on internal production severely reduces or eliminates competition as a spur for efficiency.[65]

Commitment to long-term cooperation need not imply an abandonment of competition between suppliers. In fact, Japanese auto manufacturers rely on multiple suppliers for a higher share of their externally sourced parts than do U.S. automakers.[66] The secret to fusing cooperation and competition lies in a willingness to work with a supplier to solve problems, instead of simply switching immediately to an alternative source. When a supplier's performance is subpar, Japanese assemblers do not dismiss that firm. Instead, a fraction of the supplier firm's business is shifted to a competitor for a brief period as a penalty. Supplier and purchaser work together to identify the problem and find a mutually satisfactory solution. Only if a supplier proves unwilling or unable to adapt over a substantial period of time is the relationship severed.

This in turn raises the broader issue of the basis of the Japanese supplier-purchaser arrangement. Some analysts and management executives believe that the Japanese type of relationship cannot be replicated in other national contexts because the system is underpinned by a "cooperative spirit" that is culture-specific. A careful study by MIT's International Motor Vehicle Program, however, concludes that this is not the case:

In fact, we find no evidence that Japanese suppliers love their assembler customers any more than suppliers do in the West. Instead, they operate in a completely different framework that channels the efforts of both parties toward mutually beneficial ends with a minimum of wasted effort. . . . Cooperation does not mean a cozy relaxed atmosphere—far from it. Japanese suppliers face constant pressure to improve their performance, both through constant comparison with other suppliers and contracts based on falling costs.

The key is that "By abandoning power-based bargaining and substituting an agreed-upon rational structure for jointly analyzing costs, determining prices, and sharing profits, adversarial relationships give way to cooperative ones."[67] Undoubtedly a certain measure of trust underpins this type of arrangement. But such trust need not depend on Confucian ethics. Trust can be a reasonable, logical belief formed in response to repeated cooperative behavior.[68] The secret to the voice-based supplier system is that in committing to a long-term relationship, purchasers constrain themselves in such a way that cooperation becomes a rational means of maximizing their self-interest.

Although the auto industry provides a useful illustration of the incentives and performance outcomes associated with exit-based versus voice-based supplier systems, the point has widespread applicability. Cooperation encouraged by a long-term commitment offers potential performance benefits for supplier systems across a wide array of industries.[69] In addition, recent research on the proliferation of production networks among locationally or strategically similar firms has identified a variety of efficiency premiums associated with information sharing and other forms of cooperation.[70] These advantages, like those of the voice-based supplier arrangement, are in many instances made possible by mutual commitment to extended, continuing relationships.

◈ Markets and Constraints

The point of this discussion has by no means been to deny that freedom of choice plays a significant, and in many instances beneficial, role in economic affairs. Markets cannot function without a substantial degree of freedom on the part of economic actors. (Indeed, as the East European experience has revealed, even planned systems require a relatively large sphere of choice in order to function.[71]) The issue is not free choice versus constraints but which types of constraints are most conducive to beneficial economic behavior. What the foregoing examples suggest is that the constraints of market competition frequently are inadequate or even counterproductive. Effective, efficient performance in some important areas of economic life necessitates that actors be constrained by non- or extramarket institutions. Such constraints encourage and enable them to make decisions that, given market incentives alone, would seem irrational.

Equality and Efficiency

The Illusory Trade-Off

No one doubts that there is a direct trade-off between more equality and efficiency in a perfectly competitive static neoclassical economy operating at 100 percent efficiency. . . . But dynamic real world economies are another matter.

—*Lester Thurow*[1]

Along with liberty and democracy, equality stands as one of the most cherished social principles of the modern world. Yet it is widely held that we ought not have too much equality. The most prominent basis of anti-egalitarian sentiment is the view that equality impedes economic efficiency and that it is better for society to be unequally rich than equally poor. This belief is so ingrained as to be virtually unquestioned, even by those who are otherwise staunch ethical egalitarians. But is it correct? Is there a trade-off between equality and efficiency?

AUTHOR'S NOTE: Portions of this chapter appeared earlier in the *European Journal of Political Research* 27(2), 1995, 225-254. I thank Kluwer Academic Publishers for permission to reprint this material here.

◈ Normative Arguments

Debates over equality frequently focus on ethical considerations.[2] One of the most common objections to distributive egalitarianism contends that equalizing income requires excessive interference with individual liberty.[3] Historically, this form of opposition to equality initially stemmed from a fear that egalitarian measures would impinge upon freedom of property ownership.[4] In particular, government efforts to redistribute income would of necessity impose restrictions on the freedom to appropriate profit. Equality might even require the abolition of private ownership of property. Since the advent of authoritarian socialism in the Soviet Union, Eastern Europe, and China, the threat to freedom posed by equality has been seen as extending to encompass a broad array of liberties. Egalitarian distributive outcomes, in this view, can be achieved only via extensive political and social repression.[5]

Egalitarians have countered by arguing that the freedom to own property is intrinsically contradictory. A consequence of this freedom is that property assets will be distributed unequally; indeed, a number of individuals will own no property at all. And in a market economy, the economic freedom of those without property is severely restricted.[6] A related contention is that the libertarian objection relies on a rather limited conception of freedom, as merely the absence of coercion. True individual freedom ought to consist of positive capacities, not just the absence of barriers. In most existing societies, greater equality of resources would enhance the capability of large numbers of people to generate and fulfill informed preferences, thereby augmenting their freedom. In this sense, equality and liberty are not only compatible; they are interdependent.[7]

Two other popular objections attack egalitarianism directly, asserting that equality is an unfair distributive principle.[8] One suggests that individuals should be compensated in proportion to their contribution to the social product. That is, income should be proportionate to the economic value of one's work. This is the distributive principle implicitly favored by neoclassical economic theory.[9] Egalitarians respond that differences in the value of work are determined to a substantial degree by individuals' intelligence and talent, which in turn are largely innate and/or a result of environment. They are products, in other words, of factors over which an individual has no control. This ought to render them morally irrelevant in the determination of just rewards.[10]

The other objection to equality contends that individuals who wish to work harder or longer, or who endeavor to develop skills that increase their productivity, deserve to be recompensed for their extra effort. If work effort is a disutility for individuals but a benefit for society, it seems only fair to reward greater effort with greater compensation.[11] This is a sensible point, and one with which few egalitarians would presumably disagree.[12] Equality should apply not simply to material goods per se, but to the broader consumption-leisure trade-off. Individuals who prefer greater leisure should receive less monetary compensation than those who put forth greater work effort. But although compensation according to effort would justify some inequality, it surely would not countenance the enormous disparities in income that characterize existing societies. The distribution of income would likely be relatively egalitarian, although not perfectly so.

◈ The Equality-Efficiency Trade-Off Thesis

The most prominent argument against equality is based not on normative considerations but on a well-accepted principle of economic theory. It is widely believed, even by many ethical egalitarians, that equality is inimical to economic efficiency. Achieving greater equality of income entails sacrificing some measure of efficiency. Arthur Okun's *Equality and Efficiency: The Big Tradeoff* offers the classic expression of this thesis. In Okun's words: "Any insistence on carving the pie into equal slices would shrink the size of the pie. That fact poses the tradeoff between economic equality and efficiency."[13] Okun professes that "Equality in the distribution of incomes . . . would be my ethical preference. Abstracting from the costs and consequences, I would prefer more equality of income to less and would like complete equality best of all."[14] But he reluctantly concludes, like many others, that given the existence of a trade-off between equality and efficiency, society ought to forgo greater equality in favor of a healthy economy.[15]

Economic prosperity is determined in large measure by the degree to which investors invest and workers work. According to the equality-efficiency trade-off thesis, it is in these two areas that distributive equality hinders economic efficiency. Efforts to increase equality are said to reduce the quantity of funds available for investment and to dampen work incentives.[16]

Equalizing income involves giving more of the social product to those less well-off. It entails flattening compensation scales and/or redistributing income through taxation and government transfer programs. In the trade-off view, egalitarian institutional arrangements lessen society's supply of savings and investment. Corporations and affluent individuals have a high propensity to save and invest. Consequently, decreasing the income share of these sectors in favor of lower-income individuals, who tend to allocate a greater percentage of their earnings to consumption, will reduce the society's investment rate. In an essay on "The Tradeoff Between Growth and Equity," Kenneth Arrow remarks:

> It appears that savings by individuals is likely to rise more than proportionately with income. Hence total personal savings will fall as a result of redistribution. Further, to the extent that redistributive taxes fall on business institutions that form such a large part of the saving mechanism, there may again be a reduction in saving. . . . For these reasons, the aggregate volume of capital formation may fall as a consequence of redistribution.[17]

Equality, in effect, crowds out investment.

A similar logic is said to apply to work motivation. Work effort, according to the trade-off view, is directly determined by the prospect of pecuniary reward. To elicit hard work, substantial material payoff is required. David Hume once suggested that depriving people of this incentive by distributing the social product equally would "reduce society to the most extreme indigence, and instead of preventing want and beggary in a few, render it unavoidable to the whole community."[18] Work effort refers not only to the intensity and length of work but also to investments people make in human capital and new ideas. Engineers and other specially skilled employees must invest in years of schooling or skill training before they receive compensation. Entrepreneurs and inventors risk time, effort, and capital in creating and marketing new innovations. To encourage a sufficient quantity of individuals to make such investments, society must, it is asserted, offer a level of compensation above that of other jobs that require lesser investments. Correlatively, there needs to be a material punishment, in the form of reduced income, to discourage idleness and slack effort.[19] Absent significant material reward for success and punishment for failure, individuals cannot be effectively motivated to work hard.[20]

Few dispute the assertion that perfect equality in the distribution of income would result in substantial efficiency losses. Achieving complete distributive equality would virtually eliminate monetary incentives, which surely would substantially reduce work effort and investment. Consider, for instance, a society in which the social product is divided into an equal consumption allowance for each citizen. If the population were 10 million, the effective marginal tax rate on additional income would be 99.99999 percent, and an average earner who stopped working and investing entirely would reduce the value of his or her own consumption share by a mere 0.00001 percent.[21] Plainly, the disincentive to put forth extra effort, or any work effort at all, would be overwhelming.

But this claim is not particularly relevant to our understanding of actual, existing economies, for none has an income distribution even remotely approximating perfect equality.[22] The question is: What is the relationship between equality and efficiency at various levels of income equality? In particular, what are the efficiency effects of the current income distribution in developed economies?

The assertion that a trade-off exists between equality and efficiency is generally meant to be an empirical claim that efforts to increase equality involve a sacrifice of some efficiency, not merely a theoretical suggestion that a hypothetical state of perfect equality would be inefficient.[23] But there are reasons to suspect that equality's efficiency effects might be considerably less detrimental than assumed by the trade-off thesis, and perhaps even beneficial.

First, greater equality may increase and stabilize consumer demand, which may in turn boost investment. In focusing exclusively on the supply of funds available for investment, the crowding out thesis ignores variation in the incentives to invest. Rational actors do not simply invest whatever funds they have left after their consumption needs are fulfilled. They invest when they expect the payoff to exceed a return they could otherwise obtain from their funds. Plainly there are a variety of factors that affect the expected rate of return on any particular investment, but in aggregate terms one of the most influential components of the investment climate is consumer demand. As Keynes made clear long ago, if consumers are not buying, investors will see little reason to invest. Consumer demand and distributive equality are interrelated; in fact, the assumption behind the crowding out thesis points to this interrelation. Individuals in lower income groups have a high propensity to consume; by necessity, they spend a larger share of their income on consumption than do wealthy persons. Increasing the share of income accruing to the latter thus has a tendency to undercut consumer demand and may thereby lead to a reduction in investment.

This is not to imply that more equality necessarily leads to more investment. Consumer income levels are only one factor among several that determine consumer demand, and consumer demand is but one of the various components that determine the investment climate. Moreover, the investment climate is just one factor among several that determine the level of investment. The point is simply that in order to understand investment levels, it is necessary to look beyond the supply of funds. Augmented consumer demand may attenuate, or even outweigh, the crowding out effect (if one exists), and thereby mitigate or eliminate the asserted trade-off between income equality and investment.

The second consideration has to do with perceptions of fairness. Although some degree of inequality is surely necessary to spur work effort, excessive reward for effort or for investments in human capital may be viewed as unfair by those in the middle and at the bottom end of the distributive scale. This might lead to reduced motivation on their part, canceling out or even outweighing any extra effort put forth by those at the top. In other words, to be effective, work incentives must motivate individuals at all ends of the distributive spectrum. Otherwise, their net utility may be negligible or perhaps negative.

The point here is that the utility function for workers, as for all economic actors, extends beyond income and leisure. Beliefs and preferences are embedded in—that is to say, shaped by—a wide range of social institutions and norms.[24] Norms of fairness are likely to affect employee motivation, and it seems reasonable to suspect that the income distribution within firms and within nations has a bearing on the degree to which they are seen as being in compliance with such norms.[25] It is likely that fairness norms vary somewhat across countries.[26] A particular degree of income inequality may be viewed as less objectionable by, say, U.S. workers than by their Swedish counterparts. But if norms regarding income distribution differ less across countries than do levels of inequality, which seems quite possible, then differing levels of inequality could result in differing degrees of work effort.

Figure 3.1 illustrates—in highly stylized fashion—the three principal contending theses on the relationship between income equality and economic efficiency. Thesis (1) represents the trade-off view. Thesis (2) contends that equality has little impact on efficiency, although it admits a trade-off at high levels of equality. Thesis (3) depicts the heterodox view. It, too, suggests a sharp trade-off at high levels of equality. But it predicts exactly the opposite at lower levels; that is, relatively inegalitarian countries should be able to increase efficiency by increasing equality.

◈ Prior Research

Previous research on the relationship between equality and efficiency suffers from several flaws.

A host of studies have assessed the effect of tax and transfer programs on labor supply and saving patterns in the United States.[27] Many of these have found a negative impact of transfers, but the magnitude of the effect is unclear. More important, this research has not analyzed the impact of tax and transfer

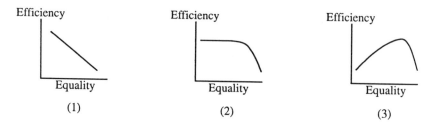

Figure 3.1   Equality and efficiency: Contending theses

programs on aggregate economic outcomes. Detrimental effects of equality on labor supply or savings may be so small as to have no influence on overall economic performance, or they may be offset by other positive effects of income equalization.

A number of studies have examined the relationship between transfer spending and economic performance across countries,[28] but the findings of this research have conflicted. And as we shall see (Figure 3.2 below), transfer spending is only modestly correlated with income equality, making it at best a questionable proxy. In addition, these studies focus exclusively on growth, which is only one component of economic performance.

A variety of studies have advanced the view that there is no trade-off between equality and efficiency.[29] But they have generally relied either on anecdotal evidence or on bivariate analyses that fail to control for relevant factors. And they, too, have tended to use economic growth as the lone performance measure.

The only careful empirical analysis of the relationship between income distribution and economic performance is a recent study by Torsten Persson and Guido Tabellini.[30] The authors examined the effect of inequality, measured as the pre-tax income share of the richest fifth of the population, on per capita growth in gross domestic product (GDP) during 20-year intervals between 1830 and 1985. For the nine developed countries for which such data were available, inequality was found to have a negative impact on growth. Persson and Tabellini also examined a group of 56 nations during the period 1960-1985, this time using the income share of the middle population quintile and relying on cross-sectional analysis. Once again the data indicated an association between inequality and slower growth. Persson and Tabellini's analysis, however, is limited by the fact that they use pre-tax income data of questionable reliability and that they too look only at economic growth.

Despite the issue's important policy implications, then, we know relatively little about the empirical relationship between equality and efficiency in developed market economies.

◈ A Note on Data and Method

To get an empirical handle on this question we can look at comparative country data on the relationship between income equality and various components of economic performance. The aspects of performance most directly at issue in the trade-off thesis are investment and productivity. These are reasonable proxies for, respectively, the willingness of investors to invest and of workers to work. I also consider productivity growth, output growth, trade performance, inflation, and unemployment as further indicators of performance success. After investigating the effects of income equality, I examine the impact on economic performance of two indicators of equal opportunity: unemployment levels and gender equality in job access. Finally, I look briefly at recent developments in the United States.

Descriptions and sources for all quantitative data used in this and the following chapters are listed in Appendix A.

Seventeen nations are included: Australia, Austria, Belgium, Canada, Denmark, Finland, France, Germany, Italy, Japan, the Netherlands, New Zealand, Norway, Sweden, Switzerland, the United Kingdom, and the United States. These countries were chosen to control for level of economic development; included are all members of the Organization for Economic Cooperation and Development (OECD)[31] that throughout the 1960-1990 period had a level of per capita GDP at least 50 percent as large as that of the world's richest nation (the United States or Switzerland, depending on the year).[32]

The analysis is cross-sectional. That is, I compare data across countries using period averages.[33] Because of the limited data available for income equality (discussed below), the analysis here is confined to the period 1974-1990. Later in the chapter, when I turn to equality of opportunity, I examine the entire 1960-1990 period. The same is true of Chapters 4, 5, and 6.

I present the data initially in the form of scatterplot charts. In each chart one of the variables is equality (horizontal axis) and the other is a measure of economic performance (vertical axis). The data points in these charts represent averages for each particular country during the time period in question. Each chart also has a "best-fit" line that describes the relationship between the variables. The steeper the slope of the line, the stronger the association between the variables; the flatter the line, the weaker the relationship. I also list the correlation coefficient (r) for each pair of variables. This figure is a simple statistical measure of the degree to which the variables are associated.[34] The closer the correlation is to 1 (or –1 for inversely related variables), the stronger the association; the closer it is to 0, the weaker the relationship. Later on I turn to regression analysis.

How do we know whether a relationship between two variables is a meaningful one or just a result of chance? After all, any two sets of numbers selected randomly are likely to show *some* association. The likelihood of a result due strictly to chance is accentuated when the number of data points is small, as is the case here. To avoid reaching false conclusions, social scientists typically require that there be no more than a 10 percent probability that an association between variables is due to chance; those that satisfy this requirement are deemed "statistically significant." In statistical lingo, we say they are "significant at the 10 percent level." With 17 cases, the correlation coefficient must be at least .32 (or –.32) to be significant at this level; with fewer cases, the coefficient must be higher. This is for a so-called "one-tailed" test of significance, which is used when theoretical considerations suggest a particular direction to the relationship.[35] I will indicate significant correlations with an asterisk (*). (Significance at the 5 percent and 1 percent levels will be denoted by two and three asterisks, respectively.) Social scientists are prone to fetishize significance levels. It is important to understand that the 10 percent probability requirement is an arbitrary one. Correlation or regression coefficients that do not meet this requirement may nevertheless be genuine; we merely have less confidence that they are.

The best available data on income distribution come from the World Bank, which reports the shares of national income accounted for by quintiles of households in our countries.[36] These data are derived from random surveys of each country's population, administered by the national statistical authority in the individual nations. The figures cover total after-tax household income, including wages and salaries, self-employed income, investment income, property income, and current public and private transfers. Unrealized capital gains income is not included.[37]

The earliest and only year for which data are available for the full set of countries is 1980. (The actual year varies slightly from country to country.) I use the 1980 figures as proxies for the average level of equality obtaining in each nation during the entire period from 1974 to 1990, under the assumption that relative levels of equality did not change appreciably during those years. Some fluctuation of the income distribution within each nation undoubtedly occurs. Developments in the United States, discussed later in the chapter, illus-

Table 3.1 Income Equality, Circa 1980

| | Year | Share of Household Income | | Poor/Rich Quintile Ratio |
		Poorest Fifth %	Richest Fifth %	
Japan	1979	8.7	37.5	.232
Netherlands	1981	8.3	36.2	.229
Belgium	1979	7.9	36.0	.219
Sweden	1981	8.0	36.9	.217
Germany	1978	7.9	39.5	.200
Switzerland	1978	6.6	38.0	.174
Norway	1979	6.2	36.7	.169
Finland	1981	6.3	37.6	.168
France	1979	6.3	40.8	.154
Italy	1977/86[a]	6.5	42.4	.153
United Kingdom	1979	5.8	39.5	.147
Denmark	1981	5.4	38.6	.140
Canada	1981	5.3	40.0	.133
United States	1980	5.3	39.9	.133
New Zealand	1981	5.1	44.7	.114
Austria	1980	5.5	49.7	.111
Australia	1975/85[a]	4.9	44.7	.110

NOTE: For data sources see Appendix A.
a. Figures are averages for the years listed.

trate this. The question, however, is whether these fluctuations alter a country's level of equality relative to that in other countries. It seems likely that there has been some alteration in relative levels during the past two decades, but I assume the changes were sufficiently modest so as not to substantially affect the results of the analysis. Comparison with the limited World Bank data available for earlier years suggests that this assumption is a reasonable one. In addition, cross-country variation in wage dispersion and government transfer spending, both of which contribute to income distribution trends, appears to have been relatively stable during the 1970s and 1980s.[38]

The measure of equality used here is the share of national income accruing to the poorest 20 percent (quintile) of households divided by that going to the richest 20 percent.[39] Table 3.1 shows these income shares and the corresponding quintile ratio figure for income equality for our 17 nations.

As Figure 3.2 suggests, there are two principal ways in which countries attempt to equalize income.[40] First, payment scales within and across firms can be flattened, so that the variation in citizens' pre-tax income is low. This

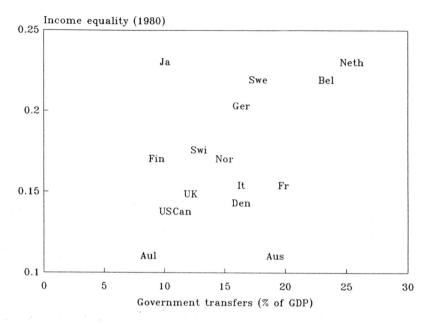

Figure 3.2 Government transfers and equality, 1974-90
NOTE: Correlation = .42. For data sources see Appendix A.

is the primary mechanism through which Japan has achieved its level of distributive equality, which is the best among developed nations according to the quintile ratio measure.[41] The second means of equalizing distributive outcomes is via taxation and government transfers. Progressive taxation and extensive social and welfare programs are the chief instruments used by countries such as the Netherlands, Belgium, and Sweden, which are next behind Japan in their degree of income equality. In Japan, by contrast, government transfers are minimal. France and Austria also spend a large fraction of national income on welfare and social programs, but their pre-tax income differential is rather severe, so their after-tax level of equality is very low. Countries such as Australia, Canada, and the United States feature wide differences in compensation along with minimal transfer spending; consequently they are among the least egalitarian of industrialized nations.

Let us see, then, what the evidence has to say regarding the relationship between equality and efficiency.

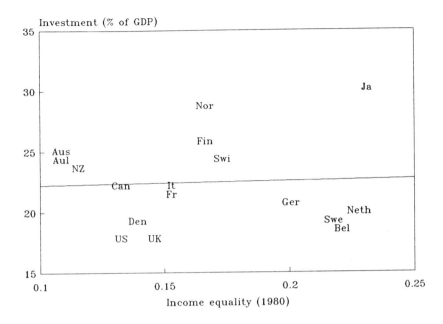

Figure 3.3 Equality and investment, 1974-90

NOTE: Correlation = .04. For data sources see Appendix A.

◑ The Comparative Record

Equality and Investment

Does income equality crowd out investment? One provisional means of assessing the crowding out thesis is to look at the relationship between equality and savings across countries. If variation in the share of income accruing to the well-to-do is a key determinant of differences in national savings rates, we should find equality to be negatively associated with savings. But that is not the case. The correlation between equality and gross savings for our 17 countries from 1974 to 1990 is positive, not negative ($r = .30$).[42]

Figure 3.3 shows the relationship between equality and investment during the period 1974-1990.[43] As the chart reveals, developed economies have not experienced a trade-off between equality and investment. The comparative evidence with regard to investment does not appear to support the equality-efficiency trade-off thesis.

Equality and Work Effort

What about work effort? Here again there is reason for skepticism toward the assertion that equality has detrimental effects. Surveys and econometric studies suggest that differential marginal tax rates have relatively little impact on work effort.[44] In the face of higher taxes, individuals, especially those with higher incomes, often maintain their present work patterns or work more in order to sustain their previous standard of living. Sometimes labor supply decreases, but the loss tends to be minimal. Income transfers have been found to reduce the supply of labor, both because nonearned income increases and because, in many programs, transfer payments are reduced as earnings from work rise. But again the labor supply effect is not large.[45] Because progressive tax and transfer programs are a key component of egalitarian measures in many countries, their apparent lack of substantial negative impact on labor supply suggests a potential compatibility between equality and strong work effort. Although the issue here primarily concerns marginal differences in the amount of work effort individuals put forward, it is also worth noting that the correlation between income equality and labor force participation for our 17 countries during the period 1974-1990 is –.09, which suggests little if any relationship between a country's income distribution and the rate at which its citizens participate in the paid labor force.

The best available indicator of work effort is labor productivity, defined as output (GDP) per worker. In assessing the effects of various causal factors on productivity, the analysis throughout the book is confined to the 1974-1990 period. Pre-1973 productivity levels were largely a function of prior development and World War II devastation. In addition, relying on exchange rates to compare levels of output can be misleading, because exchange rates often inaccurately represent the real purchasing power of money in different nations. The OECD has developed a set of "purchasing power parities" to correct for this problem, but they are available only for the 1970s and 1980s.

Differences in output per worker may stem in part from differences in the amount of capital available to work with. Hence, ideally we would like a measure of output per labor *and* capital input. Unfortunately, data on capital stock levels are available for only 11 of our countries.[46] As it turns out, the correlation between capital stock per worker and labor productivity for these 11 nations during 1974-1990 is only .13, suggesting that capital stock levels may account for only a very small portion of cross-national differences in productivity. For this reason, I proceed using labor productivity as a proxy for work effort—that is, without controlling for capital stock—with the proviso that the results should be treated with caution.

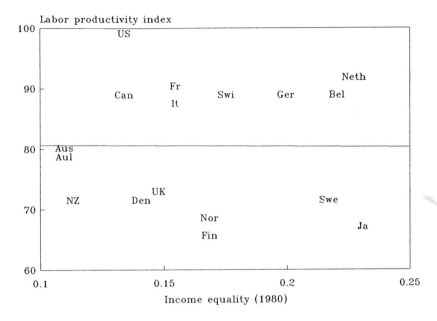

Figure 3.4 Equality and productivity, 1974-90

NOTE: Correlation = –.01. For data sources see Appendix A.

Figure 3.4 shows the comparative evidence on the relationship between equality and labor productivity. Although one of the least egalitarian countries, the United States, has the highest average level of productivity, overall there is no association between the two variables. The data suggest, in other words, that differences in income distribution across developed nations may well have no effect on work effort.

Equality and Other Performance Indicators

Let's turn now to some other indicators of economic performance. Perhaps these will reveal the heretofore hidden accuracy of the trade-off argument. If equality reduces investment and work effort, as the trade-off thesis suggests, then it should also negatively affect other aspects of performance. The evidence does not appear to support these assertions, however, so we should not expect to discover such a pattern.

Indeed, there is reason to suspect that greater equality may be associated with *better* performance. By stabilizing consumer demand, it may help to reduce the intensity and duration of business cycle downturns. The demand-accentuating impact of equality may also lead to stronger growth in an economy without necessarily increasing the ratio of investment to GDP. Healthy demand may encourage higher rates of investment, in turn leading to increased output and sales. In these circumstances investment as a share of national output would remain constant, but the economy's growth rate would be higher.

Perhaps more important is the role of fairness, discussed earlier. As R. H. Tawney observed in his classic treatise on equality: "Efficiency rests ultimately on psychological foundations. It depends, not merely on mechanical adjustments, but on the intelligent collaboration of contentious human beings, whom hunger may make work, but mutual confidence alone can enable to cooperate."[47] Egalitarian distributive arrangements may foster a greater willingness on the part of the workforce to do what is necessary to succeed in international competition—for example, flexible adjustment of production to new demand patterns, accommodation to the introduction of productivity-enhancing technology, sacrifice of present consumption in favor of investment and market share. If widespread, these sorts of actions could lead to faster growth, better trade performance, and lower inflation and unemployment.

The best indicator of economic progress is productivity growth. Consistent with the above hypothesis, the cross-national evidence displayed in Figure 3.5 shows a clear and statistically significant positive relationship between equality and productivity growth during the 1974-1990 period.[48] If anything, greater equality appears to contribute to productivity growth, not to retard it.

Along with productivity growth, growth of output—generally referred to simply as economic growth—is the most widely used indicator of economic success. The measure used here is growth of real GDP per capita. A per capita measure is a better indicator of advance in living standards than the simple measure of growth often used in economic analysis. (Unless otherwise noted, all figures for growth throughout the book refer to the per capita measure.) Figure 3.6 shows that growth provides no support for the trade-off thesis. Its association with equality for our 17 countries is again positive, although the correlation is weaker than that for productivity growth and is not significant.

What about trade performance? National trade balances (defined as the value of exports minus that of imports, as a share of GDP) are considered by some to be the indicator par excellence of economic competitiveness.[49] Given that trade now amounts to 25 to 50 percent of GDP in most developed countries, successful performance is indeed determined to an increasing

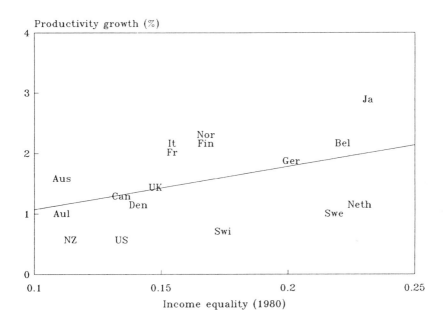

Figure 3.5   Equality and productivity growth, 1974-90

Note: Correlation = .43, significant at the 5% level. For data sources see Appendix A.

degree by how well a nation fares in direct competition with its foreign rivals. Proponents of the trade-off thesis will find no solace in the evidence regarding trade balances. As Figure 3.7 shows, the association between equality and trade performance is very strongly positive. Nations with greater equality have tended to fare better in maintaining a healthy trade balance.

Next, let's look at inflation. If distributive equality does indeed buoy consumer demand, as suggested earlier, the possibility exists that its impact will be too strong, resulting in too much spending chasing too few goods—the classic conditions of demand-pull inflation. On the other hand, to the extent that the workforce perceives the income distribution as relatively fair, egalitarian countries may be less vulnerable to cost-push inflation caused by wage hikes that exceed productivity increases. The correlation between equality and nominal wage changes in the manufacturing sector (the only sector for which longitudinal data on wages are available) during 1974-1990 is −.38*, suggesting an association between equality and wage restraint. Not surprisingly, then, Figure 3.8 reveals that the more egalitarian countries have had better success

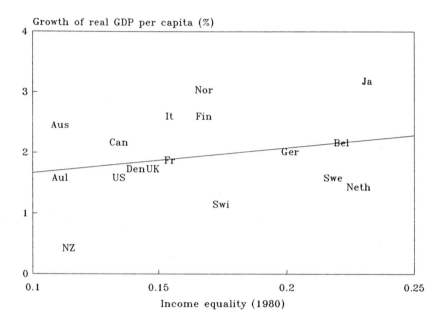

Figure 3.6 Equality and growth, 1974-90

NOTE: Correlation = .25. For data sources see Appendix A.

at keeping price increases in check, whereas those with less equality have suffered higher inflation levels.

A final indicator to consider is unemployment. As Figure 3.9 shows, most of the countries with less income equality feature consistently high rates of unemployment, whereas several of those with more egalitarian income distributions have achieved low unemployment levels.[50] There are some exceptions to this pattern, however, and the correlation between the two variables is weak. We may thus surmise that there is probably no genuine relationship between income equality and joblessness.

◙ Three Objections

At this point, the skeptical reader might understandably wish to press three important objections, each suggesting that the conclusions I have drawn from the data here are erroneous. The first potential complaint is that the analysis has been

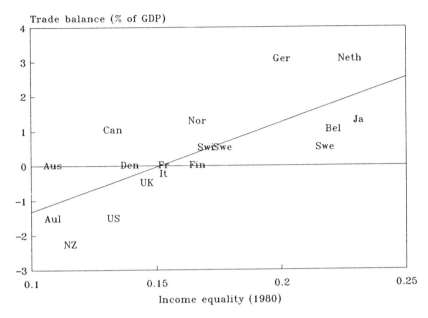

Figure 3.7 Equality and trade performance, 1974-90

NOTE: Correlation = .74, significant at the 1% level. For data sources see Appendix A.

biased by Japan's extraordinary performance during the past three decades. In particular, Japan's rates of investment, productivity growth, and output growth have been much higher than those of any other developed nation. For this reason, Japan should perhaps be considered a statistical outlier and discarded from the data pool. What would the data show if Japan were excluded? Table 3.2 lists the correlation coefficients with and without Japan. The change does make a difference. The coefficients for investment and unemployment switch sign, and those for productivity growth and output growth are smaller.

Still, these results offer little in the way of support for the trade-off thesis. Although negative, the correlation between equality and investment is not statistically significant. Hence we cannot confidently reject the possibility that it is due to chance. The same is certainly true for unemployment. The coefficient for labor productivity turns positive, and those for productivity growth and output growth remain so. Furthermore, the direction and magnitude of equality's association with trade performance and with inflation are not affected by the exclusion of Japan.

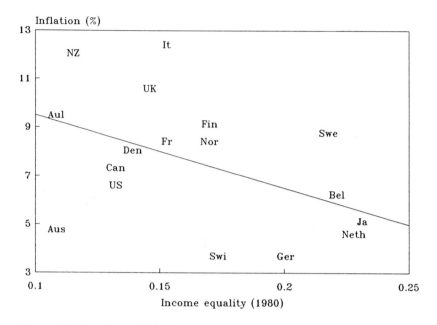

Figure 3.8 Equality and inflation, 1974-90
NOTE: Correlation = –.46, significant at the 5% level. For data sources see Appendix A.

Second, it may be objected that evidence supporting the trade-off thesis is hidden by my failure to control for other factors that affect economic performance. To see if this is the case, we can examine regression equations in which equality and other relevant variables are used to predict our performance indicators.[51] A regression equation is simply an equation for a best-fit line through a set of data points.[52] It can be constructed with any number of independent, or predictor, variables. Here the equations take the following form:

$$\text{Economic performance} = \text{constant} + B_1 \text{ equality} + B_2 X_2$$
$$+ B_3 X_3 + \ldots + B_i X_i$$

X_2, X_3, and so on represent factors that might be expected to influence national economic performance. We are interested here in B_1, the coefficient for equality. Like correlation coefficients, regression coefficients tell us the direction and strength of the relationship between an independent variable (in our case, income equality) and a dependent variable (economic performance).

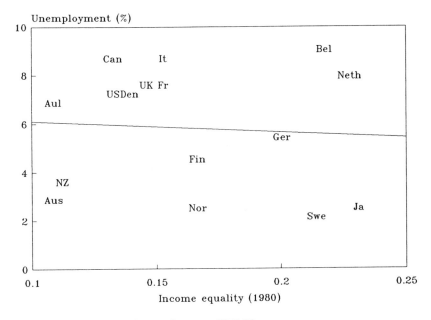

Figure 3.9 Equality and unemployment, 1974-90

NOTE: Correlation = −.08. For data sources see Appendix A.

Table 3.2 Equality and Economic Performance, 1974-90: Correlations With and Without Japan

	Including Japan	*Excluding Japan*
Investment	.04	−.27
Productivity	−.01	.14
Productivity growth	.43**	.28
Growth	.25	.08
Trade balance	.74***	.75***
Inflation	−.46**	−.41*
Unemployment[a]	−.08	.10

NOTE: For variable definitions and data sources, see Appendix A.
a. Switzerland is not included due to lack of data on unemployment.
* significant at the 10% level; ** 5% level; *** 1% level.

By including other variables in the equation, we can determine the effect of equality on performance outcomes holding these additional factors constant. Of course, numerous factors influence each of our performance indicators. It is neither possible nor desirable to include all of them in the equations here.[53] I include only those that theoretical considerations or empirical findings strongly suggest to be relevant, and that do not represent pathways through which equality might have its effect.[54]

Real interest rates are included in the equations for investment, productivity and output growth, and unemployment. High interest rates indicate, to a large extent, a policy choice in favor of price stability. They reduce the demand for investment and may thereby dampen growth and heighten unemployment.[55]

To control for the "catch-up" effect, I include a variable in the equations for investment, productivity growth, and output growth representing each country's level of per capita GDP in 1974. By copying the technological advances of leader nations, less developed countries are able to grow more quickly with similar levels of investment and work effort.[56] Faster growth of income in turn makes possible higher investment levels, and less developed nations may invest at higher rates in any case in an attempt to catch up.

The only control variable added to the equation for productivity levels is unemployment. As we shall see later in this chapter, there are theoretical reasons to suspect that the level of unemployment is positively related to work effort.

Trade performance is likely to be influenced by dependence on the world market. Economic actors in countries heavily reliant on exports and imports may be more willing and able to flexibly accommodate changing demand patterns; such nations might thereby prove more successful in international trade.[57] On the other hand, countries with large domestic markets (e.g., the United States, Japan, Germany) may be able to achieve strong trade balances by using the importance of their home markets for smaller export-dependent nations to manipulate the terms of international trade in their favor. Whichever of these hypotheses is more accurate, we would like to know the effect of equality on trade performance net of degrees of economic openness. I therefore include a variable in this equation representing each nation's average of exports and imports as a share of GDP.

The equation for inflation includes a variable representing the rate of unemployment. According to a prominent line of economic thought expressed in the Phillips Curve, nations confront a trade-off between unemployment and inflation. Low unemployment fosters wage militancy by reducing the cost of job loss to workers, thereby contributing to cost-push inflation.[58]

Over the long run, inflation is a function of money supply increases that exceed the growth of production.[59] Presumably, then, a variable should be included in

Table 3.3 Equality and Economic Performance, 1974-90: Coefficients for Regression
Equations With Control Variables

	Including Japan	*Excluding Japan*
Investment	.04	−.22
Productivity[a]	.03	.07
Productivity growth	.37**	.31*
Growth	.17	.08
Trade balance	.67***	.67***
Inflation[a]	−.46**	−.41*
Unemployment[a]	−.17	−.02

NOTE: Coefficients are standardized. For variable definitions and data sources, see Appendix A.
a. Switzerland is not included due to lack of data on unemployment.
* 10% level; ** 5% level; *** 1% level.

the equation for inflation representing change in the money supply. But actually, that depends on the view one holds regarding the causes of money supply growth. According to orthodox economic logic, monetary authorities determine the rate of money supply increase autonomously. If so, it is necessary to control for money supply changes in the analysis. An alternative view is that central bank decisions regarding the money supply tend to be made in response to economic trends, such as changes in wages or investment demand.[60] For instance, in order to avoid a recession, monetary authorities may be forced to accommodate wage militancy by permitting a substantial expansion of the money supply. A careful empirical study of money supply patterns in 12 of our countries finds considerable support for this interpretation.[61] This suggests that institutional factors such as income equality will affect inflation in part *via* changes in the money supply. I thus estimate the equation for inflation both with and without a variable representing change in the money supply.[62]

Along with the real interest rate, the equation for unemployment includes a variable controlling for labor force participation. Nations with low levels of labor force participation should, all else being equal, be able to achieve lower rates of joblessness. Then again, high levels of labor force participation may encourage countries to implement measures, such as active labor market policy, to reduce friction in the job matching process and assure effective integration of their citizens into paid work.

Table 3.3 presents the regression results. It shows the standardized coefficients for equality in the equations. Like correlation coefficients, these typically range between 0 and 1 (or −1 for inversely related variables). The equations were calculated first with Japan included and then with it omitted.

The coefficient for investment is very small and again turns negative when Japan is excluded. The correlation and regression results with Japan omitted from the data thus suggest that higher levels of equality indeed may have a detrimental effect on investment rates. In neither case is the coefficient close to statistical significance, however, which means that this apparent association could well be a result of chance. For productivity the regression coefficient is positive but nonsignificant with or without Japan included. This is consistent with the correlation evidence in indicating no impact of equality on work effort.

For productivity growth and output growth the coefficients remain positive, and the former is statistically significant whether or not Japan is included. This suggests that, controlling for the catch-up effect and interest rates, equality is associated with stronger productivity growth. Adding the control variables has no effect at all on equality's relationship with trade performance. The coefficients retain their positive sign and remain significant at the 1 percent level irrespective of Japan's inclusion. For unemployment, the coefficients remain negative, suggesting that if equality affects the rate of unemployment at all, it does so in a beneficial way. But here the coefficients are relatively small and not significant.

The results for inflation are shown with the money supply variable left out of the regression equation. The coefficient is negative and significant whether or not Japan is included. With the money supply variable added, the equality coefficient remains negative but is no longer significant. Equality is associated with slow money supply growth during the 1974-1990 period ($r = -.37*$). A plausible interpretation of developments during these years is therefore the following: Equality induced wage moderation, enabling monetary authorities to pursue a sustained tight money policy, which resulted in low inflation rates in egalitarian countries. Alternatively, central banks in the more egalitarian nations may have made autonomous decisions in favor of tight money, thereby forcing wage restraint. But why would monetary authorities in egalitarian countries be more likely than those in less egalitarian nations to pursue such a policy? Is this simply a random correlation? Probably not. Central banks should be more prone to choose a policy of tight money if they have confidence that wage earners will cooperate by restraining wage demands, and income equality offers workers an incentive for such cooperation. Thus, regardless of the exact causal chain, there is good reason to suspect that differences in income distribution have had real effects on cross-national variation in inflation rates.

On the whole, these findings are relatively consistent in rejecting the thesis of a trade-off between equality and efficiency. Most of the correlation and regression coefficients for income equality have the opposite sign to that predicted by the trade-off thesis, and those with the predicted sign are small and not statistically significant.

A third potential objection to these findings is one of reverse causality. I have assumed a particular direction of causality between the variables, but the causal relationship could in fact lie in the opposite direction. It is conceivable that, instead of equality supporting successful performance, the reverse is true.[63] In other words, the findings here may reflect the fact that those countries that have performed well economically during the past two decades have been better able to equalize the distribution of income. Evidence confirming the trade-off thesis could be hidden by this process. The plausibility of reverse causality is heightened by the fact that income equality is measured at only a single point in time, and in the middle of the period being anayzed.

Looking at numbers can tell us little, if anything, about the direction of causality between two variables. Yet there *is* a way to get a handle on this issue. If strong economic performance leads countries to distribute income more equally, rather than the other way around, we would expect the richest nations to be more egalitarian and the poorest to be less so. Figure 3.10 shows that this is not the case. The chart plots national wealth (an index of GDP per capita) with income equality for our 17 countries for the year 1980.[64] Contrary to the reverse causality hypothesis, the data indicate that several of the richest countries are among the least egalitarian (the United States, Canada) and some of the least wealthy are among the most equitable (particularly Japan). Overall, there is no relationship between wealth and income distribution. It is unlikely, then, that my findings are muted by this objection.

Based on the available data, then, I conclude that greater distributive equality than presently exists in most, if not all, developed countries is compatible with an efficient, successful national economy. And some of the evidence suggests that increasing equality might well *enhance* performance in a number of nations.

◈ Equal Opportunity

Let's push a little further. To this point I have been concerned exclusively with equality in the distribution of income. Yet when people speak of equality they often refer not to end-state equality, but to equality of opportunity. Indeed, as an ethical principle, this latter conception of equality has enjoyed much wider acceptance, at least in the United States, than has distributive equality.

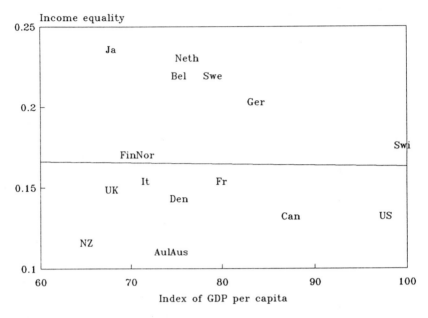

Figure 3.10 National wealth and equality, 1980

NOTE: Correlation = –.02. For data sources see Appendix A.

What does equal opportunity consist of? That is not an easily answerable question, but I submit that its central component is equal access to jobs. To say that individuals have an equal chance in life is to suggest, in large part, that they have comparable chances of obtaining well-paying, satisfying work.[65]

Equalizing opportunity can be a costly and market-eclipsing process. Therein lies the chief potential source of conflict between equality of opportunity and economic efficiency. Reducing jobless rates, for example, typically requires government funding for public employment schemes or for incentives to elicit increased hiring by the private sector. Funding for training, retraining, and job search services is also critical to equalizing access to jobs. Equalizing access to education entails redistributing funds from wealthier schools and school systems to poorer ones and perhaps also raising the level of spending on education in order to provide a level chance for the less advantaged. These measures involve higher levels of government spending and/or government efforts to redistribute finances. In the market liberal view, such government meddling often reduces efficiency. In addition, low unemployment levels may reduce incentives for hard work. And equalizing job opportunities between women and men and among racial or ethnic groups may require some type of affirmative action policy, which diminishes firms' freedom and flexibility. For these reasons, the market liberal perspective tends to assume, if only implicitly, a trade-off between equal opportunity—or, more accurately, the process of equalizing opportunity—and economic efficiency.

On the other hand, a number of economic advantages stem from conditions of equal opportunity. Most important, talents and skills are wasted when access to education and high-paying jobs is asymmetrically distributed. Institutionalized inequities—such as sustained involuntary unemployment, unequal pay for women and men, and unequal educational opportunity—discourage individuals from making investments in human capital and prevent society from taking full advantage of its human resources.[66] In addition, barriers to opportunity contribute to "the poverty and the social alienation that breed drug use and criminality and, in turn, divert significant resources to the unproductive tasks of guard labor."[67] It is quite possible that, on the whole, the beneficial effects of measures to equalize opportunity may offset or even outweigh the potential costs.

To assess the relationship between equal opportunity and economic performance, it will help to operationalize the notion of equal access to jobs in a set of measurable indicators. I look at two here: general access to employment (rates of unemployment) and gender equality in labor market access (pay comparability between women and men and female labor force participation). These by no means cover everything that is meant by equal access to jobs, but they get at a good bit of what is embodied in that notion. The figures are shown in Table 3.4 and explained below. As before, I compare national averages for each indicator of equality with various measures of economic performance—investment, productivity, productivity growth, output growth, trade balances, inflation, and unemployment. Here the time period covered extends back to 1960. To avoid overloading the text with an unwieldy mass of charts, in this section I include only a few scattergrams. For the most part I show only the correlation and regression coefficients.

Job opportunity undoubtedly depends in part on educational opportunity. Equal access to education requires, most fundamentally, equalizing the quantity and quality of educational resources available to students.[68] Unfortunately, there is no satisfactory indicator of equal educational opportunity for which comparative data exist. One possibility is the share of the adult population with a secondary school degree. In many nations, however, a nontrivial share of adults receive their principal education and training through vocational training and/or apprenticeship programs. There is little reason to

Table 3.4   Equality of Opportunity, 1960-90

	Unemployment %	Female/Male Pay Ratio[a]	Female Labor Force Participation[b] %
Australia	4.5	.76	48.3
Austria	2.3	na	51.0
Belgium	6.0	.69	43.7
Canada	6.9	.61[c]	50.3
Denmark	4.4	.81	63.3
Finland	3.4	.73	67.0
France	4.9	.86[d]	51.1
Germany	3.4	.71	51.1
Italy	7.2	na	37.8
Japan	1.8	.51	56.1
Netherlands	4.8	.73	33.9
New Zealand	1.9	.68	43.0
Norway	2.0	.78	53.2
Sweden	2.0	.83	66.4
Switzerland	na	.67	53.8
United Kingdom	4.9	.64	54.6
United States	6.0	.61[c]	54.2

NOTE: For data sources see Appendix A. na = not available.
a. Average for the years 1965, 1975, and 1985 in manufacturing.
b. As a percent of women ages 16-64.
c. All workers.
d. Nonagricultural employment.

think that this method is a less effective form of job preparation than completing secondary school; indeed, it may be more effective. Secondary school graduation rates are thus a misleading guide to equality of educational opportunity. We could, perhaps, add together the shares of secondary school graduates and participants in vocational training or apprenticeship programs, but reliable comparative data on the latter do not exist.

Another potential indicator is the degree of disparity in funding among schools. Money isn't everything in education, but it does matter a great deal.[69] Unfortunately, we lack comprehensive data on the extent to which educational resources are equally distributed within countries. Available figures for the United States suggest a rather wide disparity in funding among schools and school districts.[70] But we have no useful measure of the overall degree of inequality in this distribution within the country as a whole. Nor are comparable data for any such measure available for other nations. As a substitute, we might consider total educational expenditures as a share of GDP. But higher levels of spending are by no means necessarily related to egalitarianism in spending.

Let us move on, then, to employment access. Recent new Keynesian theorizing suggests that a low unemployment level diminishes the incentive to work hard and, in so doing, dampens productivity. As Carl Shapiro and Joseph Stiglitz put it:

> Under the conventional competitive paradigm, in which workers receive the market wage and there is no unemployment, the worst that can happen to a worker who shirks on the job is that he is fired. Since he can immediately be rehired, however, he pays no penalty for his misdemeanor. With imperfect monitoring and full employment, therefore, workers will choose to shirk. . . . The equilibrium unemployment rate must be sufficiently large that it pays workers to work rather than to take the risk of being caught shirking.[71]

This view is shared by neo-Marxian economists. According to Thomas Weisskopf:

> The threat of the "sack" serves as the basic and ultimate means whereby capitalists can assure control over workers at the workplace as well as the bargaining table. If unemployment is relatively high, the threat of job loss provides employers with an effective device to discipline workers. Conversely, if labour markets are relatively tight and unemployment relatively low, the greater ease of finding alternative employment opportunities puts workers in a stronger position to resist efforts by their employers to speed up the pace of work or in other ways to increase work intensity.[72]

Empirical studies of U.S. industry tend to support this view.[73]

As Figure 3.11 shows, the comparative evidence appears to do so as well. High average unemployment is strongly associated with higher productivity levels. It is plausible to interpret this correlation as owing partly to a voluntary choice on the part of nations such as Sweden, Norway, and Japan. Guaranteeing (something like) full employment on a consistent basis is bound to reduce an economy's average productivity level because, at least during economic downturns, a certain share of those employed must inevitably be redundant. They are kept employed simply for the sake of keeping them employed, because Sweden and other similar nations view employment security as important for economic, political, and/or moral reasons. Hence, the extent to which lower productivity levels indicate lesser work effort among the bulk of the workforce in these countries is not clear. It is also worth noting that there is a strong inverse relationship between

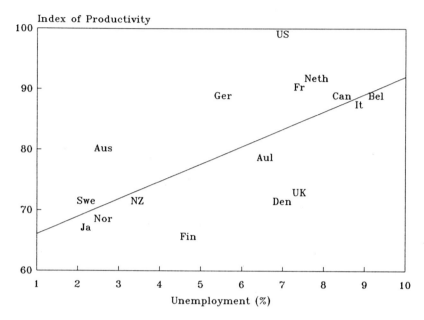

Figure 3.11 Unemployment and productivity, 1974-90

NOTE: Correlation = .66, significant at the 1% level. For data sources see Appendix A.

unemployment and labor force participation ($r = -.47**$), which suggests that even if equal access to jobs does reduce work intensity, it nevertheless may encourage a greater number of citizens to work.

What about growth of productivity? Here there is less reason to expect an equality-efficiency trade-off. New technology (machinery and modes of work organization) is one of the principal sources of productivity advance, but it also frequently threatens to eliminate jobs. Where the jobless rate is high, workers and unions may thus be more likely to oppose technological innovation. In a context of low unemployment, new jobs are more easily found, making the workforce less hostile toward implementation of new technology.

On the other hand, Gosta Esping-Andersen has argued that low unemployment enhances the economic and political power of the labor movement and thereby fosters wage militancy, which in turn discourages investment and reduces growth. Advanced capitalist economies thus "appear to converge in the incapability of ensuring both full employment and balanced economic growth."[74] This suggests that we might indeed discover a trade-off.

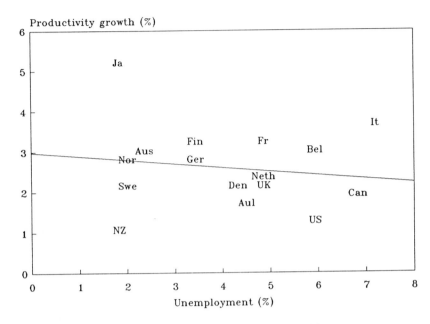

Figure 3.12 Unemployment and productivity growth, 1960-90

NOTE: Correlation = −.17. For data sources see Appendix A.

Figure 3.12 reveals that, in comparative terms, there is no apparent effect of unemployment on productivity growth. Japan features low unemployment and rapid productivity growth, whereas in New Zealand a low jobless rate coexists with very slow growth of productivity. The United States and Canada have had high unemployment and poor productivity growth, whereas Italy has achieved strong productivity growth with a very high level of joblessness. Most of the other countries fall somewhere in the middle. The correlation is negative but not statistically significant. With Japan omitted it turns positive but again is not significant. (Reliable unemployment data are not available for Switzerland, so it is not included here.)

Thomas Weisskopf has analyzed the relationship between these two variables using longitudinal data from 1958 to 1985 for the manufacturing sector in eight of our countries.[75] He finds that, over time, unemployment is positively associated with productivity growth in the United States, but negatively associated in Germany and Sweden. In Britain, Canada, France, Italy, and Japan the association is negative but not statistically significant. Weisskopf concludes, reasonably, that the effect of unemployment on productivity growth depends on the broader industrial relations context within the particular country:

> Where private and public institutions afford workers some influence over economic decision making and a significant degree of security, it is low rather than high unemployment that appears most likely to sustain high levels and rates of growth of productivity.[76]

What about the effect of unemployment on other aspects of economic performance? Table 3.5 shows the correlation and regression coefficients for the relationships between unemployment rates and our other performance indicators. For growth, trade performance, and inflation, no meaningful association in either direction is evident. The coefficients for inflation hide patterns that differ for the pre- and post-oil shock periods. A trade-off obtained during 1960-1973 ($r = -.48**$), but not during 1974-1990 ($r = .09$). The former is consistent with the traditional Keynesian notion of a Phillips Curve, whereas the latter appears to support the view of monetarist and new classical economists that no such curve exists.[77] The lack of a trade-off during the past two decades may result from a process whereby, in exchange for low unemployment, workers in some countries are willing to forgo demands for high wage increases, thus preventing the cost-push inflation predicted by the Phillips Curve.[78] Other factors having to do with the size and structure of the labor movement, which I address in Chapter 5, may also play a role in this result. As we shall see there, it was actually only in the 1974-1979 period that an unemployment-inflation trade-off was absent. During the 1980s the Phillips Curve appears to have returned.

For investment there is a strong negative correlation, suggesting that low unemployment is conducive to high levels of investment. The association holds up if Japan is omitted and if interest rates and the catch-up effect are controlled for. Esping-Andersen is correct to suggest that a low jobless rate encourages wage militancy, as we will see in Chapter 5. But that effect may be outweighed by reduced employee opposition to new technology, resulting in higher investment rates.

On the whole, then, the comparative evidence suggests that equal access to jobs is negatively related to work effort but positively associated with investment. It appears that these effects offset one another, so that unemployment has no impact on growth of productivity or output. Nor is there any relationship between unemployment and trade performance. Low unemployment does contribute to higher inflation, but I defer discussion of this issue to Chapter 5.

Table 3.5   Unemployment and Economic Performance, 1960-90: Correlation and
Regression Coefficients

	Correlation Coefficients		*Regression Coefficients*	
	Including Japan	*Excluding Japan*	*Including Japan*	*Excluding Japan*
Investment	−.55*	−.46**	−.44**	−.41*
Productivity[a]	.66***	.62***	.66***	.62***
Productivity growth	−.17	.08	.02	.18
Growth	−.13	.21	.01	.26
Trade balance	0	.08	−.03	.11
Inflation[b]	.01	−.04	.08	.03

NOTE: Switzerland is not included due to lack of data on unemployment. Regression coefficients are standardized. Regression equations include several control variables. For variable definitions and data sources, see Appendix A.
a. 1974-90.
b. Results differ for 1960-73, 1974-79, and 1980-90. See text.
* 10% level; ** 5% level; *** 1% level.

Next, let's look at gender equality in access to jobs. One indicator of equal job opportunity for women is the female/male pay ratio. The causes of unequal pay tend to be twofold: Women are overrepresented in low-paying jobs and underrepresented in high-paying positions (occupational sex segregation), and women often receive lower pay than men for similar jobs. The former is the primary factor in the compensation differential.[79] To the extent that the gendered distribution of occupations represents an unconstrained choice on the part of women to work primarily in certain types of jobs, such as those that permit intermittent employment, it does not necessarily indicate inequality of opportunity. This, indeed, is the explanation favored by some analysts for the prevalence of occupational sex segregation.[80] However, evidence suggests that for the United States at least, this theory holds little water.[81] Instead, a good deal of the segregation reflects (conscious and/or unconscious) discrimination by employers.[82] Hence, unequal compensation for women and men represents in large part an unequal distribution of chances for well-paying work.

The measure I use here is the pay ratio of women to men for full-time workers. The figure for each country is an average of the ratio in the years 1965, 1975, and 1985. For a number of our countries, such data are available only for the manufacturing sector. This is unfortunate, because the gender pay gap in manufacturing often differs from that in other sectors, and countries vary markedly in the share of total employment accounted for by manufacturing. Moreover, for Canada and the United States, it is necessary to use figures

Table 3.6 Gender Equity and Economic Performance, 1960-90: Correlation and Regression Coefficients

	Correlation Coefficients		Regression Coefficients	
	Including Japan	Excluding Japan	Including Japan	Excluding Japan
Female/male pay ratio				
Investment	−.16	.32	−.15	.30
Productivity[a]	−.10	−.37*	−.07[b]	−.13[b]
Productivity growth	−.18	.46**	−.21	.19
Growth	−.30	.32	−.34*	.16
Trade balance	−.11	.03	−.22	−.05
Inflation	.26	.25	.26[b]	.18[b]
Unemployment	−.13[b]	−.48[b]**	−.10[b]	−.43[b]**
Female labor force participation				
Investment	.10	.03	.28	.21
Productivity[a]	−.53**	−.56**	−.32[b]*	−.36[b]*
Productivity growth	.02	−.09	.22	.17
Growth	.13	.06	.28	.21
Trade balance	−.22	−.26	−.25	−.26
Inflation	.06	.08	.36[b]*	.36[b]*
Unemployment	−.39[b]*	−.38[b]*	−.44[b]*	−.42[b]*

NOTE: Results for female/male pay ratio do not include Austria and Italy due to lack of data. Regression coefficients are standardized. Regression equations include several control variables. For variable definitions and data sources, see Appendix A.
a. 1974-90.
b. Switzerland is not included due to lack of data on unemployment.
* 10% level; ** 5% level.

covering all employees, and there are no data at all for Austria and Italy. Also, for some countries the figures are based on wages, whereas others use earnings.

Because of these problems, I use an additional indicator of gender equality: the extent of female labor force participation, measured as a share of the female population ages 16 to 64. This, too, reflects the degree to which attractive job opportunities are open for women.

As Table 3.6 indicates, pay equality between women and men appears to have a detrimental effect on all but one of our performance indicators, although only one of the 14 correlation and regression coefficients is statistically significant. This result is largely a product of Japan's influence. The degree of gender pay equality in Japan is much lower than in any other developed country, and as noted earlier, Japan's performance along several measures has been much stronger than that of other nations. If Japan is excluded, most of the coefficient signs are reversed. This suggests that, on the whole, gender equality is not inimical to successful economic performance. The results for women's labor force participation support this inference.

Overall, then, the evidence suggests at worst only a modest trade-off between equal access to jobs and successful national economic performance. Low unemployment is associated with low productivity levels. But it is not clear to what extent this owes to the effect of unemployment on work incentives. In any case, the effect is offset to some degree by the association between low joblessness and high investment rates. Except for the 1974-1979 period, countries have faced an unemployment-inflation trade-off.

◙ Developments in the United States

Between 1980 and 1990, the real after-tax income of the richest fifth of the American population increased by 32.5 percent, while that of the bottom fifth fell 5.2 percent.[83] Although disturbing, this development was not unexpected. A good deal of the economic policy espoused and implemented by the Reagan and Bush administrations was premised on the notion that we had not only too much government, but also too much equality. Those favoring Reagan's tax and social spending cuts tended to believe these reforms would free up capital for investment and heighten work incentives. Both effects were to result in part from a shift of income toward the well-to-do. As John Kenneth Galbraith remarked sardonically, this was policy guided by a view "that the rich were not working and investing because they had too little money and that the poor were not working because, in the form of government benefits, they had too much."[84]

But although the fiscal and social policies of the Reagan-Bush era contributed to a trend toward inequality, they were not fundamentally responsible for it. The U.S. turn away from income equality is more long-term and structural in nature. Figure 3.13 shows pre-tax levels of equality in the United States from 1947 to 1990 (longitudinal data for post-tax income are not available). As before, equality is measured here as the share of income going to the poorest fifth of the population divided by that accruing to the richest fifth.[85] The chart reveals that equality increased moderately, if haltingly, during the first two decades after World War II. Since the early 1970s, the United States has experienced a steady decline in income equality. Pre-tax inequality is now greater than at any point in the entire postwar period.

This trend is attributable to several developments. One is a widening gap between the pay of higher- and lower-paid workers. This owes in part to a

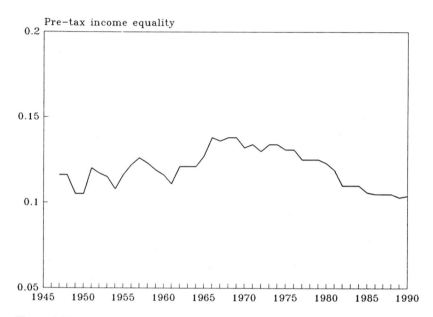

Figure 3.13   U.S. income equality, 1947-90
Source: U.S. Bureau of the Census 1990, table 10, 1993a, table B-7.

shift in the structure of jobs. Although the 1970s and 1980s witnessed a massive expansion in the number of available jobs, many of the new jobs were low-paying service sector positions. Declining unionization and an erosion in the value of the minimum wage also contributed to this shift. A second development contributing to heightened inequality is an increase in involuntary part-time work as a share of employment. A third is a higher average level of joblessness. Finally, the well-to-do during this period enjoyed a sizable increase in earnings from salaries and investments.[86]

Because of the impact of tax and transfer programs, the degree of income equality in the United States is slightly greater than that shown in Figure 3.13—although these programs achieve relatively little redistribution compared to those in other developed nations.[87] During the 1970s, the tax-transfer system became more progressive over time, which worked to offset the growing inequality in pre-tax incomes. In the 1980s, however, these programs did less to restrain the trend toward greater inequality. The tax system became less progressive and redistributive programs were slashed. Consequently, after-tax income equality declined.[88]

Figure 3.14 U.S. unemployment, 1950-90
Source: Council of Economic Advisers 1992, table B-37.

What about equality of opportunity? Unemployment has risen dramatically in the years since 1973, averaging 6.9 percent during 1974-1990 compared to 4.6 percent in the two prior decades. Figure 3.14 shows this
increase in the jobless rate. For gender equality in job access, the news is
somewhat more encouraging. As Figure 3.15 reveals, female labor force
participation has increased steadily during the past three decades. And the
gender earnings differential declined during the 1980s, after not improving at
all in the 1970s.

These longitudinal data on equality offer a further opportunity to evaluate
the equality-efficiency trade-off thesis. Given our earlier findings, it should
come as no surprise that, as income inequality increased in the United States
in the years after 1973, economic performance worsened. As Table 3.7
reveals, every major performance indicator with the exception of investment
shows a decided deterioration during this period. Of course, a host of factors
have contributed to this decline.[89] Falling income equality may have played
only a minor causal role, if any. Did growing gender equality contribute to
the U.S. downturn? Probably not. Female labor force participation has been

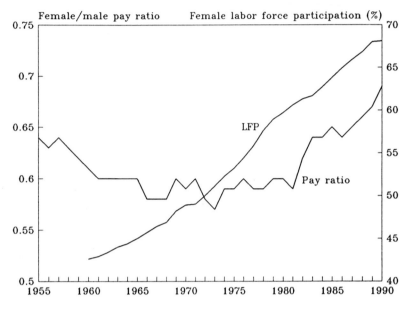

Figure 3.15 U.S. gender equity, 1955-90

Sources: U.S. Bureau of the Census 1990, table 26; OECD 1988, chart 5.12; OECD 1992, table 2.5.

Table 3.7 U.S. Economic Performance (Percentages)

	1948-73	1974-90
Investment	18.2[a]	18.0
Productivity growth	2.2	0.6
Growth	2.6	1.5
Trade balance	0.4[a]	−1.5
Inflation	2.7	6.6
Unemployment	4.7	6.9

Sources: Council of Economic Advisers 1991, 1992 for 1948-59; OECD 1992 for 1960-90.
a. 1960-73.

rising steadily during the whole of this century, not just during the period shown in Figure 3.15.[90] And the female/male pay ratio began increasing only in the early 1980s, nearly a decade after the downturn commenced. Overall, then, the U.S. experience offers no support for the thesis of a trade-off between equality and efficiency.

Indeed, aside from the effect of the jobless rate on work effort and inflation, none of the evidence examined in this chapter indicates that increasing equality requires a sacrifice in national economic success.

Too Much Government?

The legitimate object of government is to do for a community of people whatever they need to have done, but cannot do so well for themselves in their individual capacities.

—Abraham Lincoln[1]

No economic institution has come under more severe attack in the past two decades than government. Government intrusion has been widely blamed for the economic malaise that has stricken much of the developed world since the early 1970s.[2] During the height of the golden age, it was virtually taken for granted that government had an important role to play in managing economic demand, providing public goods to relieve or prevent market failure, redistributing income to assist the poor, and regulating corporate social conduct. But as the prosperity of the 1950s and 1960s was replaced by stagflation in the 1970s, a backlash occurred in elite and (to some degree) popular opinion. In 1976 *Fortune* magazine noted: "It is now clear that a groundswell is running against the power, the costs, and the inefficiencies of big government."[3] By the mid 1980s the OECD observed that "Rather than being widely regarded as a major contributor to economic growth and macroeconomic stability, the view that the growth and financing of the public sector has, on balance, stifled growth now attracts widespread support."[4]

Does the comparative record support this assertion? In this chapter I attempt to find out. I examine five types of government intervention: fiscal policy, redistributive programs, labor market policy, industrial policy, and regulation. For fiscal and redistributive policy, I use quantitative data on taxation and government spending for our group of industrialized OECD nations. As in Chapter 3 I focus on the period 1960-1990, although I again also examine the years 1960-1973 and 1974-1990 separately. For the other three types of state intervention I draw mostly upon qualitative evidence from a small set of countries, as in Chapter 2.

Although my chief concern is to examine the argument that government adversely affects economic efficiency, I go beyond that issue. Many critics of government intervention not only claim that it tends to undermine efficiency; they also insist that it frequently fails in its direct objective. Redistributive programs fail to reduce the poverty rate. Policies aimed at reducing unemployment and upgrading the labor force have no such effect. Industrial policies aiming to promote competitiveness and growth are unable to do so. Regulatory measures fail to protect the interests of consumers and workers. Sometimes the argument is, to borrow Albert Hirschman's useful terminology, one of futility; government policies are said to be incapable of achieving their goals. In other instances the argument is a stronger one—one of perversity. Government efforts are said to have the perverse effect of worsening the condition they aim to rectify.[5] I attempt to evaluate these claims based on the comparative record.

The Market Liberal View

> Government is not the solution to our problem. Government is the problem.
>
> —*Ronald Reagan*[6]

We have already encountered, in Chapter 3, two of the principal arguments advanced by critics of government tax and transfer policies. These policies are said to reduce investment, by shifting resources away from those with the strongest proclivity to save and invest, and to dampen work incentives.

Critics also claim that state fiscal intervention fuels inflation. Heightened public spending can be financed in three ways. First, tax revenues can be increased. In the market liberal view, higher taxes are directly or indirectly shifted onto product prices, as workers and employers seek to obtain the rate of growth of real wages and profits to which they have become accustomed. Assar Lindbeck has labeled this phenomenon "tax-shift inflation."[7] A second option for government is to borrow money. "We know now that inflation results from all that deficit spending," argued President Reagan in 1981. "Bringing government spending back within government revenues ... is the only way ... that we can reduce and, yes, eliminate inflation."[8] By increasing the demand for loans, government borrowing can drive up interest rates, a cost that firms may pass on to consumers in the form of higher prices. Deficit spending can also heighten inflation by producing excessive demand. The third means of financing increased state expenditures is simply to print more money. According to Milton and Rose Friedman:

> Financing government spending by increasing the quantity of money is often extremely attractive to both the President and members of Congress. It enables them to increase government spending, providing goodies for their constituents, without having to vote for taxes to pay for them, and without having to borrow from the public.[9]

In the view of monetarists, increasing the quantity of money is the principal source of inflation.

Finally, and perhaps most important, market liberalism suggests that efficiency is undermined by the way government intervention interferes with the market allocation of resources. Governments purchase and produce all manner of goods and services. They also regulate and subsidize the private sector. But unlike private actors, governments seldom function with a hard budget constraint. That is, if governments fail to produce, subsidize, and regulate in an efficient fashion, they generally do not face the threat of bankruptcy or poverty. This makes the state susceptible to inefficient decisions.[10] Moreover, as public choice theorists have insisted, politicians may be able to maximize their reelection chances by catering to the wishes of "rent-seeking" special interest groups, at the expense of the larger collectivity. In Richard McKenzie's words:

> The economy may become progressively less competitive and less efficient, dynamic, and adaptable as interest groups from all points on the income distribution take advantage of the government's transfer powers and secure their own monopoly restrictions. The end result can be the development through government of a "public bad": a reduction in the prosperity of all groups through the competitive and destructive use of transfer powers.[11]

In conjunction, these deleterious effects of government economic activity are expected to reduce investment and work effort, slow the growth of productivity and output, diminish competitiveness, and yield higher inflation

Table 4.1   Taxation and Government Spending as a Share of GDP, 1960-90 (Percentages)

	Tax Revenues		Government Expenditures	
	Average	*Change*	*Average*	*Change*
Sweden	50.7	31.8	50.3	30.4
Norway	46.6	21.8	43.3	24.7
Netherlands	46.2	15.6	49.7	21.9
Denmark	45.0	28.8	45.7	33.6
Austria	42.7	12.3	44.6	13.9
Belgium	41.7	22.0	47.0	24.9
France	41.4	11.6	43.4	15.3
Germany	41.4	8.4	43.0	13.6
United Kingdom	37.9	10.1	41.1	9.9
Finland	36.0	11.5	34.9	14.6
Canada	34.5	15.9	37.9	18.3
Italy	33.5	13.3	40.9	22.9
Switzerland	29.7	10.9	25.6[a]	13.5[a]
United States	29.3	5.5	32.3	9.1
Australia	28.8	9.9	30.3	13.6
Japan	24.8	15.8	25.9	14.8
Average	38.1	15.3	39.7	18.4

NOTE: New Zealand is not included due to lack of data. For data sources see Appendix A.
a. Includes only current disbursements of government, rather than total outlays.

and unemployment. The greater the degree of government intervention, and the faster the growth of that intervention, the larger the adverse effect on economic performance.

◈ Fiscal Policy

Let's look first at the relationship between aggregate measures of state fiscal intervention and economic performance. Table 4.1 shows data on taxation and government expenditure for 16 of our 17 countries (data are not available for New Zealand), with nations listed in descending order according to levels of tax revenue.[12] The figures are rather striking. In the majority of developed countries, taxes and spending accounted, on average, for well over a third of gross domestic product (GDP) during the past three decades. In the typical country, taxes accounted for an additional 15 percent of GDP in 1990 compared to 1960, and government spending accounted for an additional 18 percent. It is little surprise, then, that the degree to which government is

Table 4.2   Fiscal Policy and Economic Performance, 1960-90: Correlation and Regression Coefficients

	Correlation Coefficients		*Regression Coefficients*	
	Taxation	*Government Spending*	*Taxation*	*Government Spending*
Investment	−.27	−.44**	−.29	−.55**
Productivity[a]	−.19	−.02	−.05[b]	−.01[b]
Productivity growth	−.12	−.07	−.22*	−.26*
Growth	−.25	−.20	−.39**	−.45**
Trade balance	.27	.31	.18	.25
Inflation	.02	.09	.09[b]	.11[b]
Unemployment	−.28[b]	−.01[b]	−.27[b]	−.13[b]
	Change in Taxation	*Change in Spending*	*Change in Taxation*	*Change in Spending*
Investment	0	−.05	0	−.09
Productivity[a]	−.37*	−.22	−.27[b]	−.20[b]
Productivity growth	.03	.02	−.06	−.12
Growth	.11	.05	.01	−.09
Trade balance	.02	.05	−.12	−.10
Inflation	.22	.27	.24[b]	.15[b]
Unemployment	−.28[b]	−.07[b]	−.14[b]	−.04[b]

NOTE: New Zealand is not included. Regression coefficients are standardized. Regression equations include several control variables; see pp. 56-57. For variable definitions and data sources, see Appendix A.
a. 1974-90.
b. Switzerland is not included due to lack of data on unemployment.
* Significant at the 10% level; ** 5% level.

appropriating and distributing funds and the rate at which this intervention has increased have provoked a fierce attack by those wedded to the free market view. Let us see if this attack has merit.

Table 4.2 shows the correlation and regression coefficients for these four measures of government fiscal intervention as predictors of our seven economic performance indicators. On the whole, the results for *levels* of fiscal intervention suggest a fair amount of support for the market liberal view. Quite a few of the correlations are in the predicted direction, although only one is statistically significant. The regression results, in which variables such as the catch-up effect and interest rates are controlled for (see pp. 56-57), indicate even stronger support for the market liberal perspective. Most of the regression coefficients for levels of taxation and government spending have the predicted sign and are significant at or near the 10 percent level. On the other hand, with the possible exceptions of productivity and inflation, there is very little indication that high *rates of change* in fiscal intervention impair efficient performance. The signs for the correlation and regression coefficients are inconsistent, and none is close to statistical significance.

Levels of taxation and government spending are each inversely correlated with investment, productivity growth, and output growth; and the relationships appear even stronger in the regression equations. These results suggest that, as the free market view contends, high levels of government fiscal intervention may crowd out investment and thereby slow the growth of output and productivity. The correlation and regression results for productivity levels, on the other hand, indicate a lack of any relationship. Government intrusion appears not to dampen work effort.

Turning to trade performance, there is no evidence of an adverse impact of fiscal intervention. On the contrary, each of the measures representing levels of government intervention is positively associated with trade balances. The correlations are stronger for the period 1974-1990 ($r = .41^*$, $.36^*$), when international trade accelerated, than for 1960-1973 ($r = 0$, $.17$). (For an explanation of significance levels indicated by *, **, and ***, see Appendix C.) These results suggest a possible beneficial impact of fiscal intervention on trade performance. This could simply reflect the fact that the smaller European countries, which tend to have high levels of taxation and government spending, are forced to succeed in international trade because of the limited size of their domestic markets.[13] Yet when economic openness is controlled for in the regression equations, the results are similar.

Nor does it appear that high taxation and spending levels heighten inflation, as there is no association between levels of fiscal intrusion and inflation. On the other hand, there is some indication that high *rates of change* in these variables may be associated with higher inflation. The correlation and regression coefficients for both taxation and spending are positive, but they are not particularly large and are well short of being statistically significant. Previous research on this issue has discovered no relationship between these variables. David Cameron examined the effect of increases in government spending and budget deficits on inflation for 21 OECD countries between 1965 and 1981, but found that neither variable had a significant impact. Similarly, Assar Lindbeck, who argues that there are strong theoretical reasons to think that fiscal intervention will be linked to higher inflation, nevertheless found that "cross-country regressions from the post-World War II period for highly developed countries do not reveal any positive association between inflation and the size, or rate of expansion, of the government budget."[14]

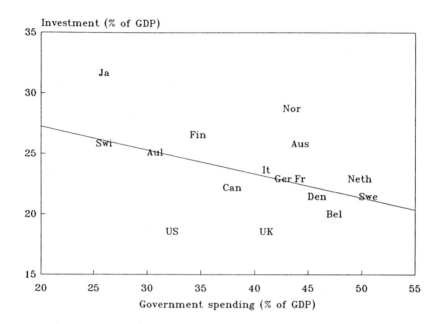

Figure 4.1 Government spending and investment, 1960-90

NOTE: For data sources see Appendix A.

Our final performance indicator is unemployment. If there is any relation between fiscal intervention and unemployment, it would seem to be a healthy one, as taxation levels show a moderate, although not statistically significant, inverse association with unemployment rates.

The comparative record, then, appears to suggest some fairly substantial support for the claim that extensive fiscal intervention undermines economic performance. Levels of taxation and/or government spending appear to be inversely associated with three performance measures—investment, productivity growth, and output growth. As in Chapter 3, however, there is reason to consider Japan an outlier among developed countries. Japan's levels of tax revenue and state expenditure have been the lowest among these nations during the past three decades, while its rates of investment, productivity growth, and output growth have been markedly higher than those of any other country. Figures 4.1 and 4.2 offer some perspective on the degree to which Japan is an outlier. (As the figures in Table 4.1 indicate, Japan is *not* an outlier

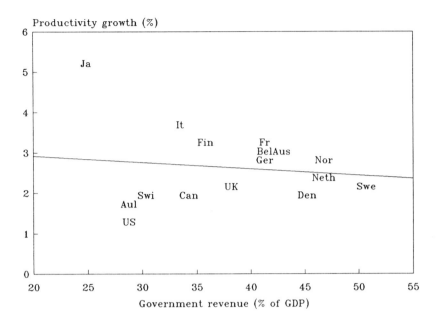

Figure 4.2 Taxation and productivity growth, 1960-90
NOTE: For data sources see Appendix A.

on the variables representing *change* in fiscal intervention.) Here again, therefore, we ought to examine the data with Japan excluded, to see if any of these associations are mere artifacts of Japan's exceptional status.

The argument in favor of omitting Japan here is not purely statistical. There is a strong theoretical rationale as well. Japan is a unique case among developed nations in that it does in fact pursue two of the principal goals typically sought by active interventionist states—income equality and government steering of the economy—but does so without high levels of taxation or government expenditure. We have already seen that Japan is one of the most egalitarian developed nations in terms of income distribution. In Japan, unlike other developed countries, this outcome is accomplished through equalization of primary—that is, before-tax—incomes. Hence there is no need for extensive state redistributive efforts. As we shall see later in this chapter, Japan also probably ranks first among our countries in terms of the degree to which its government engages in economic steering. Over the course of the

Table 4.3   Fiscal Policy Level and Economic Performance, 1960-90: Correlation and Regression Coefficients With Japan Omitted

	Correlation Coefficients		Regression Coefficients	
	Taxation	Government Spending	Taxation	Government Spending
Investment	.02	−.22	.01	−.44
Productivity[a]	−.38*	−.19	−.14[b]	−.06[b]
Productivity growth	.31	.40*	.04	.06
Growth	.25	.33	−.05	−.06
Trade balance	.43*	.48**	.34	.41*
Inflation	−.01	.07	.04[b]	−.09[b]
Unemployment	−.61[b]**	−.30[b]	−.57[b]**	−.41[b]*

NOTE: New Zealand is not included. Regression coefficients are standardized. Regression equations include several control variables; see pp. 56-57. For variable definitions and data sources, see Appendix A.
a. 1974-90.
b. Switzerland is not included due to lack of data on unemployment.
* 10% level; ** 5% level.

post-World War II period, the Japanese state has engaged in extensive promotion of particular sectors and firms in order to advance the nation's international competitiveness. But whereas other governments pursue this task via public subsidies and/or state ownership, the Japanese economic bureaucracy has relied mainly on mechanisms that do not involve state expenditure, such as selective allocation of bank credit and limits on foreign imports.

Omitting Japan substantially alters the findings, as Table 4.3 indicates. Five of the six critical correlation coefficients—for levels of fiscal intervention with investment, productivity growth, and output growth—switch sign. And in the regression equations only the coefficient for government spending as a predictor of investment remains negative and close to statistical significance. The other five coefficients all suggest no impact in either direction. Furthermore, the correlation and regression coefficients for trade performance and unemployment now indicate a favorable relationship with fiscal activism. These results offer little or no support for the market liberal thesis.

Let's look more closely at the effect of fiscal intervention on economic growth. This issue has received a good deal of attention in previous research. More than a dozen studies have been conducted seeking to determine the nature of this relationship. But many of these include both industrialized and developing countries and thus tell us little or nothing about the relationship within developed market economies alone.[15] The research focusing on the latter economies has yielded no clear finding. Some studies have concluded that taxation and/or spending impair growth, whereas others have found no evidence to support that notion. Still others have found mixed or inconsistent results.[16] What accounts for this disparity in findings?

Peter Saunders has argued that the divergence in results stems largely from differences in the particular time period and group of countries examined.[17] My findings here support Saunders's view. The time period is important because, to the extent an inverse association exists between fiscal intervention and growth, it was much stronger in the period 1960-1973 than during 1974-1990. For our 16 countries the correlations for per capita growth during these two periods, respectively, are $-.44**$ and $-.08$ for taxation and $-.38*$ and $-.06$ for government spending. It also matters which countries are included in the analysis. In particular, it makes a profound difference whether or not Japan is included, as we have just seen. Another key is which measure of growth is used. Per capita growth is a better indicator of advance in living standards; yet the simple measure of economic growth is more commonly used in analyses of this sort. For our 16 countries during the period 1960-1990, levels of taxation and spending are inversely associated with both measures of growth, but the correlations are considerably stronger for simple growth ($r = -.49**$, $-44**$) than for per capita growth ($r = -.25$, $-.20$). Studies concluding that taxation and spending reduce economic growth typically have relied on data from the 1960s and 1970s, have included Japan, and have used the simple measure of growth. Those finding no impact generally use more recent data, exclude Japan, and/or rely on the per capita growth measure. The conclusion one draws about the effect of fiscal policy on growth depends, therefore, on how one chooses to interpret the evidence.

The same can be said about the relationship between government fiscal intervention and national economic performance in general. My own view is that we certainly want to include data from the 1980s rather than just the two prior decades. Also, it is important to look not only at output growth, but at a wide variety of performance indicators. I also believe the data tell us more when Japan is omitted than when it is included. Japan is the most egalitarian and interventionist nation among industrialized democracies, whereas each of the other countries with low levels of taxation and government expenditure (with the possible exception of Finland) is relatively inegalitarian and features consistently noninterventionist government. With Japan excluded, the comparative record suggests only minimal support for the notion that high levels of fiscal intervention impede economic success.

At the same time, Japan's exceptional performance results perhaps indicate that income equalization and economic steering are most efficiently achieved without directing funds through the government. This may have to do with administrative costs. As Arthur Okun has noted, there is a "leaky bucket" effect associated with government fiscal programs; for every dollar that passes through the state, part inevitably leaks out in the form of administrative expenses.[18] It may also be partly a result of private sector efficiency relative to that of government. That is, aside from administrative costs, private actors may be able to accomplish tasks such as income equalization at lower costs than can government. That is certainly plausible, given the lack of a hard budget constraint on state officials. Alternatively, it is possible that Japan's success is a product of other factors that have nothing to do with the fact that it achieves distributive equality and state direction of the economy without high levels of taxation and government expenditure. This line of reasoning is explored in Chapter 6.

◙   Redistributive Programs

Redistributive policies have been subject to sustained and scathing criticism in recent years. A large measure of the hostility owes to a belief that tax and transfer programs undermine economic efficiency. As Irving Kristol has written:

> Efforts to redistribute income by governmental fiat have the precise effect of impairing economic efficiency and growth—and therefore of preserving poverty in the name of equality. All such schemes of income distribution imply higher rates of marginal taxation for the productive population, with a consequent diminution of work incentives and a shrinking of capital available for reinvestment. When this happens on a sufficiently large scale, the results become disastrous for everyone.[19]

These claims certainly have some intuitive merit. On the other hand, redistribution may also have some productive effects. As noted in Chapter 3, income equalization may increase and stabilize consumer demand, heighten motivation and workplace cooperation by promoting fairness, and encourage wage moderation. As Gosta Esping-Andersen has argued, expansive social security programs, which account for the bulk of transfer expenditures in all developed nations, may enhance firms' flexibility in labor deployment by facilitating early retirement. In addition, social services have become a significant source of new jobs, helping countries absorb the rapid increase in female labor market participation. The welfare state has become, as he puts it, "a major agent of labor market clearing."[20] Any adverse impact produced

Table 4.4 Government Transfers as a Share of GDP, 1960-90 (Percentages)

	Average	*Change*
Netherlands	21.5	12.3
Belgium	18.7	11.4
France	17.9	7.9
Austria	17.3	7.0
Germany	14.8	3.3
Italy	14.3	8.2
Sweden	14.2	11.7
Denmark	13.1	11.0
Norway	12.9	11.4
Switzerland	10.5	7.7
United Kingdom	10.3	5.4
Canada	9.4	4.7
United States	8.7	5.8
Finland	8.2	4.9
Japan	7.6	7.7
Australia	7.3	3.2
Average	12.9	7.7

NOTE: New Zealand is not included due to lack of data. For data sources see Appendix A.

by crowding out of investment and/or reduction of work effort may be offset, or even outweighed, by these beneficial effects.

Table 4.4 shows the figures for government transfers in 16 of our 17 countries (again, no data are available for New Zealand). Included in this total are state benefits for sickness, old age, family allowances, social assistance grants, and unfunded employee welfare benefits paid by general government. On average, one-eighth of the total output in these nations was transferred from one sector of the population to another during the period 1960-1990. And transfer payments through this period grew at a faster rate than total government spending.

There is no indication that *changes* in transfer payment levels have any impact on performance, so these results are not shown here. The correlation and regression coefficients for *levels* of transfer spending are displayed in Table 4.5. With Japan included, three of the seven correlations are in the direction predicted by the market liberal view. Among the regression coefficients, only those for investment and output growth have the expected sign, but each is statistically significant. At the same time, the results also indicate favorable associations between transfer spending levels and both trade performance and unemployment. Altogether, this suggests some support for the

Table 4.5 Government Transfers and Economic Performance, 1960-90: Correlation and Regression Coefficients With and Without Japan

	Correlation Coefficients		Regression Coefficients	
	Including Japan	Excluding Japan	Including Japan	Excluding Japan
Investment	−.24	−.06	−.42*	−.25
Productivity[a]	.33	.26	.24^b	.24^b
Productivity growth	.12	.50**	−.18	.10
Growth	−.11	.27	−.42**	−.17
Trade balance	.46**	.58***	.51*	.57**
Inflation	−.25	−.29	−.24^b	−.29^b
Unemployment	.06^b	−.09^b	−.46^b*	−.65^b**

NOTE: New Zealand is not included. Regression coefficients are standardized. Regression equations include several control variables; see pp. 56-57. For variable definitions and data sources, see Appendix A.
a. 1974-90.
b. Switzerland is not included due to lack of data on unemployment.
* 10% level; ** 5% level; *** 1% level.

market liberal thesis that extensive redistributive programs undermine the economy, but some support for the opposite view as well.

If we exclude Japan—again for both theoretical and statistical reasons—the comparative record tends to suggest a generally beneficial impact of redistribution on efficiency. The negative regression coefficients for investment and output growth persist, but they are smaller and no longer significant. Transfer spending is now positively associated with productivity growth, although the regression coefficient indicates only a weak effect at best. Most impressive, the findings for trade performance and unemployment, and possibly also productivity and inflation, strongly support the notion that higher levels of redistributive intervention are linked with superior performance outcomes. These findings call into question the market liberal view of a trade-off between redistribution and economic efficiency.

Here again previous research has focused exclusively on output growth. Three studies that include Japan found some evidence that higher levels of transfer spending reduce growth; another, which looked at the period 1952-1976, found no effect; one found evidence of a nonlinear relationship. Two other studies found, as I have here, mixed results depending on whether or not Japan is included.[21]

One of the more careful studies on the topic, by John McCallum and Andre Blais, concludes that where transfer spending exceeds a certain share of national wealth, it has an adverse effect on growth.[22] Redistributive expenditures in a number of countries may have indeed exceeded some critical threshold during the late 1970s and throughout the 1980s. For instance, in the 1980s, transfer payments averaged 27 percent of GDP in the Netherlands in the 1980s and 25 percent in Belgium, compared to an average of 13 percent for our 16 countries during the period 1960-1990. With Japan included, the correlation between transfer spending and growth for 1960-1990 as a whole is –.11, but for the 1980s it is –.37*. Omitting Japan, the correlation is .27 for 1960-1990 and –.29 for the 1980s. Similar patterns hold for investment and productivity growth.

As with fiscal policy, then, the overall conclusion drawn depends on one's interpretation of the evidence. With Japan included, there seems good reason to believe that high transfer payment levels have an adverse impact on rates of investment and output growth. If Japan is omitted, these effects are somewhat less certain, and the data strongly support a conclusion that transfer payments are associated with better trade performance and lower unemployment rates. There is a sound theoretical rationale for excluding Japan, as it is one of the most egalitarian industrialized nations despite its very low level of transfer spending. But again, the fact that Japan achieves a high degree of income equality without extensive tax and transfer programs may tell us something important about the most efficient path to distributive equity and poverty relief. And it certainly makes sense to acknowledge that there are probably limits beyond which transfer spending begins to have detrimental effects on economic performance.

Redistributive programs are frequently attacked not only for undermining the economy, but also for their alleged inability to reduce the incidence of poverty. It is particularly in the United States that this charge has been leveled. The cynicism toward social welfare programs—which include Social Security, Unemployment Insurance, Aid to Families with Dependent Children (AFDC), Food Stamps, Medicare and Medicaid, and an assortment of other measures—stems from a simple fact. As Figure 4.3 shows, while transfer spending as a share of national wealth doubled between the late 1960s and the early 1980s, the percentage of the population in poverty did not decline during that time. What explains this apparent lack of impact?

By most accounts redistributive policies *have* helped to alleviate poverty in the United States. The trouble is, since the late 1960s their effect has been offset by the sudden stagnation of growth in productivity and real incomes, a dramatic rise in the rate of unemployment, and widening wage inequality.[23] The pretransfer poverty rate grew steadily during this period, rising from 18 percent in 1968 to 24 percent by the mid 1980s.[24] Had it not been for the growth of transfer programs during that time, these developments might have caused a much more substantial increase in the posttransfer rate of poverty

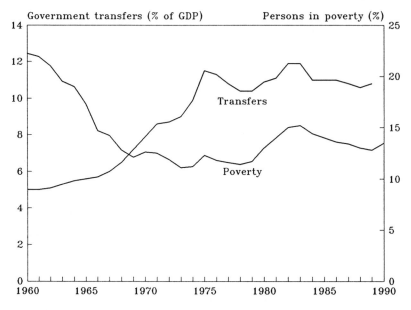

Figure 4.3   U.S. government transfers and poverty, 1960-90
Sources: OECD 1992, table 6.3; U.S. Bureau of the Census 1993b, table 2.

than actually occurred. Furthermore, the bulk of the increase in transfers went to the elderly; for the rest of the population transfer payments rose only slightly (in inflation-adjusted terms). Between 1968 and the mid 1980s the poverty rate for persons over 65 fell from 25 to 13 percent, while for the rest of society it rose from 11 to 16 percent.[25] This, too, suggests that redistribution has had a beneficial impact.

At the same time, it is hard to disagree with the assertion that our redistributive programs should be accomplishing more. In fact, in comparative terms, the U.S. transfer system is uniquely ineffective at reducing poverty. Figure 4.4 shows pretransfer and posttransfer poverty levels for eight nations in 1985. The poverty line for each country is set at 40 percent of the median income, which approximates the official U.S. standard. The chart reveals that the pretransfer poverty rate is actually lower in the United States than in many other countries. But our tax and transfer system does a comparatively woeful job at reducing the rate. Thus, the posttransfer U.S. poverty rate is more than double that of the other nations.[26]

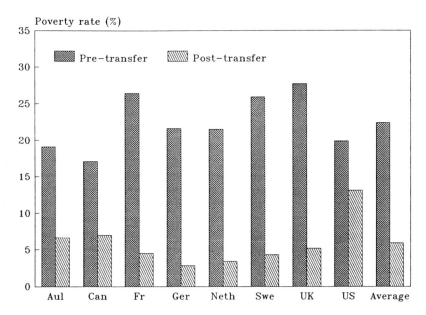

Figure 4.4 Transfer system effectiveness, 1985
Source: Smeeding 1992.

Why is the U.S. redistributive system so ineffective? According to critics, part of the problem is that transfer programs seldom reach those most in need.[27] On the surface, this argument would seem to have some merit. The bulk of transfer payments in the United States go to the middle class rather than the poor. Using data from the Congressional Budget Office, Neil Howe and Phillip Longman have calculated that in 1991 more than half of the various entitlements (including direct outlays and tax benefits) dispensed by the federal government went to households with incomes over $30,000.[28] The solution seems obvious: target government aid at the poor.

Judging from the comparative record, however, lack of targeting would not appear to explain the ineffectiveness of U.S. social welfare policy. Most European nations rely less on targeted programs than the United States does. And for good reason. Means-tested programs, such as AFDC and Food Stamps, tend to be highly vulnerable to cutbacks during periods of political backlash against government spending. Universal programs, like Social Security, are more resistant to conservative attack, even though they are less cost-effective at reducing the incidence of poverty. The U.S. experience during the 1980s illustrates this trade-off. Although the Reagan administration wanted to reduce all transfer programs, popular pressure allowed spending reductions only on targeted policies. Universal programs such as Social Security were effectively off-limits. European and U.S. experience consistently demonstrates that universal transfer programs are more politically sustainable than targeted policies. As a result, they tend to be more effective, over the long run, at helping the needy.[29]

Another line of reasoning asserts that the failure to reduce poverty is a product of the redistributive programs themselves. Alexis de Tocqueville once remarked that "Any permanent, regular administrative system whose aim will be to provide for the needs of the poor, will breed more miseries than it can cure, will deprave the population that it wants to help and comfort."[30] Contemporary adherents of Tocqueville's view contend that transfer programs have been structured so as to encourage welfare dependency. Individuals are faced with an incentive to stay on welfare rather than enter the workforce.[31] Indeed, according to Charles Murray, the best-known proponent of this argument, this is an inherent feature of government programs:

> Social programs in a democratic society tend to produce net harm in dealing with the most difficult problems. They will inherently tend to have enough of an inducement to produce bad behavior and not enough of a solution to stimulate good behavior; and the more difficult the problem, the more likely it is that this relationship will prevail.[32]

It is certainly true that welfare recipients face incentives to remain on welfare. But is that because the benefit levels in the United States are too generous? Or is the problem that we offer too little support to those who work in low-wage jobs? Every other developed nation has some type of national program that guarantees health care to all citizens, and most offer a subsidy to all families with children to help defray the cost of child care. The United States has neither, and although some employers provide these benefits, many do not. Poor single mothers who receive income support through AFDC also receive Medicaid benefits. For the typical single mother on AFDC, therefore, the costs of entering the workforce include not only the loss of her welfare payments, but also the cost of purchasing health insurance and child care (along with transportation).[33] Reducing benefit levels might encourage some single mothers to leave the welfare rolls, but it would not help lift them out of poverty. Accomplishing the latter requires increased government support for those with low-wage jobs.

What about the stinginess of the U.S. transfer system? This too may help explain its relative ineffectiveness, but it certainly does not tell the whole story. As a share of GDP, the United States spends more on transfer programs than does Australia, and nearly as much as Canada and Britain (see Table 4.4 above). Yet the transfer system in each of the latter three countries is much more effective than the U.S. system at reducing poverty (Figure 4.4). Among these nations with meager redistributive programs, the difference in transfer system effectiveness appears to be largely a function of specific programs.[34] For instance, in the United States the floor for supplemental Social Security payments to the elderly is set at 35-38 percent of the nation's median income, whereas the floor for equivalent programs in Canada and Australia is 52-56 percent of median income. Canada provides a special widows' benefit to assist elderly women living alone, who comprise the largest single poverty group. The United States has no such program. In addition, each of these other nations offers a universal child allowance. Because payments are independent of work effort, they act as an income supplement, and thus do not discourage people from working. By contrast, in the AFDC program, which is the closest thing the United States has to a child allowance, any earned income by the recipient reduces the benefit level. Instead of supplementing earnings, and thus helping lift individuals out of poverty, the U.S. transfer system thereby creates a trade-off between earned income and welfare income. The poor must rely on one or the other. Unfortunately, for many people neither by itself is sufficient to enable an escape from poverty.

Contrary to critics' objections, then, the comparative evidence suggests that redistributive programs tend to be quite effective at reducing the incidence of poverty. The United States is an exceptional case, in part because of its particular incentive structure and partly due to its stinginess in specific areas.[35]

◈ Labor Market Policy

Along with its generous welfare state, Sweden's economy is best known and most widely admired for its very low rate of unemployment and its highly skilled workforce. These latter achievements are largely the result of the world's most comprehensive and effective labor market policy. That policy has two interconnected components: an employment service and government-sponsored training.

As we saw in Chapter 2, there is a high probability of market failure in the area of human capital. Both employers and workers encounter powerful incentives to underinvest in skills training. The future payoffs from such investment are uncertain, and employers face the threat of workers moving to another firm after benefiting from training. Job matching is also susceptible to market failure. In standard economic theory, employers who need workers and workers who need employers hunt for one another; eventually they find each other and the labor market is in equilibrium. At any given moment there may be workers who are unemployed and jobs that need to be filled, but that circumstance is only temporary. Unemployment is *frictional.* Although this model captures a good deal of what goes on in labor markets, it ignores the substantial informational barriers to quick and effective job matching. Workers and employers cannot always quickly and easily locate one another. Moreover, economies are constantly in flux; certain industries decline as others rise. The skills of displaced workers looking for jobs may not match those needed by the firms looking for workers. Unemployment in these circumstances is *structural.* Given the market failure in human capital and in job matching, government assistance can improve labor market performance. It does not automatically help, as critics are wont to point out.[36] But it *can* help.

Swedish employment policy is administered by a National Labor Market Board, but its functions are largely decentralized and carried out by local boards.[37] The policy consists partly of traditional job creation and relief work to employ displaced workers, but its main thrust involves training and job placement. Firms must notify their local board in advance whenever employees are to be laid off, and they must notify the agency of any job openings lasting more than 10 days. Workers who are displaced or who leave their job by choice can receive subsidized training through the employment service. The service then helps place workers in new positions. About 20 percent of all job openings in the Swedish economy are filled through the employment service.[38]

The payoffs of this program are substantial. The high level of coordination achieves a better match between workers and employers than the market can accomplish by itself.[39] The policy also helps ensure a highly trained labor force. Officials keep in close communication with firms and with officials in other areas regarding trends in skill needs. Training is free for displaced workers and is universally available; eligibility is not means-tested. The training programs are full-time (40 hours per week) and last from 2 to 72 weeks.

There is an element of compulsion in the system; after a short time, displaced workers can receive unemployment compensation only if they participate in a retraining and placement program. Although desirable in efficiency terms, this sort of coercion seems politically feasible only where workers can receive genuine skill improvement and where they have a substantial prospect of getting a good job within a short period of time. Swedish labor market policy helps ensure that these conditions prevail.

It is not only displaced workers who receive training through the labor market program. Training and retraining services are also available to currently employed workers. The entire system is financed by a tax, to which companies contribute approximately 2.5 percent of their annual payroll. Training of current workers is a preventive strategy, aimed at avoiding unemployment rather than simply dealing with its effects.

Sweden's employment policy has enabled the country to keep unemployment at a very low level (an average of 2.0 percent between 1960 and 1990) despite having the highest rate of labor force participation among developed nations (78 percent during that period).[40] Swedish policymakers recognized early on that Keynesian demand management would not be sufficient to hold unemployment at such a low level without provoking excessive inflation. Active labor market policy was considered necessary to achieve what demand manipulation could not.

The system heightens productivity by permitting a high degree of labor flexibility. Labor mobility between firms and industries is greatly facilitated. And within firms, employee opposition to the introduction of new technologies and forms of work organization is reduced. Workers with (de facto) employment security are less threatened by innovations that may displace particular jobs.

Labor market policy in the United States contrasts starkly with that of Sweden.[41] Consider training first. As we saw in Chapter 2, American workers are, by international standards, poorly trained. This is partly a result of the fact that, due to the incentives noted earlier, employers are reluctant to spend money on training. But it also reflects the inadequacy of government programs. Government support for worker training in the United States has been directed primarily through a series of public training assistance programs— the 1962 Manpower Development and Training Act (MDTA), replaced by the 1973 Comprehensive Employment and Training Act (CETA), in turn replaced by the 1982 Job Training Partnership Act (JTPA). Funding for federal training programs such as these is insufficient to reach more than a minuscule portion of the workforce. Because of limited finances, these programs are intended to focus on the most economically disadvantaged. Although MDTA and CETA were somewhat successful in this regard, JTPA's structure of incentives—in which private training organizations are paid according to the number of trainees who graduate or obtain jobs—is such that it encourages screening. Local JTPA programs systematically select the most promising candidates for training while weeding out the untalented and discouraged.[42] A thorough study concludes that "There is no compelling evidence that the Job Training Partnership Act system, on balance, makes much difference for the pattern of employment, earnings, and productive capacity of the American workforce."[43] Even if they were more effective, the fact that programs such as JTPA operate at the margins of the labor market considerably limits their usefulness as a tool for upgrading the skills of U.S. workers.

Vocational schooling makes a similarly minor contribution to overall training. Less than 30 percent of students who take vocational courses in high school use their acquired skills in their future jobs, and postsecondary vocational-technical schools reach less than 5 percent of American students. Community colleges play a more prominent role. These schools account for half of all first-year higher education enrollments in the United States, and two-thirds of community college students are involved in vocational programs. But community college training programs are weakened by their lack of integration with the needs of local labor markets. Also, in part because of an absence of standardized curricula, students tend to take courses sporadically rather than pursuing a coherent degree program, and dropout rates are high.

In the area of job matching the United States also fares poorly. The American labor market is commonly thought to be among the most flexible in the world. Many displaced workers are able to quickly locate and obtain another job with equivalent pay. But a sizable number of the unemployed are not able to do so. A survey by the U.S. Bureau of the Census in the mid 1980s discovered that about 40 percent of workers losing their job suffered a long period (over a year) without being able to find a new job paying at least three-quarters of their former earnings level.[44]

The United States lacks an effective employment policy to help remedy these deficiencies in the private labor market. The focus of employment programs has been overwhelmingly oriented toward public job creation as a remedy for unemployment. This stop-gap strategy does reduce the number of unemployed, but it does little to enhance the underlying health of the labor market or the economy. The Job Service (or Employment Service) is the agency in charge of job matching, but it receives little funding and is poorly coordinated. In the words of one commentator, "the reputation of the Employment Service is deservedly abysmal, and it seems unable to perform its mission for even low-level blue collar work."[45] Furthermore, like the training system, U.S. employment policy tends to operate at the margins of the labor market, serving more as a welfare service than an integral complement to the labor market. The systems in nations such as Sweden and Germany, by contrast, "are much more tightly integrated into the day-to-day functions of the labor market and the industrial relations system, and they serve a broader cross section of the population."[46]

Swedish labor market policy may function more effectively than its U.S. counterpart, but does this difference have real effects on economic performance? One way to assess the impact of active labor market policies on performance outcomes is to use country data on program expenditures. The OECD has recently conducted such an analysis, yielding inconclusive results.[47] The study rightly notes several severe problems with drawing conclusions based on spending figures. Some aspects of active labor market policy, including the interaction of its various components, are not adequately accounted for by budgetary figures. And in many countries the budget devoted to labor market measures is more a response to than a cause of labor market performance. Consequently, I shall rely on a less exact, but probably less misleading, mode of assessment.

The best single indicator of labor market performance is the unemployment rate. Looking at unemployment alone tells us little, however, because nations may be able to achieve low jobless rates at the expense of other desirable goals. If labor market policy affects economic outcomes, its impact should be apparent in the way countries are able to manage the potential trade-offs between such goals. One way to hold down unemployment, for example, is by limiting the size of the labor force (e.g., by discouraging women from working, limiting foreign guest workers, and so on). Figure 4.5 charts average labor force participation rates with unemployment for 16 of our countries (unemployment data are not available for Switzerland) between 1960 and 1990. Successful labor market performance also requires not only that citizens be employed, but that they be employed in decent-paying jobs. A useful measure of the latter is the degree of wage dispersion between industries. Figure 4.6 shows this (the interindustry coefficient of variation in hourly earnings adjusted for part-time employees, expressed as a percentage) for the year 1985 with unemployment. Finally, Figure 4.7 shows unemployment together with productivity growth. Because productivity refers to output per employed person, countries with lower rates of unemployment may, all else being equal, exhibit lower rates of productivity growth.

Plainly, Sweden's record is superior to that of the United States. Indeed, as noted earlier, Sweden has been the most successful industrialized nation at integrating its population into the workforce while maintaining low jobless rates. Other nations with particularly strong records in this area include Japan, Norway, and Finland. Sweden has also been the most successful at holding unemployment in check without resorting to mass employment in low-wage

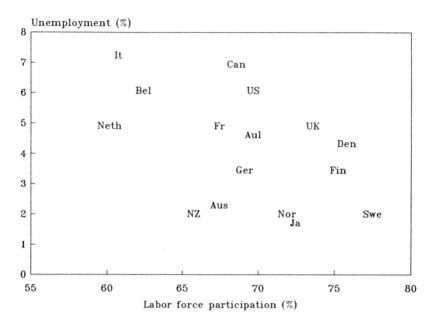

Figure 4.5 Labor force participation and unemployment, 1960-90
NOTE: For data sources see Appendix A.

jobs; its level of interindustry wage dispersion is the lowest among the 16 countries. The next best performers here are Norway, Germany, and Denmark. In terms of combining high productivity growth with low unemployment, Sweden is not at the top. Yet it is among the best performers, along with Japan, Norway, Austria, Finland, and Germany. Here the U.S. record is perhaps the least enviable among developed countries.

What accounts for the success of these top labor market performers? Japan is an exceptional case, because of its lifetime employment system and firm-based training (discussed in Chapter 2).[48] The other six countries that do well on at least one of the combined indicators all have fairly extensive labor market programs. Austria and Germany focus more heavily on training, whereas Norway, Finland, and Denmark accentuate the job matching aspect along with public employment or job subsidies. As we have seen, Sweden is strong in both training and job matching.[49] By no means can labor market policy fully explain the success of these nations. Other factors, including fiscal and monetary policy and union size and structure (discussed in Chapter 5),

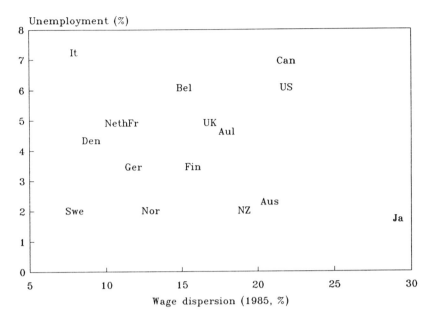

Figure 4.6 Wage dispersion and unemployment, 1960-90

NOTE: For data sources see Appendix A.

have no doubt contributed. Moreover, several countries with reasonably extensive labor market policies, including the Netherlands and the United Kingdom, have been less successful at achieving desired labor market performance. Based on the comparative evidence, then, it would appear that an active, coherent labor market policy may be a necessary (outside of Japan) but not a sufficient condition for labor market success.

These findings suggest that current wisdom about labor market performance is mistaken. In recent years a growing number of observers have argued that the U.S. labor market, which is characterized by minimal regulation and substantial job turnover, has proved superior to the rigidity-plagued labor markets of European nations.[50] The key difference is said to lie in job creation. Between 1960 and 1993 employment rose by 84 percent in the United States (and by 46 percent in Japan), compared to just 6 percent in Europe. In 1973 roughly 65 percent of the working age population (those between 15 and 64) was employed in both Europe and the United States. By the early 1990s the share had increased to 75 percent in the United States but fallen to 62 percent

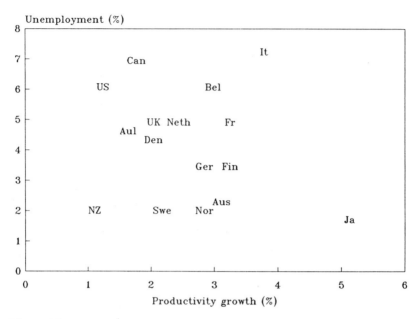

Figure 4.7   Productivity growth and unemployment, 1960-90
NOTE: For data sources see Appendix A.

in Europe. This lack of new jobs is widely believed to be the fundamental cause of Europe's unemployment problem. The jobless rate in Europe jumped from an average of 2.4 percent in 1970, to 6 percent in 1980, to nearly 12 percent by 1994. Europeans are also more likely to stay unemployed longer. Around 50 percent of U.S. jobless find work within a month, compared to only 5 percent of those in Europe.[51]

On the other hand, a relatively high proportion of the jobs created in the United States are low-paying ones.[52] Thus, pay inequality is a good deal more severe in the United States. Europeans in the lowest pay decile earn 68 percent as much as the median worker, whereas their American counterparts earn just 38 percent of the median. In addition, the jobless in Europe are more likely to receive unemployment compensation, and that compensation typically replaces a higher percentage of the worker's former income. Unemployment also strikes a smaller share of the workforce in Europe. In the late 1980s, an average of 2 percent of U.S. employees became jobless each month, compared to just 0.4 percent of Europeans.[53]

To a number of observers, this suggests a trade-off. In Europe, those on the margins of the labor market are likely to be among the long-term unemployed. In the United States, they are more likely to be stuck in a low-wage, dead-end job. But this view overlooks the substantial variation in labor market performance across Europe. (The figures just cited also include some of Europe's poorest countries—such as Greece, Turkey, and Portugal—so they are not entirely accurate for the group of European nations I have been examining.) The data shown here, especially those in Figure 4.6, suggest that some nations have been able to manage this apparent trade-off more successfully than others. Except in Japan, an effective labor market policy appears to have been a key to this success.

◈ Industrial Policy

Industrial policy consists of government intervention to supplement market forces at the microlevel. In contrast to fiscal and monetary policies, which are broad, arm's-length measures, industrial policy is targeted to specific problems and in some cases to specific industries and firms. In this sense, industrial policy encompasses labor market and regulatory policy, although it is usually thought of as a separate form of government activism.

On efficiency grounds, industrial policy's justification rests on the prevalence of market failure.[54] There are a number of instances in economic life in which the structure of market incentives is such that the invisible hand does not produce efficient performance. Frequently this is a result of problems related to "externalities," lack of competition, and barriers to information.

A prominent instance of market failure concerns the provision of finance to firms. One aspect of the problem is that individuals may prioritize consumption over saving to such an extent that capital is exceedingly expensive. Another, which we encountered in Chapter 2, has to do with the allocation of finance, stemming from a gap between rate of return and social benefits. Capital may be steered disproportionately toward investments with high short-term payouts for individual investors, rather than long-term gains in growth and employment for society as a whole. In addition, by focusing simply on rate of return, capital markets may ignore the spillover benefits that certain industries have on other sectors of the economy. Semiconductors, for example, are the key component for almost every type of electronics product, from computers to televisions to telecommunications to robots. Automobiles are another example. Auto assemblers purchase raw materials, components, and equipment from thousands of supplier firms. Success in such "linkage" industries may produce broader payoffs via their upstream and downstream ties to other sectors and firms. Of course, different countries will have different linkage sectors, depending on which industries they specialize in. For the United States and Japan they may include semiconductors and automobiles, for Germany machine tools and chemicals, for Italy textiles, and so on.

A second important instance of market failure concerns research and development (R&D). Private firms face a variety of incentives to underinvest in R&D. One is uncertainty. It is impossible to know ahead of time whether a technology can be successfully developed and the extent to which it will result in profits for the developer. Another is that knowledge is often nonexclusive. It can be difficult to prevent other firms from obtaining and appropriating the benefits of one's research. Of course, patents and copyrights help to protect inventor property rights, but they are less than perfect at preventing piracy.

Market failure also occurs in the transfer of technology. Small and medium-size firms, in particular, often cannot keep up with the latest technological advancements. Acquiring such information can be costly and time consuming, and implementing new technology requires a degree of expertise not always present in such firms.

Another instance of market failure involves cooperation among firms. Collaborative efforts in research or production can yield substantial benefits to firms and economies. Knowledge interaction effects can be exploited, risk pooled, scale economies realized, and wasteful duplication of effort avoided. But because of the costs involved and the risk of exploitation, cooperation between firms may not occur without some outside inducement.

The prevalence of market failure suggests that an economy relying exclusively on markets would operate far below its potential efficiency. It also has important implications for trade between nations. In the orthodox model of international trade, all countries are assumed to have access to the same technology, so comparative advantage in industries is determined by national endowments of natural resources and production factors. Countries with fertile soil for growing bananas produce and export bananas; those with rich iron ore deposits manufacture and export steel; those with lots of labor relative to capital specialize in labor-intensive goods; and so on. But the theory has limited relevance to real-world trading conditions. For most products comparative advantage is not inherited; it is created. Cost and quality differentials in labor, equipment, and knowledge are not determined by static endowments; they are created by gaining a dynamic edge in technology, efficiency, and/or skills.

At least in theory, government intervention in the form of industrial policy can help prevent or compensate for market failures and thereby increase allocative efficiency and social benefits. The market liberal view contends that government action is unlikely to succeed in this objective, for the reasons noted earlier:

1. There is a disjunction between government expenditures and revenues, so efficiency incentives are weak.
2. Government action is susceptible to hijacking by rent-seeking special interests, to the detriment of the general welfare.[55]

What does the comparative record say? There is no hard and fast means of evaluating industrial policy on a comparative basis, for the simple reason that industrial policy encompasses such a wide array of objectives, in pursuit of which governments use a multiplicity of policy instruments. I am forced to rely, therefore, on anecdotal evidence.

The country best-known for use of a proactive industrial policy is, of course, Japan. The chief function of Japanese industrial policy has been to promote the development of key sectors. Japan's economic agencies—led by the Ministry of International Trade and Industry (MITI)—have supplied firms in targeted industries with subsidies and low-interest loans through the Japan Development Bank, the Japan Export-Import Bank, and other government financial institutions. They have offered firms special tax incentives, such as accelerated depreciation privileges, low tax rates on profits, and exemption from tariffs on imported production inputs. MITI has imposed quotas and tariffs on imports that compete with the products of these industries and has restricted foreign direct investment. Preferential treatment has been given to firms in these sectors in the authorization of patent and know-how contracts. Quasi-public agencies have been created to facilitate the purchase of goods produced in these sectors. In several instances MITI has initiated and helped fund research consortiums among the leading firms in an industry. Perhaps most important, these various measures are designed to signal to private financial institutions that certain industries and firms should receive favorable treatment. During the 1950s and 1960s MITI focused its support on traditional "heavy" industries such as steel, chemicals, ship building, and automobiles. Since the early 1970s the direction of assistance has shifted toward knowledge-intensive sectors, such as semiconductors, computers, telecommunications, high-definition television, biotechnology, and aerospace.

At a more general level, the Japanese government has pursued a policy of "indicative planning" or "signaling," which consists of collecting information from industry associations and firms about projected technology, production, and demand trends and distributing it to other sectors and firms. This provides companies and the state with more information on which to base decisions than is available from prices alone.

> MITI conducts or commissions countless study groups, industry committees, and reports concerned with new technologies, trends in international competition, and future issues. These are conducted with the input of the best Japanese experts, academics, high-level industry representatives, and government officials. The reports are broadly disseminated and publicized and are widely covered in the press. The major function of such studies is to awaken firms to emerging trends and problems, and cajole them into responding.[56]

The Japanese government—in collaboration with local prefectures, trade associations, and universities—also provides small and medium-size firms with access to a nationwide public system of technological assistance.[57] Japan has 185 consulting and research centers, staffed by 7,000 people (including more than 5,000 engineers). These centers offer research services, technological advice, testing, and training. Other public agencies and cooperative organizations provide loans, credit guarantees, and equipment leasing programs to encourage technological modernization in small and midsize companies.

The state has also engineered the concentration and modernization of several industries, particularly those in which a large number of firms operate at a smaller-than-optimum scale and produce an excessively wide variety of products in small quantities. The converse danger is that firms may overinvest, creating excess capacity. For industries in which this problem obtains, the government has in certain instances attempted to engineer cooperation among the firms in setting investment levels.

Finally, the Japanese government has provided assistance to declining industries, such as coal and ship building during the 1970s. This support is usually combined with state-led formation of a temporary cartel to organize reduction of capacity and output.

A number of analysts credit industrial policy with playing an important role in Japan's postwar economic success.[58] Others assert that, on the contrary, industrial policy has played little or no role in that success. Some of these critics point to the fact that the actual amount of Japanese government grants and loans to the private sector has been relatively small. Moreover, the "sunrise" industries supposedly favored by the state—steel, semiconductors, and so on—have been given no more aid than industries such as agriculture, energy, and textiles.[59] This argument ignores the fact that the Japanese economic bureaucracy has channeled funds to industry chiefly in an indirect fashion, via private banks.[60] Since World War II Japanese firms on average have relied on external financing for half of their investment resources, and bank loans have accounted for roughly 75 percent of those external funds.[61] Japanese banks are capable of supplying such funds partly because they, in turn, can borrow from the Bank of Japan. By encouraging low interest rates and guaranteeing loans in a selective fashion through the Bank of Japan, MITI is able to significantly influence the direction of financial resources and thus to support key industries of its choosing. Also, as noted earlier, even minor government grants provide a signal to private financial institutions that the economic bureaucracy deems a sector worthy of support. This encourages private finance to direct funds toward these industries.

A second point often made by skeptics is that several Japanese industries— including watches, cameras, motorcycles, bicycles, and tape recorders—have achieved rapid growth and become world leaders without much in the way of government assistance of any kind. This is said to indicate that the real cause of Japan's success has been factors such as intense competition, entre- preneurial zeal and foresight, flexible labor markets, a high domestic savings rate, and prudent but stimulative macroeconomic policies.[62] But this is not a genuine counterargument, for no one asserts that industrial policy has been essential to the success of all Japanese industry. The contention is merely that it has played an important role in the performance of a number of key sectors. Even so, industrial policy may have indirectly furthered the growth of non- priority industries as well. As Andrea Boltho suggests:

> It must be remembered that industrial policy gave general encouragement to large firms. Given the conglomerate nature of many of Japan's dominant "keiretsu" groups . . . government help to them may well have spilled over from priority to non-priority sectors. Considerations of industrial structure must also be taken into account. The nature of many of the sectors that grew spontaneously seems in some sense dependent on the more basic branches that MITI nurtured. It is plausible to argue that the planned growth of steel or chemicals, by spurring the economy into a self-sustained growth process, made possible the unplanned growth of radios and tape recorders.[63]

A third line of criticism has been advanced by David Friedman.[64] Friedman contends that Japanese firms have become world leaders not by reducing costs or making use of advanced technology, but rather by offering customers a varied line of specialized products. This has enabled them to find market niches alongside mass producers and to adjust more rapidly to changes in demand. Rapid product modification is a result, not of industrial policy, but rather of the proliferation of small firms using flexible methods of production.

Thus, Friedman asserts, "Japan's economic success can be explained primarily as the result of a greater diffusion of flexible manufacturing strategies in the country than in other nations."[65]

Friedman focuses on the automobile and machine tool industries, and he makes a persuasive case that the success of Japanese producers in these two sectors indeed owes in good measure to their use of flexible production. In neither case has state assistance been overwhelming, and Friedman details how attempts by MITI to concentrate these two industries and to push them toward greater standardization of products were blocked by the firms. On the other hand, MITI has supplied assistance of various kinds to firms in each of these industries, and a number of analysts suggest that this aid was crucial to the success of these companies.[66] Particularly critical was the early prohibition on foreign ownership and imports in the Japanese market. This permitted Japanese firms to get a foothold in the market and gave them sufficient time to develop their flexible, lean production systems.[67] Industrial policy and flexible production are certainly not incompatible. For Japanese firms in these two industries, they appear to have played a mutually supportive role in enhancing performance.

There has clearly been much more to Japan's postwar economic achievements than industrial policy (see Chapter 6). No one would deny this. But arguments contending that industrial policy has played little or no role in that success appear to be misguided.

Japan is not the only nation to have successfully pursued industrial policy. Among developing nations, South Korea and Taiwan have both engaged in substantial government steering. These countries are commonly viewed as among the most successful newly industrializing countries at raising productivity and spurring sustained growth. Although orthodox economists frequently attribute this success to a faithful commitment to laissez faire, the record suggests otherwise. The governments of both countries have made extensive use of loans, subsidies, tax incentives, import protection, technology assistance, and other measures to direct their nations' development toward particular industries and away from others. Each has also maintained strict control over finance, limiting foreign ownership and restricting capital outflows, in order to assure national control over industry. Careful analyses indicate that industrial policy has had an important hand in these East Asian "miracles."[68]

Among developed countries, France is perhaps the best-known practitioner of industrial policy next to Japan.[69] France has a long tradition of an autonomous, interventionist state. Following World War II, a Planning Commission was formed to guide an export-led, modernizing growth strategy. The commission used its influence over the granting of tax advantages and the issuance of industrial bonds and bank loans and credits to stimulate preferred industries and firms. Aiding the commission were the nationalized Bank of France (under the direction of the Ministry of Finance), which controlled the flow of funds in the economy; modernization commissions, the Planning Commission's links to particular branches of industry; a national agency for the collection and analysis of economic data (INSEE); and a special school (ENA) set up to centralize recruitment to the senior civil service and to train future planners. As in Japan, the French government has also engaged regularly in indicative planning.

For the first several decades after the war, industrial policy yielded substantial dividends in France. Through selective intervention and indicative planning, the French state helped turn what was a relatively backward economy at the end of the war into a strong economic performer by the 1970s. In the late 1960s and early 1970s, however, the state planning apparatus made several poor choices with regard to the steel, computer, and supersonic transport industries. Also, unlike the Japanese government, which in most cases has used industrial policy to promote domestic competition, the French government's principal aim was to create national champions in targeted sectors. As Stephen Cohen, Serge Halimi, and John Zysman note:

> When the French state intervened in the Gaullist years in pursuit of detailed objectives, it used administrative power to shape a series of national champions, one or at most two French companies in a sector that could be internationally competitive. The champion would be protected at home to be competitive abroad. The core of the notion was to use political power to override market developments and push them in a different direction.[70]

In the conditions of fierce international competition, economic stagnation, and volatile product demand that characterized the 1970s, these monopolistic firms became less competitive than before. In addition, the planning apparatus came into conflict with the political wing of the French state, as various groups that were less favored by state-led growth (those in small- and medium-sized business and in declining sectors) began to organize to pressure the government for help. As a result of these developments, the French government partially disbanded the planning bureaucracy during the 1970s, weakening its internal coordination as well as the state's links with industry. It continued to intervene on a significant scale, but no longer quite as effectively.

Surprisingly, the United States is also the home of several industrial policy success stories. Three of America's most competitive industries—commercial aircraft, computers, and semiconductors—owe their strength in no small measure to proactive government assistance.[71] In these sectors' early stages, the federal government, particularly through the Defense Department, provided a guaranteed market and substantial amounts of funding for R&D, thus enabling risky, long-term research projects. Since the 1930s the government has regularly funded more than 75 percent of R&D in the American aircraft industry, and during the 1950s and 1960s nearly 80 percent of industry sales were to the government. In the fifties and early sixties roughly half the funds devoted to computer R&D in the United States were provided by the government, and up until the mid 1950s government purchases accounted for 50 percent of U.S. computer sales. The federal government also funded about one-quarter of semiconductor R&D in the 1950s and was the principal customer for the new integrated circuit in the early 1960s, accounting for 95 percent of sales. In each of these industries government research support spurred innovation, and large, continuous government orders enabled U.S. firms to move quickly down the learning curve and achieve economies of scale.

American agriculture is another case in which proactive government assistance has made an important contribution to competitiveness.[72] Although the U.S. agricultural sector is today the most productive in the world, in the 1800s it was a relatively high-cost, low-productivity industry. In the early part of this century, the federal government began to allocate large quantities of funds to state land grant colleges to support basic agricultural research. State experimental stations helped to further develop this research. Agricultural extension agencies were set up beginning in 1914 to provide information and technical assistance to farmers. The Rural Electrification Agency brought electricity to farms across the country. A variety of public and quasi-public financial institutions—including the Farm Credit System, the Commodity Credit Corporation, and the Farmers Home Administration—were developed to assist farmers in purchasing productivity-enhancing equipment. This provision of technological innovation, advice, and capital played a crucial role in generating the dramatic productivity advances that occurred in American agriculture.

Needless to say, government pursuit of industrial policy has nowhere been an unmitigated success. Plenty of instances can be cited in which government efforts have gone awry. The most common objection to industrial policy is that it has a tendency to turn into "lemon socialism," to focus on propping up declining industries and firms or supporting uncompetitive but politically powerful constituencies. Although it is certainly true that this type of intervention is widespread, this criticism misses a fundamental point. Support for declining or weak industries—in the form of subsidies, import protection, and so on—occurs no less frequently in laissez-faire oriented nations than in interventionist ones. For better or worse, the political temptation has proven too strong for governments in all developed countries. In an attempt to stave off or cushion decline, Japan has offered subsidies and protectionism for its farmers and its coal mining industry, European nations for their ship builders and steel firms, and the United States for its steel, auto, and textile companies, among others. Although it is not possible to make a firm judgment, there does not appear to be any correlation between a nation's degree of proactive government intervention and its reactive support for uncompetitive sectors.

The question, then, is: Does proactive industrial policy work? On the whole, the answer would seem to be yes. If the effects of industrial policy show up in aggregate economic performance data, they should do so most vividly in indicators of dynamic efficiency—in particular, rates of productivity growth. Among the 17 developed nations I have been examining, Japan has had the highest rate of productivity growth during the past three decades and France the fourth highest (see Appendix table B.3). Although this is undoubtedly due in part to other factors and processes, the fact that the two foremost practitioners of industrial policy are among the most dynamically successful economies would seem to warrant at least a provisional conclusion that industrial policy has had beneficial effects. The phenomenal growth rates achieved by South Korea and Taiwan compared to other developing nations support this assessment.

Of course, like any other policy tool, industrial policy may succeed when done well but can also fail when done poorly. Comparative experience suggests several keys to success. It helps to have a centralized, autonomous government agency through which to implement affirmative government assistance. Japan's industrial policy has been greatly facilitated by the fact that the relevant ministries are highly cohesive and largely autonomous from the elected parliament.[73] And it is no coincidence that industrial policy successes in the United States have been engineered through the Defense Department and the Department of Agriculture—two relatively stable, independent agencies. Another key to industrial policy success in nations such as Japan and South Korea has been reliance on the market to guide intervention. The state's role in implementing an industrial policy is to supplement the market, not to displace it; governments do a better job of smoothing out market failure than of replacing markets. Market processes should inform government choices, and firms receiving state assistance should face a quid pro quo: success in market competition.[74] Finally, close cooperation between government officials and private sector actors is essential. Making effective decisions about when, where, and how to intervene requires sound information, which in turn depends on the degree to which government agents communicate with business and labor.

◈ Regulation

Government regulatory activity is of two types. Economic regulation consists of rules governing prices, output, service, and entry in industries such as energy, finance, telecommunications, and transportation. In the United States this type of regulation began a century ago and is supervised by industry-specific agencies such as the Securities Exchange Commission, the Federal Communications Commission, and the Interstate Commerce Commission. Social regulation, which began in force in the late 1960s, aims to promote consumer and worker safety and environmental protection. Its principal governing agencies include the Environmental Protection Agency, the Occupational Safety and Health Administration, the Food and Drug Administration, and the Consumer Products Safety Commission.

Regulation has been a focal point of recent attacks on government.[75] Only welfare policy has come in for harsher criticism. During the late 1970s and throughout the 1980s, excessive regulation was widely identified as a central culprit behind the post-1973 downturn. William Simon argued in 1978 that

> The evidence clearly indicates that the regulatory process has run amok. . . . Most existing regulation is so irrational that it should be wiped out by law, along with the bureaucracies that have spawned it. This is a disease of government; it is not government. The costs to American industry of this incredible torrent of governmental edicts and rulings are so immense and of so many kinds that they defy the imagination.[76]

President Reagan advised Congress in 1981 that "American society experienced a virtual explosion in government regulation during the past decade. . . . The result has been higher prices, higher unemployment, and lower productivity growth."[77]

One particularly influential study by Murray Weidenbaum and Robert DeFina contended that the direct and indirect costs of regulation to the U.S. economy in 1979 were $100 billion, or 4 percent of the country's GDP.[78] This amount appeared staggering in and of itself, but the study also suggested that it represented an increase of $35 billion compared to 1976. Regulatory costs were apparently growing at an alarming rate. Surely the effect was to crowd out productive investment. Several empirical analyses identified government regulation as a key cause of the productivity slowdown that occurred in the 1970s.[79] With the rise in regulatory activity during the Bush administration, critics again sounded the alarm. One estimate claims that the costs of regulation to the U.S. economy totaled $500 to $600 billion per year by 1992.[80] This amounts to roughly 10 percent of the GDP.

The chief critique of economic regulatory activity is that it tends to reduce competition. It does so by restricting entry, limiting price flexibility, and imposing costly requirements on firms. Regulation may benefit the existing firms in an industry by protecting them from (further) competition, but it may also have an adverse effect on efficiency and on the interests of consumers.[81] Some critics advocate complete deregulation of affected industries.[82] Yet although some of the criticism of regulatory activity is quite justified, the U.S. experience with deregulation suggests that the appropriate solution is not laissez faire. It involves, instead, a different form of government activism.

The airline industry offers a useful illustration. Between 1938 and 1978 air transportation was heavily regulated by the federal government through the Civil Aeronautics Board (CAB). The board regulated entry into the business, determined which routes existing airlines could serve, and dictated fares for those routes. To maximize consumer satisfaction, the CAB attempted to ensure that as many towns as possible were served and that fare prices did not rise too high. Critics contended that by minimizing competition, industry regulation eliminated incentives for cost reduction, with a consequent adverse impact on the interests of consumers.

In 1978 the critics, led by Alfred Kahn, then head of the CAB, succeeded in deregulating the airline industry. Entry, route, and price restrictions were abandoned. What have been the effects? Productivity appears to have improved, in large part due to the creation of "hub-and-spoke" routes and the airlines' ability to adjust fares to maximize the number of seats filled per flight. According to Kahn, as of 1988 fare prices per mile had declined 30 percent (in inflation-adjusted terms) since deregulation.[83] According to a study by the National Academy of Sciences, the rate of growth of passenger trips doubled between 1978 and 1989, compared to an increase of 50 percent between 1968 and 1977.[84] This signifies, it would seem, that on the whole consumer satisfaction with the industry increased following deregulation.

On the other hand, prices fell almost as much in the decade prior to deregulation as they have since then. And the shift to hub-and-spoke operations has increased the miles a passenger must fly for a typical trip; estimates of the average increase range from 5 to 30 percent.[85] Although there has been no decline in the number of towns served (thanks in part to the government-subsidized Essential Air Services program), the time required for many flights has risen, as formerly direct routes now require a connection through a hub. Any assessment of deregulation's impact must also factor in its effect on employees. The Association of Flight Attendants estimates that real wages for its members fell 20 to 40 percent in the decade following deregulation.[86]

Competition increased dramatically after 1978, with a multitude of smaller carriers leaping in—frequently to service minor routes but also to compete with the large carriers on major routes. But before long the industry began to grow substantially more concentrated. The eight largest airlines held 81 percent of the domestic market in 1978; by 1989 their share had increased to 92 percent.[87] Contrary to the expectations of the deregulators, large carriers used their scale and other advantages to drive out smaller industry players. Consequently, low fares and broad service could go by the wayside.

Sustaining whatever gains have come from airline deregulation may now require increased government activism—in particular, stricter antitrust scrutiny and perhaps a limited degree of price regulation—to ensure competition and prevent the major carriers from abusing their monopoly power. This is a qualitatively different type of state intervention than occurred previously, but it is intervention nonetheless. The key is to steer a course between the type of heavy-handed regulation that characterized the CAB prior to 1978 and the complete laissez faire that has reigned in the past decade and a half. On this point some of the principal proponents and critics of deregulation agree.[88]

The banking industry offers a second illustration. In the 1930s, U.S. banking institutions were partitioned by the government into two tiers, with *banks* permitted to make all manner of commercial and consumer loans and *savings and loans* (S&Ls or thrifts) limited to offering home mortgage loans. The federal government insured deposits of banking institutions up to a certain amount; in exchange, the rate of interest these institutions could pay on deposits was restricted, and they were subject to strict capital standards (specifying the percentage of assets a banking institution must keep on hand), which were monitored by government regulators. By the late 1970s savings and loans, and to some extent banks, had come under severe strain. High inflation and the development of money market funds, which could offer higher rates of return, were turning depositors away in droves. In 1980 Congress phased out interest rate ceilings for thrifts and banks. Yet the health of the S&L industry did not improve; in fact it worsened appreciably. In 1982 the Reagan administration, Congress, and state governments further deregulated the thrifts, allowing them to invest in virtually any type of venture and opening ownership of savings and loans to anyone.

The result, as is well-known, has been catastrophic. Taxpayers are now faced with bailing out more than 1,000 failed thrifts at a cost of more than $500 billion (including interest payments). Many blame deregulation for this course of events. But the arguments for sustaining the multifarious restrictions on U.S. banking institutions are actually rather weak. Innovations in financial services have made it difficult for thrifts to survive relying solely on home mortgage loans for revenue. Given the growing international competition in banking, a strong case can be made for permitting, indeed encouraging, the type of unification of the banking industry that effectively occurred with the deregulatory measures of 1980 and 1982. Allowing banks to underwrite securities and sell insurance is the next logical step in undoing the institutionalized division of the U.S. financial services industry.[89]

The S&L disaster is primarily a result not of deregulation per se, but of government's failure to distinguish between regulation and supervision. Along with its deregulatory measures, the federal government raised the limit on federal deposit insurance from $40,000 to $100,000, lowered capital standards, and substantially reduced its monitoring of thrifts. It is one thing to widen firms' options in an attempt to increase their competitive abilities. It is quite another to give them a free ride. Higher guaranteed deposit insurance levels, minimal capital standards, and lax enforcement encouraged all manner of crooks to enter and exploit the thrift industry, leaving us with the costly mess we face today.[90] Deregulation of banking can work only if accompanied by strict enforcement of capital standards and a reduction of deposit insurance levels.[91]

Thus, the principal lesson of the U.S. experience with deregulation of the airline and banking industries—and other industries as well[92]—is that the relevant question concerns not whether government should intervene, but how it should intervene.[93]

In the area of social regulation, critics are divided into two camps. The American business community has tended to oppose outright most government efforts to improve the environment and the safety of workers and consumers. Extraordinary efforts have been devoted to blocking or delaying passage of new legislation, and compliance with regulatory laws has often been resisted.[94] Consequently, the process of social regulation in the United States has tended to be highly confrontational. This contrasts with most other developed nations, where regulatory decision making and enforcement are more cooperative.[95]

Based on his extensive comparative survey of the causes of economic success, Michael Porter contends that regulatory standards can actually enhance performance by forcing firms to innovate and upgrade quality.

It might seem that regulation of standards would be an intrusion of government into competition that undermines competitive advantage. Instead, the reverse can be true in many circumstances. Stringent standards for product performance, product safety, and environmental impact contribute to creating and upgrading competitive advantage. They pressure firms to improve quality, upgrade technology, and provide features in areas of important customer (and social) concern.[96]

Porter finds no evidence that stringent regulatory laws undermine firms or industries. Business opposition may thus be shortsighted in many instances.

Other critics of social regulation focus on the means chosen to achieve regulatory goals. In the United States, both environmental and worker safety regulation are vulnerable to the charge of being ill-conceived. Charles Schultze was one of the first to point this out, in a seminal 1977 book entitled *The Public Use of Private Interest.* Schultze wrote:

> Once the decision to intervene has been taken, there remains a critical choice to be made: should intervention be carried out by grafting a specific command-and-control module—a regulatory apparatus—onto the system of incentive-oriented private enterprise, or by modifying the informational flow, institutional structure, or incentive pattern of that private system?[97]

U.S. social regulatory policy has typically chosen the command-and-control option, which consists of requiring industry to adopt the "best available technology" for eliminating particular types of pollution or workplace hazards.

Weaknesses of the command-and-control strategy are manifold. The regulatory standards tend to apply only to new products or factories, thereby encouraging overuse of old technologies and plants that are both less efficient and more harmful. This strategy offers no incentive for further reduction in pollution or workplace hazards below the required level. Once the standard has been met, there is no inducement for continued improvement. Firms are thus discouraged from researching better mechanisms for pollution control and worker safety; knowing they will soon be forced to adopt the new technologies, they prefer to stick with the old ones they may already have in place. The command approach is also difficult and costly to devise and enforce. It requires detailed knowledge by administrators about the benefits and costs of particular technologies and extensive inspection to ensure compliance. Finally, the command-and-control strategy encourages business to fight new regulatory measures as hard as it can. Perversely, the stringency of proposed regulations thus leads to underregulation in many areas.

As with industrial policy, a more effective approach to social regulation is to rely on incentives rather than dictates.[98] Regulatory goals can be better achieved, at less cost, by adopting measures that permit greater flexibility while still constraining business to conform to the desired pattern of behavior. Regulatory policies should be aimed, in Robert Reich's words, at "organizing and maintaining decentralized markets that can align the publicly desirable with the privately profitable."[99]

An example of the incentive-based approach to social regulation is the creation of a market in pollution permits—an emissions trading program.[100] Companies currently emitting harmful substances into the air or water would have to buy a permit allowing them to do so. Congress, or the relevant executive agency, could decide the overall quantity of pollution to allow and sell a corresponding number of permits. Any company wishing to begin emitting pollutants, or to increase its level, would have to purchase the necessary quantity of permits from another company that is able and willing to reduce its emissions. The system would provide a forceful incentive to reduce pollution emissions; firms that do so will profit by selling their permits. Government could reduce the overall quantity of allowable emissions whenever it so desired by buying back and retiring the relevant quantity of permits. Conservation groups could also purchase permits in order to reduce pollution, just as they currently purchase development rights in land to protect natural habitats. The 1990 Clean Air Act Amendments created an emissions trading program to deal with sulfur dioxide emissions, which cause acid rain. The strategy may soon be extended to other pollutants.

For pesticides and other toxic substances, taxes could help discourage use by firms. In the area of workplace safety, the chief concern of regulators would be companies' results in preventing injuries and deaths, rather than their compliance with a myriad of rigid standards. Again, taxing or penalizing injuries and deaths is the logical solution. This would give firms flexibility to choose the most effective means of compliance. Of course, using these sorts of incentives can constitute only part of an overall social regulatory strategy. The most dangerous toxic emissions and substances should be banned outright. Regulators would have to make sure that polluters do not congregate too heavily in a single area. And dangers to workers from harmful substances (such as asbestos or vinyl chloride) would have to continue to be prevented through technology standards, because the effects tend to appear long after the causes and are often difficult to judge.

For all their potential advantages, such market-based strategies do nothing to ease the burden and cost of regulatory *enforcement*. A reasonable solution here is to turn over the bulk of responsibility for monitoring to the workforce. In many industrialized countries, worker health and safety committees are a standard feature of companies; in most of Europe they are statutory.[101] These committees have authority to inspect workplaces and to respond to dangerous substances or circumstances, even to cite employers for violations. The task of monitoring and enforcement simply cannot be effectively carried out by a government administrative agency. Even with more than 1,000 inspectors, the Occupational Safety and Health Administration is able to visit only 2 percent of the 6 million workplaces in the United States each year.[102] Although the chief concern of safety committees tends to be workplace dangers to employees, they could be used to monitor compliance with environmental standards as well.

It is important to recognize that the social regulatory standards imposed in the United States during the past 25 years have had some substantial benefits. The United States has achieved significant reductions in both levels and emissions of several major pollutants, including sulfur dioxide, carbon monoxide, lead, and nitrogen dioxide. Transportation emissions were cut from 123 million metric tons in 1975 to 4 million in 1986. Automobile fatalities in 1983 were only 70 percent as high as they would have been without safety standards. The rate of workplace deaths was cut in half between 1970 and 1990, and the rate of injury and illness on the job also fell during that period.[103] Yet, this progress should hardly be considered satisfactory. According to the National Institute for Occupational Safety and Health, more than 5,000 workers are killed every year due to on-the-job accidents. Out of hundreds of toxic air and water pollutants and workplace substances, the federal government has regulated only around a dozen of each.[104]

Regulation of corporate social conduct, particularly regarding the environment, is one of the most popular types of government intervention among the public. In a recent Gallup poll, for instance, a majority of citizens in 20 out of 22 nations said they favor environmental protection, even if it hurts economic growth. In the United States, a 1989 *New York Times*/CBS poll found 80 percent agreeing that "protecting the environment is so important that standards cannot be too high, and continuing environmental improvements must be made regardless of the cost."[105] Protecting consumers, workers, and the environment effectively and with the least economic cost should, naturally, be the primary aim of policymakers. The United States could benefit from broader coverage and more stringent standards, together with a shift toward incentives rather than directives as a means of achieving the desired goals.

◈ Markets and Government

> In general, the assertion that the government can do no better than the market
> is simply false.
>
> —*Joseph Stiglitz*[106]

Markets are the most ingenious, effective mechanism ever devised for allocating economic resources and spurring their efficient use. But markets also have a number of inherent weaknesses. They are unstable, subject to cycles of boom and bust. They tend to foster income inequality, leaving a sizable segment of the population in poverty. They discourage investment in skills training and do a mediocre job of matching workers looking for jobs with employers looking for workers. They encourage misallocations of capital and an inadequate supply of research and development, and they impede technology transfer and cooperation among firms. Finally, markets do an unsatisfactory job of protecting the health and safety of workers, consumers, and the environment. It is these types of failure that rightly induce governments to intervene.

Overall, I have found little support for the market liberal thesis that government intervention undermines economic success. The evidence regarding the effects of taxation, government spending, and transfer programs is mixed, and the conclusion depends largely on one's view as to whether Japan ought to be included in the data. I have argued that there is good reason to omit Japan as an exceptional and misleading case. If we do so, the evidence suggests a lack of any adverse impact of fiscal or redistributive intervention on economic performance, except perhaps at very high levels. Certainly no trade-off is evident for labor market policy and industrial policy. If anything, greater state activism in these areas generally enhances economic efficiency. Regulatory policy in the United States could be improved by reform, but that does not mean it should be reduced. Similarly, the charges of futility and perversity leveled against each of these types of state intervention appear largely unfounded.

Needless to say, government intervention does not always and everywhere generate benefits—economic and/or social—for society. But the comparative evidence suggests that it often does.

Labor Organization
and the Common Interest

Paradoxically, unions are all the more difficult to bargain with in the name of
the public interest because labor power is so fragmented. . . . One giant union
with the power to settle for all would tend to exercise some social responsibility.
But many small or relatively small unions, each dominating its own market,
have been able to gain more for their members than a single big union could.

—Fortune magazine[1]

The labor union is an institution created by working men and women to redress
a severe power imbalance in economic life. It aims to bring a little democracy to
the workplace. Generally speaking, the same is true of works councils. But
according to the market liberal view, democracy comes with a price tag, because
labor organizations are an impediment to economic efficiency. There is a trade-
off, in other words, between democracy and efficiency. In recent decades this
view appears to have gained increasing prominence among the citizenry as well
as the policy-making establishment in the United States. According to Gallup
polls, by the early 1980s only 55 percent of the American public approved of
unions, while 35 percent disapproved; in 1957, 76 percent had indicated approval
versus only 14 percent disapproving. In the late 1970s and early 1980s polls
consistently found that 50 to 75 percent of the public believed unions are "too

powerful."[2] During the 1980s an antiunion orientation was institutionalized in U.S. government policy, with the executive branch offering direct and indirect support for an employer attack on American unions.

Unions and works councils are believed to undermine efficiency in three ways.[3] First, they may block the introduction of new technology. Technological innovation often raises productivity, but it also frequently displaces jobs, at least in the short run. Hence labor organizations, which represent the interests of workers whose employment is threatened, are expected to oppose management's desire to implement new technologies, thereby reducing investment and productivity growth.

Second, unions and works councils are thought to disrupt the market for labor by replacing exit with an alternative mechanism for workers to express their preferences—voice. Firms may suffer a deadweight loss associated with the time and effort spent negotiating wage levels, work rules, and grievances, or lost due to strikes.

Finally, according to standard economic theory, unions frequently bargain for and succeed in obtaining wages that exceed marginal productivity levels. The line of reasoning here follows on Adam Smith's legendary remark that "People of the same trade seldom meet together, even for merriment and diversion, but the conversation ends in a conspiracy against the public, or in some contrivance to raise prices."[4] Smith was referring to collusion among industrialists, but a number of economists believe the point applies to collusion among laborers as well. With higher wage costs, firms must either shed labor, raise prices, or find themselves with a diminished quantity of funds available for reinvestment. The first response raises society's jobless rate. The second leads to higher inflation. In the third case, reduced investment slows growth of productivity and output and increases unemployment levels.

How does the market liberal perspective on labor organization stand up to empirical scrutiny? The past decade has witnessed a spate of research on the relationship between unionism and economic efficiency within the United States. This chapter brings comparative cross-country data to bear on the question. As in Chapters 3 and 4, I focus on the period 1960 to 1990. The analysis here is entirely cross-sectional, as longitudinal data on unions and works councils are insufficient to permit an examination of trends over time.

◈   Technological Innovation

Ever since the English Luddite movement of the early 1800s, labor organization has been associated, at least in the popular mind, with opposition to new technology. Although frequently enhancing productivity and thus general standards of living, technology—which refers not just to machines, but also to techniques of organizing the work process—at the same time often poses a threat to near-term employment. For this reason, unions and works councils are commonly assumed to be hostile toward technological innovation.

A number of empirical studies have been conducted on the impact of unions on technological change within the United States. In a thorough survey of the research on introduction of physical capital, Jeffrey Keefe concludes:

> The statistical literature strongly suggests that unionized facilities are more technologically modern than nonunion ones. However, once differences in size and other characteristics thought to influence technological diffusion are taken into consideration, there is probably no union effect on technological progressiveness. The studies of union policies indicate that, in most cases, unions welcome technological modernization—sometimes encouraging it, most often accepting it, infrequently opposing it, but usually seeking to protect their members.[5]

Adrienne Eaton and Paula Voos come to a similar conclusion in their review of literature regarding the introduction of new work practices:

> We find that while the nonunion (or relatively less unionized) companies use profit-sharing to a greater extent than do companies in which a substantial number of employees are organized, union companies are significantly more likely to use team production systems, quality of worklife committees, and quality circles. Because this last group of programs, along with gainsharing, is more likely to produce substantial gains in productivity than is profit-sharing, we conclude that if anything, the union sector leads the nonunion sector with regard to workplace innovations which substantially contribute to improved economic performance.[6]

One reason why unions don't inhibit technological progress in the United States may be that they have limited ability to do so. A 1986 survey by the Bureau of National Affairs found that only 25 percent of sampled American labor contracts included restrictions on implementing new technology. And in most of those cases only advance notice and discussion with the union were required. Sometimes management had to agree to retrain workers, but almost never did unions have any sort of veto power over decisions regarding new technology.[7]

What about other nations, where unions and/or works councils have greater strength and reach? In Germany, for example, many firms must secure the approval of a company works council, which is often closely linked to the union representing the firm's workers, before introducing new machines or modes of work organization. In Sweden and Japan, negotiation with a union is generally required, although union approval is not usually necessary. Contrary to the market liberal view, it does not appear that these limitations on managerial prerogative impede technical advance in these countries. For instance, as of the late 1980s, the diffusion rate of robotics technologies, advanced machine tools, and flexible manufacturing systems was higher among firms in these three nations than among firms in the United States.[8] Companies based in Japan, Germany, and Sweden have also exhibited at least as much, and probably a good deal more, experimentation and success in implementing work process innovations—including teamwork, job rotation, employee participation in decision making, and profit or gain sharing—than their U.S. counterparts, in many instances with union or works council acquiescence and not infrequently with their encouragement.[9]

Unions in Britain appear to have conformed more closely to orthodox expectations. To a greater extent than labor organizations in other nations, British unions have sought, and succeeded in imposing, strong restrictions on the introduction of new machinery and work practices. This orientation is encouraged and facilitated by the extremely decentralized, craft-based structure of the British labor movement.[10]

There is an additional reason why labor organization may not result in slower technological advance. Even where unions or works councils do oppose the introduction of new technology, they frequently have the effect of encouraging firms to increase the rate of technological progress. Compensation for unionized workers is generally higher than for nonunionized workers.[11] By making labor more expensive relative to capital, unions give firms an incentive to increase the capital intensity of production. They function as a benevolent constraint (similar to those discussed in Chapter 2), discouraging employers from using low-wage labor as a substitute for capital and thereby inducing technological progress.

There is no single quantitative indicator of the rate of technological modernization for countries. Hence, we cannot directly assess the impact of unions and works councils on technological advance across developed nations. As a useful proxy, we can look at rates of investment and productivity growth.

Workers may influence decisions about the introduction of new technology through three mechanisms. The traditional form of worker organization is the union. A simple measure of labor organization prominence is the share of the workforce that is unionized, for which good cross-national data are readily available.[12] In a number of nations, works councils rather than unions have primary responsibility for bringing employee views to bear on decisions regarding new technology.[13] Works councils are workplace-based institutions of employee representation that are distinct in status and function from unions. Councils differ according to strength and bargaining rights, with some limited to information and consultation whereas others (such as German councils) have the right

Table 5.1   Unions, Works Councils, and Codetermination

	Labor Index	Union Density (%)				Works Councils	Codeter- mination
		1970	1980	1990	Average		
Sweden	1.73	68	80	83	77	1	1
Denmark	1.55	60	76	71	69	1	1
Austria	1.21	62	56	46	55	1	1
Norway	1.20	51	57	56	55	1	1
Germany	.70	33	36	33	34	1	1
Finland	.56	51	70	72	64	1	0
Belgium	.24	46	56	51	51	1	0
Netherlands	.24	38	35	26	33	1	0.5
Italy	−.42	36	49	39	42	0.5	0
France	−.59	22	18	10	17	0.5	0.5
New Zealand	−.64	na	56[a]	45	50	0	0
Switzerland	−.72	30	31	27	29	0.5	0
Australia	−.74	50[b]	48	40	46	0	0
United Kingdom	−.78	45	50	39	45	0	0
Canada[c]	−1.03	31	36	36	34	0	0
Japan	−1.12	35	31	25	31	0	0
United States	−1.36	23[d]	22	16	20	0	0

NOTE: For data sources see Appendix A. Union data refer to employed union membership as a share of the total employed labor force. na = not available.
a. 1985.
b. 1976.
c. Data are for total recorded union membership, which includes self-employed, unemployed, and retired union members.
d. 1977.

to negotiate with management. Eleven of our 17 nations have legislatively mandated works councils. Typically the law requires councils in firms above a certain size. In Germany the size limit is five employees, so the share of the workforce represented by councils exceeds that covered by unions. A final mechanism through which workers may influence technology decisions is code-termination, whereby employees elect a share of their firm's board of directors. Like works councils, codetermination is mandatory in a number of European countries for firms above a specified size (25 in Sweden, 500 in Germany).

In analyzing the impact of labor organizations on technological change, I use a composite index of scores for union density, works councils, and codetermination. The density score is an average of each nation's unionization rate for the years 1970, 1980, and 1990. For works councils and codetermination, a country is coded as 1 if the institution is prominent, 0.5 if intermediate, and 0 if absent. The scores for the three dimensions were standardized, summed, then standardized

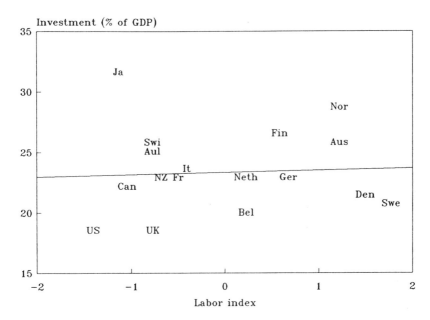

Figure 5.1 Labor index and investment, 1960-90

NOTE: Correlation = .05. For data sources see Appendix A.

again. Table 5.1 shows the labor index along with the individual scores for union representation, works councils, and codetermination.

According to the market liberal view, labor impediments to technological advance should dampen investment rates and productivity growth. Figure 5.1 suggests, however, that in comparative terms, labor strength appears to have had no such adverse effect on investment levels during the past 30 years. Some countries with relatively weak labor organization, such as Japan and Switzerland, have invested at fairly high rates. But the United States, with the lowest labor score, has the worst investment performance among developed countries. Several nations with strong labor movements, including Norway, Austria, and Finland, have strong investment records, whereas others, such as Denmark and Sweden, have invested less than the average. As shown in Table 5.2, a regression equation controlling for the catch-up effect and real interest rates shows a coefficient effectively equal to zero for the labor index.

What about productivity growth? Recent research on union effects on productivity growth across industries and firms in the United States has

Table 5.2 Labor Index and Investment, Productivity Growth, and Productivity Levels, 1960-90

	Correlation Coefficients	Regression Coefficients
Investment	.05	.02
Productivity growth	.08	−.13
Productivity[a]	−.39*	−.14[b]

NOTE: Regression coefficients are standardized. Regression equations include several control variables; see pp. 56-57. For variable definitions and data sources, see Appendix A.
a. 1974-90.
b. Switzerland is not included due to lack of data on unemployment.
* Significant at the 10% level.

yielded no clear finding.[14] Figure 5.2 reveals no indication that high levels of labor organization have slowed growth in productivity across nations. As with investment, among both strong and weak labor countries, we find some with a record of relatively high increases in productivity and others with slower growth. In a regression equation the coefficient is negative but not significant.

◈ The Market for Labor

A second way in which labor organizations may potentially undermine economic efficiency is by disrupting the market relationship between workers and management. In particular, unions and works councils may heighten labor-management conflict, resulting in production lost due to work stoppages. They also increase the time and effort devoted to negotiation over matters such as work rules and grievance settlements; this may constitute a deadweight loss for firms.

The standard market mechanism for communicating preferences is exit.[15] Consumers, for instance, express their preferences by choosing among various products to buy. Sales levels tell producers whether the quality and price of their products is satisfactory. Producers are thus able to make appropriate adjustments without ever having to communicate directly with a customer. The neoclassical model of the labor market assumes that the same basic process applies to the relationship between workers and employers. Dissatisfied workers express their preference by exiting—that is, by quitting and moving to another firm. In response, firms either find other workers whose preferences are satisfied by the conditions and pay the firm currently offers, or they alter the price and quality of employment. In theory, this permits a

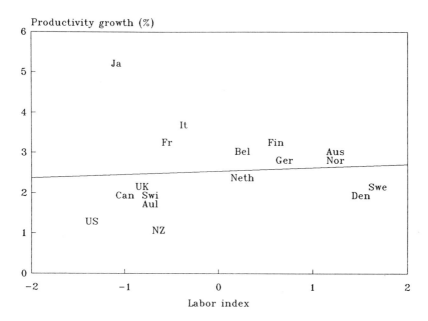

Figure 5.2   Labor index and productivity growth, 1960-90
NOTE: Correlation = .08. For data sources see Appendix A.

frictionless labor-management relationship with little time "wasted" on face-to-face communication and negotiation.

Labor organizations interfere with the market for labor by giving workers an alternative mechanism for communicating dissatisfaction: voice. This creates two potential sources of efficiency loss. First, it enables workers to express discontent by withholding their labor, via strikes and other sorts of work stoppages. Second, there may be costs associated with the time and effort spent negotiating contractual matters and addressing worker complaints through formal grievance procedures. The impersonal communication rendered by the market is, at least in theory, less time consuming and therefore more efficient.

Cross-country data can give us some insight into the former issue. If labor organizations increase the propensity of workers to engage in strikes, nations with larger and stronger unions should exhibit higher strike figures. (Authority to strike typically rests with unions.) The evidence indicates that this is not the case. Figure 5.3 suggests no association between unionization and days lost due to labor-management conflict during the period 1960 to 1990. (Data

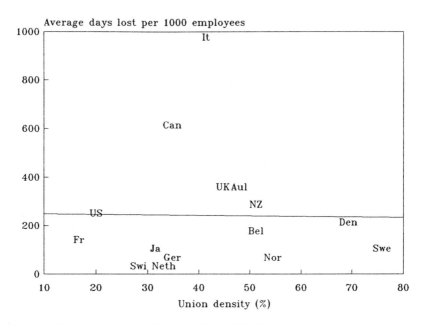

Figure 5.3   Unionization and labor conflict, 1960-90

NOTE: Correlation = –.01. For data sources see Appendix A.

are not available for Austria and Finland.) The market liberal hypothesis is further refuted if we compare encompassing versus localized union movements, a distinction elaborated in the next section (see Table 5.3 below). For the former, the average annual number of days lost per 1,000 employees due to work stoppages was 115; for the latter it was 339. This large difference owes in part to Italy's extremely high strike rate. But even if Italy is excluded, nations with localized union movements still averaged 259 days lost per year, more than double the average for countries with encompassing unions. This finding is consistent with the results of earlier research.[16]

What about the efficiency effects of time and effort spent on negotiation and grievance resolution? Richard Freeman and James Medoff have argued that union and/or works council efforts to communicate with management through voice instead of exit may enhance, rather than impair, company performance.

First of all, voice at a workplace should reduce the rate of quitting. Since lower quit rates imply lower hiring and training costs and less disruption in the functioning of work groups, they should raise productivity. In addition, the likelihood that workers and firms will remain together for long periods of time should increase the incentive for investment in skills specific to an enterprise, which also raises productivity.[17]

Unions and works councils can reduce worker exit by imposing grievance and arbitration systems, which allow employees to appeal managerial decisions, and by making seniority an important factor in pay and promotion. Formal grievance mechanisms heighten workers' ability to resolve dissatisfaction over job conditions without having to quit. Seniority provisions directly increase the opportunity cost of quitting. Empirical studies of U.S. firms conclude that American unions do indeed reduce quit rates among employees.[18] Research on employee turnover in other developed nations—including Japan, Canada, Britain, and Australia—yields the same finding.[19]

Second, "through the voice/response mechanism, the collective bargaining apparatus opens an important communication channel between workers and management, one likely to increase the flow of information between the two and possibly improve the productivity of the enterprise."[20] We have no way of determining directly whether the face-to-face labor-management communication made possible by unions and works councils is more effective than exit at conveying information. But even most economists readily admit that the quantity and quality of information provided by markets may be incomplete. And recent empirical and theoretical studies increasingly stress the payoffs firms can achieve by making use of nonmarket information provided directly by economic agents, whether employees, investors, suppliers, or customers.[21]

Given these considerations, the results shown in Figure 5.4 are somewhat surprising. There appears to be an inverse relationship between labor organization and productivity across our 17 countries. When we control for unemployment, however, the regression coefficient for the labor index is small and far from statistical significance (Table 5.2 above). This is consistent with the results of studies of interindustry differentials within the United States, which seldom find unionized sectors to have lower productivity than nonunionized sectors.[22]

◈ Wages

The conventional economic view suggests that unions frequently drive wages above marginal productivity levels, thereby contributing to inferior

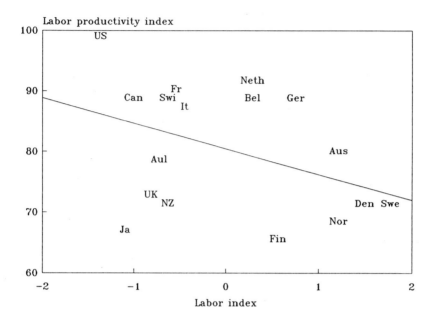

Figure 5.4 Labor index and productivity, 1974-90
NOTE: Correlation = –.39, significant at the 10% level. For data sources see Appendix A.

aggregate economic performance. If there must be unions, small, localized unions—representing a single firm or plant—are considered preferable. Localized unions are expected to exhibit greater flexibility and accommodation in negotiating compensation levels. In Assar Lindbeck's words: "Decentralized bargaining at the level of individual firms . . . is, in the long run, the system most conducive to wage moderation, as local unions then have to consider the economic situation of each individual firm separately."[23] Or as Henry Simons put it:

> No insuperable problem arises so long as organization is partial and precarious, so long as most unions face substantial nonunion competition, or so long as they must exercise monopoly powers sparingly because of organizational insecurity. Weak unions have no large monopoly powers.[24]

Larger, more encompassing unions, with greater size and strength, are expected to be more aggressive and rigid in wage bargaining. In a competitive international economy, then, nations with more powerful unions should exhibit inferior macroeconomic performance results.

During the 1980s the scholarly popularity of this view subsided considerably, as a new perspective on the relationship between labor organization and economic performance took hold.[25] The new view suggests that strong, coordinated union movements are prone to wage moderation rather than militancy. I call this view *institutional* because it takes into account the way the incentives facing labor organizations differ according to their size and structure and the economic and political context in which they act. The institutional perspective has three different, although related, versions.[26]

Three Versions of the Institutional View

Simple linear model. The key to all three versions of the institutional view is the existence of externalities in the wage bargaining process that result in locally optimal actions producing collectively suboptimal outcomes. Aggressive wage demands, if won, in many instances will be passed on by firms in the form of higher prices, which may contribute to inflation, thereby nullifying the wage gains. In addition, the country's firms may price themselves out of the international market, resulting in some having to shut down, leaving workers unemployed. High wage increases may also reduce the profit available for reinvestment, which is a key source of future wage gains. Encompassing unions, which bargain for large portions of the workforce, can and must take these considerations into account. They are constrained by their organizational status to do so. Hence, they are likely to moderate wage demands.

According to what I call the simple linear model, localized unions have less incentive for restraint. Inflation's public good (or bad) properties are most commonly said to encourage narrow, localized unions to push for large wage increases.[27] The incentive structure facing such unions approximates that of a prisoner's dilemma, as depicted in Figure 5.5. Aggressive bargaining for a localized union (union A in the figure) is rational on purely defensive grounds; if workers in other firms win high wage increases, there will likely be considerable economy-wide price inflation, so it needs a comparable wage increase just to break even. And if it succeeds in getting a high wage raise while other unions do not, the result will be higher pay in conjunction with low inflation, which is the optimal outcome among the various possibilities.

Rather than a prisoner's dilemma, the incentive structure may in some instances resemble that of a game of "deadlock," in which a noncooperative solution is favored by one party (or both) no matter what the other's preferences

Other localized unions

		Aggressive	Restrained
	Aggressive	High wage increase for A High inflation	High wage increase for A Low inflation
Union A			
	Restrained	Low wage increase for A High infliation	Low wage increase for A Low inflation

Figure 5.5 Localized union bargaining strategies and payoffs

are. That is, localized unions may prefer mutual defection to mutual coopera-tion, because obtaining a high wage increase with high inflation may be viewed as preferable to a low wage increase with low inflation. Since the raison d'être of a worker organization is to win gains for its members, if wage moderation offers no identifiable payoff it may be difficult to justify. In other words, if real wages are likely to be the same irrespective of union bargaining strategy, organizational (as opposed to economic) considerations might lead localized unions to demand high wage increases.

The simple linear version of the institutional view thus offers a set of predic-tions diametrically opposite to those suggested by the conventional economic perspective. Localized unions, which enjoy the organizational freedom to pursue the narrow concerns of their own members, often find it in their interest to bargain aggressively for high wage increases. Encompassing unions, because they are constrained to take into account the interests of a large mass of workers, tend rationally to moderate wage demands. This moderation may be disrupted by wage drift—that is, by firm-level affiliates of an encompassing labor organization bargaining for wages in excess of centrally established levels.[28] But encompass-ing unions should be expected to take this into account and to further restrain their own demands accordingly.[29]

Parabolic model. A second version of the institutional view, first elaborated by Lars Calmfors and John Driffill, accepts the point about the impact of encompassingness and centralized wage setting, but contends that extreme decentralization also leads to wage moderation. Wage militancy is said to occur in intermediate cases, where wage bargaining is conducted primarily at the industry level. The relationship between labor organization and wage outcomes is thus parabolic rather than linear.[30]

The major addition of the Calmfors-Driffill model concerns the potential effects of wage demands on employment. When a localized union wins a high wage increase from its firm, one of two things typically happens: either that increase is passed on to consumers in the form of higher prices or the firm is left with less profit to reinvest. Each may make the firm less competitive, reducing sales and leading to job cutbacks. In terms of welfare maximization, a job and a pay hike are lexicographically ordered; that is, a wage raise is possible only if one has a job to begin with. Given this consideration, it is rational for a local union *not* to push for substantial pay increases, for fear that such a strategy will result in fewer jobs for its members.[31]

If wage settlements are conducted at the industry level, the employment effects of a high wage raise are, according to Calmfors and Driffill, substantially less. Because negotiated wage levels apply to all firms across an industry, all can afford to raise prices without losing sales.[32] Hence there is little incentive for wage moderation.

The same logic applies to centralized unions that encompass a variety of industries. Here again firms can afford to raise prices in response to high wage increases, because the price rise will occur throughout the economy and consumers, in the Calmfors-Driffill model, have no available substitute for the more expensive products. All else being equal, encompassing unions would therefore exhibit extreme wage militancy. But as the simple linear model points out, economy-wide wage increases have immediate inflationary effects (whereas industry-wide increases may not). This discourages wage militancy by encompassing labor organizations.[33]

The Calmfors-Driffill model thus posits a hump-shaped relationship between centralization and wages: restraint by decentralized and centralized labor movements and militancy where wages are negotiated primarily at the industry level. It follows that the relationship between centralization and aggregate economic performance is U-shaped.

Political model. A third version of the institutional view holds that wage restraint by encompassing unions is contingent upon the presence of a leftist government and/or low unemployment. Peter Lange and Geoffrey Garrett argue that a leftist government is needed to offer labor the certainty that foregone wages will be reinvested, rather than invested abroad or wasted on consumption or speculation.[34] Colin Crouch suggests that leftist government helps "push centralized economic interests into a cooperative rather than a combative logic."[35] Others contend that encompassing unions restrain wage demands as part of a "political exchange" for low unemployment, a higher social wage, and/or greater input into policy making.[36]

Most analysts suggesting that the political context matters implicitly contend that, of the four possible combinations of labor organization and political context, the only one conducive to wage restraint is that of encompassing unions with a left-dominated government. An exception is Lange and Garrett, who suggest that wage moderation will also occur where localized unions operate in conjunction with a government dominated by a conservative party (or a coalition of such parties) that pursues free market policies.[37]

> If labor is particularly weak organizationally and in politics, it is likely that something akin to the pure play of the market will ensue. . . . Even though workers' expectations about their future material interest would dictate militancy in the market, their organizational and political weakness reduces their ability to disrupt the capitalist growth process.[38]

In the Lange-Garrett model, therefore, wage moderation occurs in "coherent" political-economic contexts: where encompassing labor movements coexist with leftist governments and where localized unions are combined with rightist governments.

Figure 5.6 summarizes the predictions of the simple linear, parabolic, and political versions of the institutional view.

An Unemployment-Mediated Linear Model

Each of these three models has a crucial theoretical flaw. The weakness of the simple linear model is noted by Calmfors and Driffill—namely, its neglect of the employment effects of wage militancy by localized unions. This gives localized unions a strong incentive to restrain wage increases.

But this point is only partially correct, for it overlooks the impact of variation in the unemployment context. The threat of job losses is likely to deter wage militancy by localized unions only in conditions of substantial unemployment.[39] If the economy is at or near full employment, it is much less difficult for workers to find another job if they are displaced. A localized union in these circumstances need not be so concerned about the effects of wage increases on its firm's competitiveness. The prisoner's dilemma applies, and its incentive to restrain wage demands is minimized.

The Calmfors-Driffill parabolic model has two additional flaws. First, it assumes a closed economy. Their hypothesis that industry-level bargaining engenders wage militancy depends on an assumption that as long as all firms within the industry raise prices, none suffers, because consumers have no available substitute for their products. But in an integrated world economy

Simple Linear Model

Labor organization	Wage bargaining strategy
Encompassing	Restrained
Localized	Aggressive

Parabolic Model (Calmfors-Driffill)

Level of wage bargaining	Wage bargaining strategy
Centralized	Restrained
Intermediate	Aggressive
Decentralized	Restrained

Political model (Lange-Garrett)

		Partisan orientation of government	
		Left	Right
Labor organization	Encompassing	Restrained	Aggressive
	Localized	Aggressive	Restrained

Figure 5.6 Alternative versions of the institutional view

that is not true. If all German automakers raise prices to compensate for high wage increases, they will (likely) lose sales to Japanese and U.S. competitors. As a result, the jobs of German autoworkers will be threatened. In an open economy with international competition, therefore, the potential employment effects of wage militancy are the same whether bargaining is conducted at the firm, industry, or national level.[40] Of course, not all industries are exposed to foreign competition. But many are—especially those that are unionized.

In any case, in several countries where wage bargaining formally occurs at the industry level—including Germany, the Netherlands, and Belgium—a high degree of union concentration, along with wage leadership on the part of important industries and collective bargaining extension practices, renders the wage setting process highly coordinated.[41] Miriam Golden has argued that the degree of labor movement concentration, or unity, is as or more important than centralization in producing the incentives and capacities associated with organizational encompassingness.[42] Where the number of labor organizations engaging in or guiding wage bargaining is small and these unions do not compete with one another for members, coordination among unions in the wage bargaining process is greatly facilitated, even if there is little formal centralization of decision making.

The German case is a good illustration. Germany has a single dominant national labor federation, the DGB. Although wages are negotiated at the industry level (i.e., bargaining is not highly centralized), the DGB encourages other industries to follow the pattern set by the large metalworkers union, IG Metall, and they typically do so. Moreover, extension laws extend collective bargaining coverage to nonunion firms. IG Metall thus faces the incentives and constraints of an encompassing organization; it is effectively bargaining for a very large share of the workforce. As Wolfgang Streeck notes, the metalworkers union

> knows that the other sectors will likely follow its lead, and that the employment of its members depends to a large extent on the propensity of businesses in these sectors to invest. IG Metall is thus forced by self-interest to conceive its collective bargaining strategies in a macro-economic framework.[43]

Also helpful is the fact that both blue- and white-collar workers, and both private- and public-sector employees, are represented by the DGB; this contains competitive bargaining among these sectors of the labor force. Overall, the degree of coordination achieved is similar to that in nations such as Norway or Sweden, which have traditionally featured highly centralized wage bargaining. In effect, then, the labor movements in Germany, the Netherlands, and Belgium, which are classified as intermediate cases by Calmfors and Driffill, behave like encompassing organizations.

The political model's weakness is that it underestimates the incentives imposed on encompassing labor movements by their organizational character. As it happens, encompassing unions often do coexist empirically with leftist or labor governments that pursue full employment. This was almost universally true during the 1960s and 1970s. But the notion that this empirical correlation is of causal importance seems mistaken. Given that encompassing unions are forced by their organizational structure to take into account the long-term interests of the broad mass of workers, neither leftist government nor low unemployment would appear necessary to spur wage moderation. Indeed, encompassing unions should exhibit greater restraint under conditions of *high* unemployment. In a context of international competitive pressure, high wage increases throughout an economy result in not only inflation, but also job losses. If a substantial share of the workforce is already unemployed, new jobs for the displaced will be all the more difficult to find (assuming the

Unemployment context

		Low	High
	Encompassing	Restrained	Very restrained
Labor organization			
	Localized	Aggressive	Restrained

Figure 5.7   An unemployment-mediated linear model of union bargaining incentives

cross-border mobility of labor is limited). The organizational character of encompassing labor unions forces them to internalize such effects, thereby encouraging wage restraint. Combined with the threat of high inflation, the prospect of increasing an already high jobless rate should lead encompassing unions to moderate wage demands even more than they would in a low unemployment context.

These considerations imply a revised set of expectations regarding the relationship between labor organization and wage behavior. I suggest that the structure of incentives facing unions is as follows: In a context of low unemployment, encompassing labor movements can be expected to restrain wage demands, whereas narrow, localized unions have much less incentive to do so. In a context of high unemployment, wage moderation by localized unions is quite reasonable, and the pressure on encompassing unions to restrain wage demands should be even further accentuated. Wage behavior, in other words, is a linear function of both labor organization and the unemployment context. Figure 5.7 summarizes these incentives.

Which, if any, of these four models is best able to account for variation in wage behavior and macroeconomic performance across nations?

What Do the Comparative Data Tell Us?

Variables. Unions vary according to structure and size. The former refers to the degree of centralization and/or concentration of the union movement; the latter refers to union density, or the share of the labor force that is unionized. Table 5.3 provides data for each of these dimensions. The indexes for union concentration and centralization are from David Cameron; they represent his scoring for the "organizational unity of labor" and "confederation power in collective bargaining," respectively.[44] Concentration is an inverse function of (a) the number of national labor confederations and (b) the number of unions affiliated with each of the confederations. Centralization denotes the

Table 5.3 Dimensions of Union Structure and Size

	Union Concentration	Union Centralization	Union Density (%)
Encompassing			
Austria	1.0	.8	55
Sweden	.8	.7	77
Norway	.8	.7	55
Finland	.8	.6	64
Denmark	.8	.4	69
Germany	.8	.2	34
Belgium	.6	.6	51
Netherlands	.6	.6	36
Localized			
Australia	.4	.3	46
New Zealand	.4[a]	.3[a]	51
United Kingdom	.4	.3	45
Canada	.4	.0	34
United States	.4	.0	20
Italy	.2	.2	42
France	.2	.0	17
"Oddballs"			
Switzerland	.6	.4	29
Japan	.2	.1	30

NOTE: Concentration and centralization indexes are from Cameron 1984, table 7.6. Density data are averages for 1970, 1980, and 1990; see Table 5.1.
a. Score not provided by Cameron. Assigned the same score as Australia here.

degree to which central confederations (a) consult with unions about wage negotiations prior to collective bargaining, (b) participate directly in collective bargaining, (c) possess the right to veto negotiated settlements, and (d) control the distribution of strike funds for unions.[45] Cameron's indexes are the most widely used in the literature and likely the most accurate.[46]

A number of researchers combine these three dimensions into a unitary index, often labeled *corporatism*.[47] Rather than follow this approach, I shall use Cameron's union concentration index. The rationale for this choice is as follows. In the realm of wage bargaining, union structure matters more than size. As noted earlier, in several countries with relatively low levels of unionization, including Germany and the Netherlands, extension laws extend union wage settlements to nonunionized workers.[48] Collectively bargained wages thus tend to cover a larger portion of the workforce than is indicated by union density figures.

How, then, should we operationalize labor movement structure? As noted earlier, centralization and concentration each encourage unions to act as encompassing organizations. We could, therefore, average the scores for these two variables to create an index of encompassingness.[49] But concentration and centralization are functional substitutes, rather than merely complements; each is sufficient, but not necessary, to generate the incentives and capacities characteristic of an encompassing organization. A country such as Germany, which has a highly concentrated but also relatively decentralized labor movement, would thus be scored too low by averaging the scores for concentration and centralization. Instead, it makes more sense to take the higher of the two scores for each nation. As it happens, for all of our 17 countries the Cameron score for union concentration is equal to or higher than the score for centralization. Taking the highest score for each country thus amounts in practice to simply using the union concentration index. Cameron does not provide a score for New Zealand. I have assigned it the same score as Australia, as Calmfors and Driffill do.[50]

Analyses of the relationship between labor organization and economic performance typically assume that the former is a constant over time. Recent research on this topic suggests that this is not an unreasonable assumption. There has indeed been relatively little change in labor movement concentration in our 15 nations during the past several decades.[51] Change has occurred in some countries, but developments have offset one another so that the overall degree of concentration has not shifted. In Sweden and the other Nordic nations, for instance, the share of union members accounted for by the largest confederation has declined in the 1980s; but at the same time the number of affiliates to the major confederations has decreased.[52] I therefore follow the pattern in the literature of using a uniform labor organization index throughout the entire time period.

Wage-setting institutions in Japan and Switzerland differ profoundly from those in our other 15 countries. These two nations have low-density, fragmented union movements, but as David Soskice has noted, the wage-setting process in each is actually highly coordinated.[53] This coordination is engineered by encompassing, cohesive employer federations, typically with union cooperation. Several analysts have argued that in Japan and Switzerland, as in other nations with relatively weak, decentralized union movements, "market discipline" produces wage moderation.[54] But this view ignores the extensive coordination that characterizes the wage bargaining process in these two nations. To the extent they exhibit wage restraint, it is, arguably, a result of cooperation among encompassing employer organizations rather than the discipline of the market.[55] Because of this peculiar institutional arrangement, Japan and Switzerland are properly considered in a different light than the other countries. I therefore exclude them from most of the analysis. Switzerland cannot be included in any case due to a lack of reliable data on unemployment, which is a key variable in my model.

The performance indicators I examine are nominal wage changes and inflation. The former can be operationalized in two ways. One is wage increases. The other is change in unit labor costs, which refers to change in wages minus change in productivity. The correlations between these two measures for our 15 countries during 1960-1973, 1974-1979, and 1980-1990 are .79, .96, and .98, suggesting that the choice of which to use makes relatively little difference. I prefer the unit labor cost measure, because it is wage increases in excess of increases in productivity that are likely to have deleterious effects on macroeconomic performance.

Unfortunately, available data on wage changes cover only the manufacturing sector.[56] For this reason, many investigators have been hesitant to use these data. Indeed, most previous research has analyzed only the association between labor organization and economic performance, taking it for granted that the purported causal link, wage restraint, occurs as hypothesized.[57] But although only a third or so of the workforce is employed in manufacturing in most industrialized countries, the manufacturing sector traditionally plays the role of wage leader, with other sectors following, to a greater or lesser degree, the patterns set there. Wage developments in manufacturing thus represent a reasonable, although plainly imperfect, proxy for developments in the nation as a whole.

Empirical studies frequently find that wage demands are influenced by the expected rate of inflation.[58] Some would therefore argue that we should be looking at real, rather than nominal, wage trends. I use nominal figures here for two reasons. First, a prominent line of research suggests that workers and unions often focus on nominal wage levels.[59] Second, and more important, wage increases are frequently as much or more a cause of inflation than a consequence. To suggest, for instance, that nominal wage (or unit labor cost) increases have tended to be relatively high in Italy or Britain because inflation has been high is to put the cart before the horse. If rapid wage gains cause rapid price increases, which then contribute to further rapid wage increases, it makes little sense to attribute the wage patterns to inflation. This sort of tug-of-war sparked by wage pressures has been a common feature of inflationary episodes, particularly that of the mid-to-late 1970s.[60] The correlations between nominal unit labor cost changes in manufacturing and economy-wide price inflation for our 15 countries are very strong: .70 for 1960-1973, .94 for 1974-1979, and .91 for 1980-1990. (For real unit labor cost changes, by contrast, they are −.07, .14, and −.33.) A wage-push perspective, which underlies all theories linking labor organization to macroeconomic performance, views this association as largely a product of wage developments influencing prices, rather than vice versa.

Most previous research in this area has treated unemployment as one of the principal outcomes of differences in labor organization.[61] But although associations, in some cases quite strong, have indeed been found between various measures of labor organization and unemployment performance, the connection between these variables, if genuine, does not appear to be a result of wage restraint. The correlations between unit labor cost changes and unemployment for our 15 countries during 1960-1973, 1974-1979, and 1980-1990 are −.52, .19, and −.13. If wage behavior had the causal effect on unemployment posited by most observers, these correlations should be strongly positive. Furthermore, recent investigations suggest convincingly that cross-country variation in unemployment levels is determined largely by state policy.[62]

Another possible performance indicator is growth. This is the variable for which the Lange-Garrett political model has been found to have explanatory success.[63] Growth, however, is affected by so many factors that its theoretical link with wage behavior is tenuous. The data support this skepticism. The correlations between unit labor cost changes and per capita growth for our three time periods are .13, −.13, and .11.[64]

Examination of the raw data and regression analysis indicate that none of the four institutional models is of any utility in accounting for variation in wage changes and inflation during the 1960-1973 period. Although the 1960s are considered by some to have been the heyday of corporatism and coordinated wage bargaining,[65] structural differences in national labor movements do not appear to have contributed to varying economic performance during that decade. This finding justifies the emphasis in the literature on the post-1973 period.

The raw data. Table 5.4 shows the comparative data on wage behavior and inflation for the periods 1974-1979 and 1980-1990. These two periods are analyzed separately here, unlike in previous chapters, because several important changes in government partisanship and unemployment context occurred around 1980. For ease of exposition, labor movements and the unemployment context are each grouped into two categories: encompassing and localized, and high and low. For labor organization the cutoff is .5 on Cameron's concentration index (see Table 5.3 above). For unemployment I use 6 percent.

Table 5.4 Labor Organization, Unemployment Context, and Economic Performance (Percentages)

	1974-79				1980-90		
	Unemployment	Change in Nominal Unit Labor Costs	Inflation		Unemployment	Change in Nominal Unit Labor Costs	Inflation
Encompassing/low unemployment				**Encompassing/high unemployment**			
Austria	1.7	7.4	6.3	Belgium	10.9	2.8	4.7
Belgium	5.7	10.3	8.4	Denmark	8.1	5.7	6.5
Denmark	5.1	12.5	10.8	Germany	6.7	2.9	2.9
Finland	4.4	12.4	12.8	Netherlands	9.6	2.2	2.8
Germany	3.4	4.4	4.7	Average	8.8	3.4	4.2
Netherlands	4.9	7.1	7.2				
Norway	1.8	9.9	8.7	**Encompassing/low unemployment**			
Sweden	1.9	10.3	9.8	Austria	3.3	4.1	3.8
Average	3.6	9.3	8.6	Finland	4.7	6.7	7.2
				Norway	3.0	6.9	7.9
Localized/high unemployment				Sweden	2.4	7.3	8.1
Canada	7.2	10.4	9.2	Average	3.4	6.3	6.8
Italy	6.6	19.4	16.1				
United States	6.7	8.5	8.5	**Localized/high unemployment**			
Average	6.8	12.8	11.4	Australia	7.4	7.9	8.3
Average w/o Italy	7.0	9.5	8.9	Canada	9.2	5.3	6.3
				France	9.0	6.7	6.9
Localized/low unemployment				Italy	10.0	9.8	10.6
Australia	5.0	11.8	12.1	New Zealand	4.8	8.1	11.3
France	4.5	14.3	10.7	United Kingdom	9.2	8.8	7.5
New Zealand	0.8	14.2	13.8	United States	7.0	3.5	5.5
United Kingdom	4.2	15.0	15.6	Average	8.1	7.2	8.1
Average	3.6	13.8	13.1				
				"Oddballs"			
"Oddballs"				Japan	2.5	0.8	2.6
Japan	1.9	9.8	9.9	Switzerland	na	3.7	3.5
Switzerland	na	6.8	4.0	Average	na	2.3	3.1
Average	na	8.3	7.0				

NOTE: For data sources see Table 5.3 and Appendix A. na = not available.

One exception to the latter is New Zealand during the 1980s, which I classify as a high unemployment case. Although its jobless rate averaged only 4.8 percent during that decade, this represented such a dramatic increase compared to previous levels (an average of less than 1 percent during the 1960s and 1970s) that it is likely to have been perceived by unions as very high.

The observed patterns correspond quite well with the predictions of the unemployment-mediated linear model. Several are worth highlighting. First, encompassing labor movements in a low unemployment context and localized unions in a high unemployment context exhibited comparable wage behavior during both periods. Not surprisingly, results for inflation were likewise comparable. This suggests, contrary to the simple linear model, that localized unions are no less able than encompassing unions to restrain wages, provided the unemployment context is conducive. An exception to this pattern is Italy during 1974-1979, where extremely high wage increases occurred despite high unemployment. If Italy is omitted from the average for its group, the overall pattern conforms more closely to what the unemployment-mediated model predicts.

Second, the four countries with localized unions in a low unemployment context exhibited substantial wage militancy during the 1974-1979 period. Consequently, they suffered much higher average inflation levels than did nations in the other groups. The differing wage behavior of localized unions in high and low unemployment contexts again illustrates the weakness of the simple linear model. In failing to take into account the importance of the unemployment level, this model ignores an important mediating factor in labor organization's effect on wage developments.

Third, during the 1980s encompassing labor movements were more successful than their localized counterparts at achieving wage restraint within a high unemployment context. Belgium, Denmark, Germany, and the Netherlands exhibited considerable moderation in that decade; nominal unit labor costs increased much less rapidly than in the seven high unemployment nations with localized unions. As a result, the former enjoyed substantially lower levels of inflation than the latter, despite similar unemployment rates.

Finally, among countries with encompassing labor movements, wage increases during the 1980s were more moderate in circumstances of high unemployment and rightist government than in a low unemployment/leftist government context. In Belgium, Denmark, Germany, and the Netherlands, unemployment averaged nearly 9 percent and leftist parties held, on average, less than 20 percent of the cabinet seats during the 1980s. In Austria, Finland, Norway, and Sweden, the jobless rate averaged only 3.4 percent and parties of the left held 60 percent of the cabinet positions.[66] Yet the former group of countries exhibited a noticeably superior degree of wage moderation. This directly contradicts the political model's assertion that wage restraint by encompassing unions is a product of some sort of political exchange with government. This hypothesis was impossible to assess empirically during the 1960s and 1970s because encompassing unions almost invariably coexisted with sympathetic governments and low unemployment. But developments in the 1980s suggest that it is mistaken. As the unemployment-mediated model contends, the combination of encompassing unions with a high unemployment context produces greater wage restraint than the other three institutional configurations. The pronounced difference between the wage behavior of encompassing unions in a high unemployment context and their counterparts in a low unemployment environment also once again emphasizes the advantages of a model that incorporates unemployment as a mediating factor in the relationship between labor organization, wages, and macroeconomic performance.

Regression results. To further assess the explanatory utility of the four institutional models, I estimate regression equations for each. The encompassingness index is the only causal variable in the equations for the simple linear model. The equations for the unemployment-mediated model include this index along with a variable representing the average unemployment rate during the time period in question. If the unemployment-mediated model is superior, adding the unemployment variable should yield a larger coefficient for the labor organization variable. The coefficient should be larger because, according to the model, encompassing unions are not universally more likely than localized unions to exhibit wage moderation. They are more likely to do so only given a particular unemployment context. Thus, for instance, the model predicts that encompassing unions in a low unemployment context and localized unions in a high unemployment environment should exhibit comparable restraint; but given a low (or high) unemployment context, encompassing labor movements should exhibit greater moderation than localized unions (see Figure 5.7 above). Controlling for unemployment should thus produce a stronger effect for labor organization. Adding the unemployment variable should also increase the amount of variation in wage changes and inflation explained by the model. This is indicated by the magnitude of the regression equation's adjusted R^2, which usually varies between 0 and 1. The adjusted R^2 should be higher for the unemployment-mediated model because unemployment matters; including it should heighten the model's explanatory power.[67]

Calmfors and Driffill provide their own combined ranking of labor movement centralization and concentration. To test their parabolic hypothesis, they then rearrange the ranking so that the most and least centralized cases are ranked first, the next most and least centralized are ranked second, and so on. I use their revised ranking as the sole causal variable in the equations for their model.

Lange and Garrett test their political model using an interaction regression equation with three main causal variables: a labor organization variable, a

Table 5.5 Regression Results

	1974-79				1980-90			
	A	B	C	D	E	F	G	H
Change in nominal								
unit labor costs								
Cameron LO (–)	–.72***	–.63***			–.81***	–.41*		
Unemployment (–)	–.18				–.64**			
Calmfors–Driffill LO (+)			.27				.12	
Lange-Garrett LO (+)				.08				.22
Government								
partisanship (+)				–.24				.41
Interaction (–)				–.12				–.82
Adjusted R^2	.32	.35	.00	–.16	.33	.11	–.06	–.16
Inflation								
Cameron LO (–)	–.69**	–.57**			–.92***	–.47**		
Unemployment (–)	–.23				–.73***			
Calmfors-Driffill LO (+)			.32				.18	
Lange-Garrett LO (+)				.22				–.07
Government								
partisanship (+)				.41				.64
Interaction (–)				–.82				–.33
Adjusted R^2	.26	.27	.03	–.16	.47	.16	–.04	–.08

NOTE: Standardized coefficients. LO = labor organization. Signs in parentheses indicate the predicted coefficient signs. Japan and Switzerland are not included (see pp. 135-136). For variable definitions and data sources, see Table 5.3 and Appendix A.
* 10% level; ** 5% level; *** 1% level.

government partisanship variable, and a multiplicative combination of these two. Their labor organization index has two components: centralization, which is the average of Cameron's scores for union concentration, union centralization, and the scope of collective bargaining; and union density, also taken from Cameron.[68] The labor organization index is the sum of the standardized scores for these two components.[69] Government partisanship is measured as the average share of cabinet portfolios held by leftist parties during the time period in question. Following Alvarez, Garrett, and Lange's 1991 article, I use data provided by Duane Swank for this variable.[70]

The regression results for 1974-1979 and 1980-1990 are shown in Table 5.5. Because the labor organization variable is operationalized differently in the various models and two of the models include additional variables, the coefficients are not strictly comparable. They do, however, give us an idea of the relative utility of the models. The adjusted R^2s offer a more direct means of comparison.

The parabolic (Calmfors-Driffill) model has little explanatory strength. All of the regression coefficients have the predicted sign, but none is particularly large or statistically significant. The equations explain virtually none of the variation in wage changes and inflation.

The political (Lange-Garrett) model fares no better. The labor organization coefficient in this model is expected to be positive.[71] One of the coefficients has the wrong sign, however, and the other three are fairly small. The R^2s are all very low. If Cameron's concentration index is used instead of the Lange-Garrett operationalization of the labor organization variable, significant negative coefficients result in three of the four equations (not shown here).[72] This suggests that labor organization, as measured by union concentration, induces wage restraint irrespective of the political context.

The two linear models, the simple model and the unemployment-mediated model, perform much better. For 1974-1979, the labor organization coefficients for each model are large and significant at the 5 percent level or better. The models explain roughly a third and a quarter of the cross-national variation in wage changes and inflation,[73] respectively. For this time period the unemployment variable adds little or nothing to the model.

For the 1980s, however, the unemployment variable produces a stark difference between the two models. Although the simple model again performs reasonably well in explaining unit labor cost changes and inflation, the coefficients for the labor organization variable in the unemployment-mediated model are twice as large and the model accounts for three times as much of the variation in the dependent variables. These results suggest that, for the 1980s at least, the unemployment context clearly influences the effect of differences in labor organization on wage behavior.

To check the robustness of these results for the unemployment-mediated and simple linear models, I reestimated the equations using two alternative measures of labor organization. One is an average of the Cameron scores for union concentration and centralization. The other is an index based on 12 indexes and rankings of corporatism or labor movement encompassingness from the literature, which were standardized, summed, then standardized again.[74] The differences in results between the two models (not shown here) were similar to those obtained using the Cameron concentration index. For the 1974-1979 period, the coefficients and R^2s were similar for the two models, whereas for the 1980s they were each much higher for the unemployment-mediated model. This offers further support for the view that the unemployment context mattered during the 1980s. Its importance is not a function of the particular operationalization of union encompassingness.[75]

Why does unemployment appear to have had little or no impact on wage behavior and inflation during the 1974-1979 period? Advocates of monetarist theory contend that the simultaneous occurrence of high unemployment and high inflation in these years demonstrates the fallacy of the Phillips Curve assumption of a trade-off relationship between the two.[76] But the phenomenon of stagflation during this period may simply have been the result of an exceptional concurrence of developments, including the 1973 oil price shock, international monetary instability following the collapse of the Bretton Woods exchange rate regime in 1972-1973, a dramatic increase in foreign competition due to the rapid expansion of international trade, the emergence of locked-in inflationary expectations, and widespread policy incoherence. Most important, because of the sustained economic advance of the 1950s and 1960s, workers and unions believed the decline in demand beginning in 1973-1974 was merely temporary. Hence rising unemployment had little initial effect on wage demands.[77] It was not until the 1980s that wages adjusted. Performance patterns in the 1960s and 1980s suggest that the mid-to-late seventies may be best viewed as a temporary exception to the inflation-unemployment trade-off.

Japan, which has a low-density, fragmented union movement, experienced moderate rates of unit labor cost increases and inflation during the mid-to-late 1970s and very low rates in the 1980s. Including it in the analysis might thus be expected to improve the performance of the parabolic model, but it does not. (These results are not shown here.) The labor organization coefficients and R^2s change only marginally, and in some cases in the wrong direction. Because it experienced uninterrupted rightist government throughout the past three decades, Japan also represents a key case for the political model. With Japan included the coefficients for this model generally have the expected sign, but most are far from significant and the R^2s are very low.

Inclusion of Japan has little effect on either of the linear models for the 1974-1979 period; the coefficients for the labor organization variable remain significant at the 5 percent level and the amount of variation explained is reduced only slightly. For the 1980s, however, including Japan renders these two models useless. The adjusted R^2s fall to near zero, and none of the coefficients is statistically significant. This suggests that for the 1980-1990 period, the utility of the linear models depends upon excluding Japan from the analysis. Because of the country's peculiar institutional arrangements, noted earlier, I believe this is justified. Also, examination of the residuals

Table 5.6   Regression Results for Misery Index Levels

| | 1974-79 | | | 1980-90 | | |
	A	B	C	D	E	F
Cameron LO (–)	–.71***			–.84***		
Calmfors-Driffill LO (+)		.24			.46**	
Lange-Garrett LO (+)			.06			.27
Government partisanship (+)			.14			.86*
Interaction (–)			–.71			–1.51**
Adjusted R^2	.47	–.02	.08	.69	.15	.28

NOTE: Standardized coefficients. Misery index = inflation + unemployment. LO = labor organization. Signs in parentheses indicate the predicted coefficient signs. Japan and Switzerland are not included (see pp. 135-136). For variable definitions and data sources, see Table 5.3 and Appendix A.
* 10% level; ** 5% level; *** 1% level.

strongly suggests Japan to be an outlier. And with Japan excluded the regression estimates are very stable, considering the small number of cases.[78]

NAIRU and the misery index. According to the unemployment-mediated model, encompassing unionization lowers what economists call the nonaccelerating inflation rate of unemployment (NAIRU), the level of unemployment at which countries can achieve moderate, stable inflation. Nations with localized union movements are able to achieve either low unemployment or moderate inflation, but not both. Low unemployment induces wage militancy, leading to high inflation rates. To keep inflation in check, such countries must resort to high levels of joblessness. Nations with encompassing labor movements, by contrast, can pursue full employment without fear of runaway inflation. They can also, if they wish, achieve very low inflation levels by raising the unemployment rate somewhat.

Thus, the benefits of encompassing unionism should be most visible if we look at the sum of inflation and unemployment rates, commonly referred to as the *misery index.* Misery index levels should be substantially lower in nations with encompassing unions. This, indeed, is the case for our 15 countries. As Table 5.6 shows, the coefficients for the labor organization variable (Cameron's union concentration index) as a predictor of misery index levels are very large and significant. The parabolic and political models perform reasonably well here, with coefficients in each case having the expected sign and in several instances reaching significance. But as the R^2s indicate, these two models are much less successful in accounting for variation in misery index levels than the unemployment-mediated linear model.

Regression results with control variables. These findings clearly illustrate the advantages of the unemployment-mediated linear model compared with the three main alternatives. It is conceivable, however, that these favorable results are spurious—a product of other variables for which I have not controlled. To assess this possibility I reestimated the regression equations for the unemployment-mediated model as a predictor of average inflation rates during 1974-1979 and 1980-1990, incorporating several control variables. One is changes in the nominal money supply. Because labor organization, like other institutional factors, may affect inflation in part *via* changes in the money supply (see pp. 56-57), a good result for the model with a money supply variable included can be interpreted as providing very strong support for its explanatory capacity. A second control variable is income equality. We discovered in Chapter 3 that greater equality is associated with lower inflation during the 1974-1990 period. A third is economic openness (average of exports and imports as a share of GDP). Nations heavily reliant on exports and imports are more vulnerable to imported inflation. A fourth is change in government expenditures, which was examined in Chapter 4; the evidence there suggested a possible positive association with inflation rates.

I estimated regression equations for inflation using all possible combinations of labor organization (Cameron's union concentration index) and unemployment with these four control variables. Table 5.7 shows the results for the unemployment-mediated model alone (equation A), for the model with each of the control variables added separately (B through E), and for the best performing combination of the variables (F).

The model turns out to be quite robust. The coefficients for the labor organization variable are consistently large and significant, even with the change in money supply variable included. The best model for each time period does fairly well in explanatory terms, accounting for around two-thirds of the cross-national variation in inflation.[79]

Summing Up

These results support the general thrust of the institutional perspective on unions, wage behavior, and national economic performance, but in a different form than that posited by its currently popular versions. The central findings may be summarized as follows:

Table 5.7 Regression Results With Control Variables: The Unemployment-Mediated Linear Model as a Predictor of Inflation

| | 1974-79 | | | | | |
	A	B	C	D	E	F
Cameron LO	−.69**	−.58***	−.61**	−.66**	−.67*	−.44**
Unemployment	−.23	−.19	−.19	−.23	−.10	−.12
Change in money supply		.54***				.62***
Income equality			−.20			−.35**
Economic openness				−.05		
Change in government spending[a]					.13	
Adjusted R^2	.26	.55	.24	.19	.12	.65

| | 1980-90 | | | | | |
	G	H	I	J	K	L
Cameron LO	−.92***	−.69***	−.87***	−1.03***	−.81**	−.71***
Unemployment	−.73***	−.47**	−.68**	−.82**	−.79**	−.62**
Change in money supply		.51***				.45**
Income equality			−.10			
Economic openness				.14		
Change in government spending[a]					.41*	.33*
Adjusted R^2	.47	.69	.43	.44	.44	.65

NOTE: Standardized coefficients. LO = labor organization. Japan and Switzerland are not included (see pp. 135-136). For variable definitions and data sources, see Table 5.3 and Appendix A.
a. New Zealand is missing in equations that include the change in government spending variable.
* 10% level; ** 5% level; *** 1% level.

1. Labor organization has a beneficial effect on national economic performance. Given a particular unemployment context, encompassing labor movements are more likely than localized unions to restrain wage demands. In effect, encompassing unionization lowers the rate of unemployment at which countries can achieve moderate, nonaccelerating inflation. Nations with encompassing unions thus enjoy superior macroeconomic performance, in the form of lower misery index levels.

2. Developments during the 1980s suggest that the unemployment context matters. Countries with localized union movements can achieve a substantial degree of wage restraint by keeping the unemployment rate high, and high unemployment accentuates the degree of restraint exercised by encompassing unions. The simple linear model is thus inaccurate. The stagflationary episode of the mid-to-late 1970s may be regarded as an exception in this respect.

3. Although mediated by the unemployment context, the relationship between labor movement encompassingness and wage moderation is linear. The parabolic model favored by Calmfors and Driffill and others is not supported by the comparative data. Nor is restraint by encompassing unions conditional on the presence of leftist government or low unemployment. The empirical evidence is not consistent with the political model advanced by Lange and Garrett and implicit in the work of many others.

4. These findings apply only to the post-1973 years. For the 1960-1973 period labor organization appears not to have been a factor in varying wage developments and macroeconomic performance.

5. Finally, Japan is an important exception, at least for the 1980s. Japanese restraint suggests that employer-guided coordination of wage bargaining may serve as an effective substitute for union encompassingness, as David Soskice has recently argued.[80]

◙ The Future of Organized Labor

Overall, I have found little evidence supporting the market liberal claim that labor organizations undermine economic efficiency. Case studies and comparative anecdotal evidence suggest that unions and works councils do not generally impede technological change, reduce labor-management conflict, lower quit rates, and facilitate improved communication between management and workers. On the other hand, the cross-national correlations and regressions presented here indicate a possible, though uncertain, detrimental effect of labor strength on levels and rates of growth of productivity. The analysis in Chapter 6 suggests that this effect may be real. It is in the area of wages that unions are expected to have their most damaging effect. Yet in direct contradiction to the market liberal view, encompassing labor movements have proved more prone than localized unions to restrain wages, and in so doing they have contributed to superior macroeconomic performance in the form of lower misery index levels.

What is the future of labor organization? Works councils appear to have gained in prominence and influence during the past two decades. As Joel Rogers and Wolfgang Streeck have written:

> There is a striking convergence among developed nations, with the sole exceptions of the United States and Britain, that works councils or similar institutions,

intermediate between managerial discretion and collective bargaining, are part of a well-functioning labor relations system. . . . The consultative councils that were set up in all European countries to promote labor-management cooperation after World War II, and later fell into disuse due to union opposition and lack of employer interest, came back in modified form in the 1970s and 1980s.[81]

The prospects for unions appear somewhat less promising. Several changes now occurring in advanced capitalist economies threaten the ability of high-density, centralized union movements to maintain their encompassing character. According to some observers, the era of "organized capitalism" is coming to a close, and with it the organizational coherence and influence of encompassing unions. Decentralizing trends threaten to disrupt and even destroy the institutional settings in which these labor movements have existed and prospered during the past three decades.[82]

First, the economic downturn beginning in the 1970s has encouraged employers to search for ways to rid themselves of what they consider to be "rigidities" associated with centralized corporatist-style bargaining. At the same time, mass unemployment gives workers an interest in promoting the survival of their own firm over and above the needs of other workers. As Wolfgang Streeck has noted:

> Under crisis conditions, the rule of the market asserts itself not just over the behavior of firms but also over workers' definitions of their interests—with their interests in the economic survival of "their" employer becoming so intense that they escape union control. . . . Trade unions trying to defend neocorporatist institutions have to fight a war on two fronts: against employers pressing for decentralization, and against members who are no longer willing to believe that centralized class politics can help them keep their jobs.[83]

This development has been most marked in nations that experienced severe unemployment during the 1980s: Belgium, Denmark, Germany, and the Netherlands.

Second, heightened international competition, increased product market volatility, and the widespread availability of microelectronic technology have encouraged a shift away from standardized mass manufacturing toward production of small batches in greater varieties. Frequent, rapid changes in demand mandate that firms be able to adapt quickly and effectively. In the eyes of many corporate managers, a prerequisite for successful product specialization is that the firm retain complete flexibility in decisions regarding its deployment of labor. This too promotes decentralization of worker-employer bargaining to the level of the firm. It encourages affiliates of encompassing union movements to forsake centralized agreements in favor of negotiation with management at the company or plant level, presaging the dissolution of national or industry-level corporatist bargaining and its replacement by firm-level "productivity coalitions."[84]

Dissension among different segments of the workforce, particularly over the issue of relative pay levels, represents a third threat to union encompassingness and coordinated wage setting. One important division is between private-sector blue-collar, private-sector white-collar, and public-sector workers. Another is between highly skilled versus semi- and unskilled employees. Yet another lies between the employed and the unemployed. Conflict among these different groups has been most visible in Sweden, where several times during the 1980s the centralized wage bargaining process was disrupted by dissension within and among the major union federations.[85]

A fourth threat to encompassing labor movements lies in the growth of the service sector. Manufacturing has always been the heart of the union movement, but the share of jobs accounted for by manufacturing has been declining steadily for several decades. Union movements less willing or able to organize service sector employees face continued declines in membership.

Finally, the interests of business and labor are to some degree devolving to the subnational, regional level, with the flourishing of industrial districts such as Baden-Wurttemberg in Germany and parts of the "Third Italy,"[86] and simultaneously expanding to the supranational level, as the European Community (EC) integrates its internal market and Asian and North American trading blocs develop. Opportunities for coordinated collective bargaining at either level appear limited. The chief barrier, again, is employers' desire to confine bargaining to the individual company. In addition, regional corporatism is rendered unlikely by the fact that political authority, at times a key facilitator of negotiation between labor and employers, tends to be weak or nonexistent at the regional level. And transnational collective bargaining is further impeded by the substantial disparities of interest between national labor movements and by the fragmented nature of the EC's policy-making process.[87]

What should we make of these developments? Clearly the threat they represent to encompassing union movements is real. Still, at present it is difficult to say anything more than that their impact looks indeterminate. It is worthy of note that encompassing labor movements did not fare especially badly with regard to unionization levels during the 1980s.[88] Table 5.8 shows the change in union density for our 17 countries between 1980 and 1990. In two of the high-density countries, the unionization rate increased slightly in the 1980s, while in four others it declined by a modest amount. In Austria and the Netherlands the rate fell by around 10 percentage points.

Table 5.8　Change in Unionization Rates, 1980-90 (Percentage Points)

Encompassing		Localized	
Sweden	+3	Canada	0
Finland	+2	Switzerland	−4
Norway	−1	Japan	−6
Germany	−3	Australia	−8
Belgium	−5	France	−8
Denmark	−5	United States	−8
Netherlands	−9	New Zealand[a]	−9
Austria	−10	Italy	−10
		United Kingdom	−11
Average	−4		
		Average	−7

NOTE: For data sources see Appendix A.
a. 1985 -1990.

Reports on individual countries do identify fragmentation in the collective bargaining process.[89] But there are at least two reasons to suspect that these labor movements might continue to act like encompassing organizations, at least with regard to wages. One is the legacy of wage moderation, which may, at least for a time, influence the perceptions and actions of unions at all levels of the bargaining process. Another is that, even if a demise of formally centralized negotiations does occur, wage setting may continue to be coordinated in an informal fashion, particularly where the union movement is highly concentrated, as in Germany.[90] Employer associations may also contribute to bargaining coordination, as in Japan and Switzerland.[91] We have seen that during the 1980s, when the decentralizing trend arguably began, encompassing labor movements continued to do a better job of restraining wage demands than their localized counterparts (Table 5.4 above). It is also conceivable that the decentralizing trend is merely a temporary one, which might be reversed, particularly if a resumption of the economic success enjoyed during the pre-1973 boom were to occur.

What does the future hold for localized union movements? One conceivable scenario is that some low-density, fragmented labor movements might increase their membership and centralization, becoming more like encompassing unions. However, this does not seem very likely. High-density, centralized labor movements are products of particular historical trajectories. First, union centralization was in part a defensive reaction to the organization of employers. In Sweden, for example, a central labor confederation was created in response to the formation of a number of sectoral employer associations in the 1890s. Union density and centralization then increased dramatically during the following two decades, owing in large measure to the formation of a central employer confederation (SAF). In some cases, centralization was foisted upon unions by employers. In Denmark and Sweden, employers in exporting firms pressured local unions into centralized wage setting in order to standardize the pay structure across sectors.[92] Second, centralization of the union movement was assisted in many cases by a highly concentrated industrial structure.[93] Third, in countries that did not participate in World War I, no major split occurred between Social Democratic unions, which in other West European nations were branded as capitulationist for supporting the war effort, and Communist unions. Instead, the Social Democrats retained hegemony in the labor movement. Fourth, unions that later became encompassing entered the electoral arena at an early stage. Affiliation with Social Democratic parties and electoral success encouraged membership and centralization.[94] Finally, Michael Wallerstein has identified a negative rationale for the existence of high-density, centralized union movements in nations with small domestic markets. Because these countries are dependent on exports, no incentive exists for unions to participate in sectoral alliances with employers to demand protectionist measures or export subsidies; by inviting retaliation on the part of foreign governments, such tactics would be self-defeating. Hence unions in these nations have the least to lose in giving up their autonomy to a central confederation.[95]

The prospects for transformation of localized labor movements into encompassing ones do not appear especially promising. The various economic shifts discussed above are making it more and more difficult for even encompassing unions to avoid fragmentation and to maintain or increase membership. Furthermore, as Joel Rogers has recently argued, localized unions face strong incentives to focus on short-run concerns and to direct the bulk of their efforts toward satisfying the interests of current members, rather than toward attracting new members.[96] If competitor firms are also unionized, labor costs tend not to be a source of competitive disadvantage for employers, who may then resign themselves to the existence of unions. By contrast, if the current level of unionization is low, and particularly if there is intra-industry variation in unionization, employers may feel the optimal strategy is to attempt to roll back unions entirely. An attack strategy by employers puts unions on the defensive. It encourages focus on the narrow, short-run interests of existing membership, such as wage levels and job conditions.

It should come as no surprise, then, that a number of localized union movements have lost substantial ground in terms of representation in recent years. As Table 5.8 shows, during the 1980s unionization declined in eight of the nine nations with low-density, fragmented labor organization, and in many of these it fell sharply. Only in Canada did the level hold constant.

It is conceivable that the future of not only encompassing unionism, but unionism itself, may now be threatened by the shift toward flexible specialization. This holds particularly for low-density countries, but potentially for highly unionized nations as well. Employers increasingly perceive a need for optimal flexibility in deployment of labor and increasingly view unions as an impediment to such flexibility. In an age of fierce international competition and rapidly shifting product markets, union survival—at least in their present form—may depend upon their finding ways to enhance firm competitiveness by promoting labor flexibility.

The most promising suggestion in this vein is for unions to expand labor flexibility by organizing and administering programs that enable workers to shift easily among jobs within firms and between firms, and that protect those who move (by choice or necessity) to a new company or region. The most important example is training programs.[97] In nations with open labor markets, firms have an incentive to underinvest in training, because of the uncertainty concerning its payoff and because of the threat of losing the investment if workers move to other firms. But skills—particularly general or polyvalent, as opposed to task-specific, skills—are critical to the success of most types of specialized production. Unions can help set up training programs within and across firms and, equally important, monitor company participation to prevent free riding. Other examples of flexibility-enhancing union activities include the administration of occupational health and safety, day care services, and portable health care and pension plans. Unions may also play a critical role in facilitating successful worker participation arrangements within firms. Recent studies suggest that participatory schemes are most effective at raising productivity when implemented in conditions associated with the presence of unions, such as employment security and narrow wage differentials between workers.[98]

Of course, any or all of these programs can potentially be carried out without union assistance. The challenge facing unions is to take the initiative in organizing and implementing them. Labor movements with higher representation levels and greater centralization/concentration should have an advantage in this effort, because they have both greater resources to devote to the task and greater leverage vis-à-vis management to ensure union involvement. At the same time, participation in these sorts of activities might facilitate increased coordination within fragmented labor movements, by enabling unions to tie the interests of particular companies to the interests of their region or industry.[99]

Ultimately, unions are likely to survive for reasons having to do with democracy and legitimacy, rather than efficiency.[100] Legitimacy in the workplace depends on the establishment of rules and procedures perceived as fair by the workforce, and that is more likely to be the case when employees have a democratically elected organization to negotiate such matters on their behalf. But there is a profound difference between survival and prosperity. The degree to which unions prosper in the new economic environment will depend largely on the degree to which they succeed in helping firms and nations enhance productivity.

◈ Results and Prospects

Those who see labor organizations as an institutional mechanism providing workers with a much-needed voice in economic affairs have reason to be simultaneously encouraged and disheartened by the findings here. Contrary to the market liberal view, a good deal of evidence suggests that larger, stronger unions enhance national economic performance. At the same time, current developments appear somewhat ominous. Although works councils seem relatively secure and growing in importance, unions face a host of threats. Unions have prospered during the post-World War II period by finding ways to combine democracy and efficiency within a predominantly fordist, mass production regime. They now face the challenge of devising new strategies in order to effect this combination in a regime of flexible specialization. What the future holds is, as always, uncertain.

The Economics of Cooperation

In the four previous chapters we have discovered that, judging from the record of the world's 17 richest industrialized nations during the past three decades, the secret to a successful economy does not lie in market-guided free choice, in more inequality, in less government, or in weaker, more fragmented labor organization. The principal assertions of market liberalism have been found wanting. On the contrary, the comparative evidence suggests that certain types of constraints, greater income equality, government activism in the form of labor market and industrial policies, and encompassing union movements may each contribute to *better* performance results. But how, if at all, do these institutions and policies fit together? Do the mechanisms through which they generate their beneficial effects have any common features? What, if anything, is the key to economic success? In this final chapter, I attempt to shed some light on these matters.

For most of the past two centuries, the dominant view among economists and policymakers has been that what drives economic success is competition. The more closely a nation's markets approximate conditions of perfect competition, the healthier its economy is expected to be. Many have been skeptical of this view, of course, and recent work in comparative political economy has generated a host of alternative explanations of variation in national economic performance. Factors such as institutional sclerosis, corporatism, government intervention, state-societal arrangements, flexible specialization, financial systems, interfirm governance arrangements, labor relations institutions, and culture have been identified as critical in various accounts. Each of these explanations, however, has trouble accounting for more than a handful of cases. Seldom, for instance, is the same causal variable invoked in explaining the success of both Japan and Sweden or both Germany and Italy. Much of this work is highly insightful, but because these studies tend to focus on only a single, isolated aspect of economic life, each can offer at best only a partial account of performance variation.

I argue in this chapter that the key to national economic success lies in combining competition with cooperation. Market competition has certainly proved a powerful motor for economic progress. But markets alone could never have generated the sustained improvement in material conditions that has occurred during the past two centuries. Nor can they produce optimal economic performance in the modern international economy. Economies succeed when their institutional frameworks offer incentives for individuals and organizations to consistently engage in productive economic activity.[1] Markets often fail in this regard. Too frequently, market incentives are such that what is locally optimal does not correspond to what is globally optimal—actions which benefit individual actors (workers, employers, investors, unions, and so on) produce suboptimal outcomes for society as a whole.

The relationship between capital and labor is a classic example. Where this relationship takes the form of a spot market, costs associated with search, negotiation over the terms of the relationship, and monitoring may be high. In addition, because neither party has any certainty that the relationship will persist, each is encouraged to act with very short time horizons, which discourages a range of beneficial behavior. Partly to overcome these and other inefficiencies of spot market transactions, the capital-labor relationship in modern capitalist economies is organized predominantly within firms.

However, the firm remedies only one of many such structural inefficiencies endemic to a capitalist economy (and only partially at that). Market capitalism is by nature rife with circumstances in which locally optimal actions yield globally suboptimal outcomes. Some of these circumstances are produced by markets themselves; others are associated with institutions, such as the firm, which have supplanted market relations. Problems of institutional inefficiency plague virtually all of the key relationships among economic actors in a market-based economy. Specifically, such problems occur at three levels. At the macro level, they occur in the relations among firms in different industries, among unions, and between government and interest groups. At the meso, or sectoral, level they obtain in the relationships between purchaser and supplier firms, between investors and producers, and among competing firms. Structural inefficiencies also exist at the micro level—that is, within the firm—in the relationships between labor and management, among workers, and among functional divisions within firms.[2]

These circumstances, I shall argue, are characterized by a common feature: Obtaining the collective good requires some sort of cooperative behavior between economic agents, and this cooperation is generated by nonmarket or extramarket institutions such as long-term, ongoing relationships and formal organization. Repeated interaction is conducive to the development of trust and holds out the threat of retaliation.[3] Organizations can induce cooperative behavior by offering selective incentives or by threatening to sanction members who defect.[4] Or they can intercede on actors' behalf to make the decision for them; here cooperation takes the form of organized coordination.

The need for cooperation-inducing institutions does not automatically bring them into existence. The degree to which such institutional solutions are used varies widely across developed capitalist economies. This variation, I contend, is a key factor accounting for differences in performance success among these countries.

I proceed as follows. The first section discusses a series of important relationships among economic actors in which cooperation-inducing institutions are needed to encourage beneficial behavior. The second describes the varying degrees of cooperation obtaining in the 17 richest market economies. The third section provides an empirical assessment of cooperation's influence in accounting for differential economic performance success across these nations during the period 1960-1990. The fourth assesses developments since 1990. The fifth discusses the origins of cooperative economic institutions. The final section offers some concluding remarks.

◈ Institutions and Economic Cooperation

In this section I discuss nine important macro-, meso-, and micro-level economic relationships in which the structure of incentives is frequently such as to discourage collectively beneficial cooperative behavior. In each case, I argue, nonmarket or extramarket institutions are needed to induce cooperation. Table 6.1 provides an overview of the discussion.

Macro-Level Cooperation

Cooperation among firms in different industries. Perhaps the most forceful objection to state intervention in economic affairs is based on government's vulnerability to abuse by rent-seeking special interest groups. As Mancur Olson has cogently argued, groups that constitute only a small portion of

Table 6.1 Summary of Key Types of Economic Cooperation

Actors Cooperating	Institution(s) Promoting Cooperation	Economic Benefits
Macro level		
1. Firms across industries	Centralized business federation	Reduced rent-seeking
2. Unions	Centralized and/or concentrated labor movement	Wage restraint
3. Government and interest groups	Centralization/concentration of authority in the state and interest groups	Coherent, productive government policy
Meso level		
4. Purchasers and suppliers	Long-term commitment by purchasers	Heightened communication, greater supplier willingness to invest and raise productivity
5. Investors and producers	Long-term commitment by investors—a product of investors having large ownership stakes and a means of effectively influencing producer decision making	Extended time horizons for producers
6. Competing firms	Industry trade associations or consortiums; government incentives	Quicker agreement on standards; greater investment in R&D and employee training; assistance with financing, technology diffusion, design, accounting, marketing, etc.
Micro level		
7. Labor and management	Long-term commitment by employers (employment guarantee)	Greater willingness on the part of workers to share valuable knowledge, accept productivity-enhancing technology, and upgrade skills
8. Workers	Employee participation in decision making combined with team production and/or revenue sharing	Greater work effort
9. Functional divisions within firms	Unified teams that link the various departments along the production chain	Quicker, more effective transition from R&D to production

society have a strong incentive to direct their efforts toward obtaining redistributive gains, or social "rents," which come at the expense of the rest of society.[5] At the same time, as public choice theorists have noted, politicians may increase their chances of reelection by attempting to please as many such groups as possible.[6] If citizens and politicians act rationally, then, government will end up allocating a significant share of social resources toward fulfillment of the needs of special interests, to the detriment of the larger social welfare.

Among the various societal collectivities susceptible to rent-seeking, business has perhaps the strongest interest, and the greatest capacity, to engage in such activity. Firms and industries can benefit handsomely from government-provided subsidies, favorable tax treatment, protection from imports, and so on. Of course, business lobbyists do not always get what they want, and it is by no means necessarily the case that government support for particular industries is inimical to the general interest. But it is probably safe to assert that the more fragmented the business lobby is—the less cooperation across industry lines—the less productive its efforts will be for society.[7]

One of the most effective means of achieving such cooperation is via the organization of firms across industries into a centralized business federation.[8] As Olson notes, the more encompassing the organization, the less likely it is to seek redistributive gains. By pursuing a rent-seeking strategy, its members would be taking largely from themselves, so they rationally choose instead to try to increase the size of the social product.[9] A central organization with the authority to speak and negotiate on behalf of its members cannot eliminate lobbying by individual industry associations and firms. But it can help reduce the likelihood that specific interests will dominate policy making, both by moderating the demands of firms and trade associations and by itself lobbying on behalf of the general interest.

Cooperation among firms and industries also yields benefits in the realm of wage bargaining. As I discuss in the next subsection, cooperation between labor unions is conducive to wage restraint. The same holds for employers. Indeed, the gains from union coordination cannot occur without parallel coordination on the part of employers. Centralized wage bargaining presupposes two parties with the authority to negotiate on behalf of their constituencies.

Cooperation among unions. In the conventional economic view, if there must be unions, small, localized unions are considered preferable. Free to take into account the circumstances of their particular firm or plant, localized unions are expected to exhibit greater flexibility and accommodation in negotiating compensation demands. However, as we discovered in Chapter 5, localized unions actually face powerful incentives favoring wage militancy.

Aggressive bargaining for each individual union is rational on purely defensive grounds, because if workers in other firms win high wage increases, there will likely be considerable economy-wide price inflation, so it needs a comparable pay hike just to break even. And if it succeeds in getting a high wage raise while other unions do not, its members will have higher pay in conjunction with low inflation, which is the best outcome among the various possibilities. Regardless of what it believes other unions will do, therefore, the rational choice for a localized union is to demand a substantial pay increase.[10]

There are two ways to obtain the cooperative solution—restraint—to this wage bargaining dilemma. One is to keep unemployment relatively high. Each local union knows that a large pay increase may price its firm out of the market, resulting in a loss of jobs for its members. In a context of low unemployment, alternative jobs are readily available. But where unemployment is high, it is difficult for displaced workers to find new jobs. Thus, if wage negotiation occurs in a context of high joblessness, the incentive for localized unions to bargain aggressively is diminished. By structuring the incentives in this way, a nation with a fragmented union movement can achieve a reasonable degree of wage restraint.[11] Yet, high unemployment is a rather severe price to pay.

Alternatively, wage restraint can be achieved via union centralization and/or concentration. Where a single representative bargains for a large share of the workforce, the potential gains from defection evaporate. Individual unions no longer have the option of free riding. All get either high wage increases with high inflation or low wage increases with low inflation. Given inflation considerations alone, the choice would appear to be a toss-up, because the real wage rate (the wage increase minus inflation) is roughly the same in either case. But in an integrated world economy, centralized unions have a strong incentive to moderate wage demands. High prices reduce local firms' competitiveness in the international market, leading to job losses for the nation. If workers were as mobile as goods and money, this would pose no problem. But with a few exceptions, labor does not easily shift across national borders. Hence, union coordination tends to produce wage restraint, irrespective of the unemployment context.[12]

Cooperation between government and interest groups. Government policy is a key determinant of economic performance. Whether general in nature, such as fiscal and monetary policy, or targeted and specific, such as industrial and labor market policy, government decisions directly influence the options and incentives confronting economic agents. In this arena it is essential that

rivalry be contained. Where government and private actors work at cross purposes, the general welfare tends to suffer. Where they cooperate, the community frequently benefits.

In general, the smaller the number of parties engaged in negotiation, the
easier it is to forge consensus and the more likely the outcome will benefit all.
The larger the number, the more difficult it becomes to reach agreement and
the less likely it is that the collectivity will benefit from whatever decision is
reached. Where business and/or labor are fragmented, each firm or industry
association or union tends to press its own particular interests upon state
officials. The relationship tends to be combative and conflictual. With private
actors struggling against one another and government agencies attempting to
please as many groups as possible, state policy has little coherence. Fragmentation within government accentuates this tendency. Where state decision
making is decentralized, societal actors are presented with an array of entry
points through which to press their concerns, and government agencies
compete with one another for status and control over resources. The result is
a lack of consistency and coherence in government policy.

The United States offers a prime illustration of the counterproductive
effects of interest group and state fragmentation, as we saw in Chapter 4.
Regulation tends to be much more conflictual in the United States than in
other developed nations. For any particular piece of regulatory legislation,
different industries and industry segments (which may be differentially affected by the law) lobby against one another, while a variety of consumer
groups argue their own position. The result is that some minimal regulatory
efforts are blocked, whereas in other cases extremely stringent and obtrusive
standards are imposed on business. U.S. industrial policy is an incoherent
mishmash, as different agencies and levels of government offer supports and
impose penalties that sometimes counteract one another. Similarly, labor
market programs are caught between the desire by some proponents to have
them play an instrumental role in skill upgrading and the wish of others to
have them function simply as an adjunct to the welfare system.

Coordination within interest groups and among government agencies encourages and facilitates cooperation, heightening the potential for productive,
coherent state policies.[13] The contrast here is not between interventionist (or
"strong") and noninterventionist (or "weak") governments. In some nations,
such as Japan and France, government takes a very active hand in directing
the economy, particularly in guiding the allocation of resources among
industries. In many others the state is involved in fewer areas and plays a less
commanding role where it does intervene. Government activism can certainly
be beneficial, but economies can succeed without the degree of intervention

practiced in Japan and France. What is critical is that government and economic interest groups cooperate, so that the state acts productively where it is needed and stays out where it is not.

Meso-Level Cooperation

Cooperation between purchaser and supplier firms. The meso, or sectoral, level refers to relationships among firms connected vertically or horizontally—that is, firms that interact with one another either as competitors or as buyers and suppliers. One of the most critical relationships is between producers and their suppliers of raw materials, equipment, and parts. In the standard economic model of customer-supplier relations, transactions occur through a spot market. Relationships between purchasers and suppliers are discrete, temporary, and based largely on price.[14]

As a mechanism for the governance of buyer-supplier transactions, the market has several faults. First, there may be considerable costs associated with continuously searching for the best suppliers or customers and with bargaining over the terms of agreements. Second, because in spot market transactions little may be known about the other party, agents are vulnerable to opportunistic behavior.[15] Third, and perhaps most important, although it may be effective at minimizing supply costs in the short run, the spot market form of customer-supplier relations inhibits pursuit of a variety of practices necessary for long-term cost minimization, as noted in the discussion of the U.S. auto industry in Chapter 2. Spot market transactions ensure the buyer a great deal of flexibility, but because there is no guarantee of future transactions, they discourage communication between purchasers and suppliers and among suppliers themselves and deter suppliers from making large-scale or asset-specific investments.[16]

Cooperation between suppliers and customers can help remedy these problems. One of the most prominent ways in which firms have sought to achieve cooperation is through vertical integration. Integration permits routinization of transactions and greater availability of information, as well as increased monitoring capacity. In these ways it can reduce costs and heighten efficiency.[17] In the view of Alfred Chandler and several other researchers, the use of hierarchy is a key reason why the productivity of U.S. firms outpaced that of their foreign counterparts during the late 19th and much of the 20th centuries.[18] Vertical integration has certain drawbacks, however. Internal production requires a substantial fixed capital investment. There are tendencies toward bureaucratization and risk-averseness associated with large size.

It may be difficult for a single firm to stay at the technological forefront for all of its component needs. Finally, reliance chiefly or entirely on internal production severely reduces or eliminates competition as a spur for efficiency. Without competitive pressure, internal components divisions have little incentive to maintain superior efficiency levels.

Consequently, many firms prefer to purchase at least some, if not most, of their supply needs. The most effective customer-supplier relationships are ones based as much on cooperation as on competition. The incentive structure utilized by Japanese automakers, discussed earlier in Chapter 2, is a useful example.[19] The key to this relationship is that the auto producers commit to a long-term partnership with suppliers. In return, the automakers insist on close communication with their supplier firms and among suppliers, and they require that suppliers steadily reduce costs. Suppliers readily comply, knowing that the sharing of information poses no direct threat to their own success and that the relationship will not be severed right after they make a large investment to improve productivity. By fostering trust and a spirit of partnership, long-term relations also make suppliers more willing to absorb the strain associated with just-in-time delivery arrangements and to make investments in flexible production techniques necessary to reap benefits from such arrangements.[20] A long-term commitment does not preclude competition. If a supplier's performance is consistently unsatisfactory, some of its business is switched to a competitor for a short time as punishment. During that time the assembler firm works closely with the supplier to try to remedy the problem. But the supplier firm is not permanently dismissed unless it proves unable or unwilling to adapt over a substantial period of time. Evidence suggests that these practices pay off. The superior efficiency of Japanese auto manufacturers at least through the 1980s is virtually unquestioned, and their supplier relationships are widely regarded as a key (although certainly not the only) factor contributing to that superiority.[21]

The Japanese purchaser-supplier relationship is voice-based, as opposed to the exit-based relationship traditionally followed by the big three American auto manufacturers.[22] The contrast illustrates the advantages of using a combination of competition and cooperation, rather than relying on competition alone. The automobile industry is but one example of the usefulness of such arrangements. Voice-based relationships, often referred to as networks, are increasingly prevalent across a wide array of industries, from construction to textiles/apparel to consumer electronics, and in a variety of national settings.[23]

Cooperation between investors and producers. As we saw in Chapter 2, in the ideal-typical flexible capital market, investors are free to withdraw their capital at any given moment by simply selling their shares. Typical investors own only a small percentage of any particular company's shares, so they are in no way constrained to hold on to their ownership position if a firm is experiencing difficulties. Their disengaged relationship with the firm forces investors to rely for information on the market, which often fails to adequately calculate long-term corporate prospects.[24] There is a strong incentive to resort to exit under such circumstances, for small individual investors have little capacity to influence the company's decisions. So they sell their shares, and others do the same. The firm's stock price drops, which discourages other investors, who in turn sell their shares, causing a further decline in the company's value. Moreover, it now costs the firm more to raise new funds through equity sales because, with the price of each share lower than previously, it must sell more shares than before to raise whatever amount it needs.

In order to preempt this course of events, corporate managers have a strong incentive to prioritize short-run performance. Investments in research or in new production technologies or distribution strategies are judged by how quickly they can show a profit. Risky ventures or those likely to benefit the company only after 5 or 10 or 15 years are more likely to be rejected. That may not be bad, if productive alternatives with shorter return periods are available. But narrow time horizons on the part of management may needlessly rule out a number of beneficial strategic maneuvers. A firm's ability to take a long-term view can be a source of considerable competitive advantage, particularly in an integrated world economy.

What is needed is an incentive for investors to prioritize long-term results, along with an effective means of communicating that preference to firms. As the German and Japanese cases illustrate, cooperation between firms and their financial backers can help overcome the short-run bias of competitive capital markets.[25] The key is that providers of finance have a consequential stake in the firm's ownership (and/or loan portfolio) and that they have a means through which to exercise their views regarding the firm's course of action. Large stakes reduce the liquidity of an investment, making it more difficult for investors to exit quickly and quietly. Having a voice in company decision making encourages investors to use their position to help change the firm, as opposed to simply abandoning it. This institutional structure encourages investors to prioritize the firm's long-run performance and to communicate with the firm when things are awry. Investors make a commitment to a voice-based rather than an exit-based relationship. In Germany large universal banks fill this role, whereas in Japan it is carried out by other companies and banks linked through cross-ownership.

An alternative is for firms to be their own principal source of finance. If retained earnings are large enough, a company can fund many of its own investments instead of having to rely on external provision. This may be part of the reason why large American firms such as IBM, U.S. Steel, General Motors, and Boeing, each of which dominated its industry for a good portion of the post-World War II era, were able to make long-term investments for such a sustained period of time.[26] Internal financing is not, however, an option for many firms.

Cooperation among competing firms. The relationship between firms within the same industry (those offering similar goods or services) is that to which the standard assumption of competition's virtue applies most directly. And there is no denying the beneficial effects that competition indeed has, in stimulating improvement and guiding resource allocation. Yet even in the relations between competing firms, cooperation has an important role to play. Industry trade associations are often a key promoter of such cooperation.

One of the most basic arenas in which cooperation benefits competing firms is that of standard setting. In some industries, establishment of uniform standards is a precondition for intensive production. Of course, firms may compete fiercely to produce the product around which a standard will be set, and new developments always hold out the potential for changes in industry standards. But unless some product standards are set an industry can remain disjointed and haphazard, reducing productivity and consumer satisfaction. Even in sectors where government is the ultimate arbiter of product standards (such as energy), a speedy recommendation from the industry can accelerate the decision-making process. Trade associations often provide a catalyst for forging quick agreement on standards.

Cooperation is also sometimes a precondition for investment in research and development (R&D). As noted in Chapter 4, market incentives are such that R&D tends to be underproduced. Uncertainty is partly to blame, as firms seldom know what the results of research will be and whether they will pay off in sales and profits. The risk is heightened for small firms, for whom the costs of R&D are disproportionately large. Perhaps more important, the products of research are not always appropriable. That is, they can often readily be copied by competitors, so that any gains accruing to the firm conducting the research are only temporary and may be insufficient to compensate for the costs of the research effort. Patents aid in protecting inventor property rights, but they are frequently less than perfect at doing so.[27]

Collaboration can help overcome this disincentive to R&D investment. Joint research allows risk to be pooled and helps protect against free riders. In addition, knowledge interaction effects can be exploited and wasteful duplication of effort avoided.[28] Because of the costs and uncertainty involved, however, cooperation between firms may not occur without some outside, extramarket inducement. Trade associations can assist by facilitating communication between firms and by providing resources and selective incentives for joint action. Most sectors of German industry have established cooperative industrial research groups, which pool funds to finance R&D and technology diffusion.[29] Small firms benefit especially from these organizations, of which there are more than 100. The German machine tool industry, to cite just one example, has thrived in recent years in large part because of a variety of cooperative activities spurred by its trade association.[30] Among the most important has been a series of joint research projects connecting firms with each other and with university researchers. In some cases government enticement may be critical. The highly successful VLSI project among Japanese semiconductor and computer producers, which was organized and partially funded by the Japanese government, is an exemplary case of state-led multi-firm research collaboration.[31] Japan's government uses a variety of policies—including loans and subsidies, favorable tax and regulatory treatment, and rapid depreciation allowances—to encourage cooperative R&D. As of the mid 1980s nearly a third of all Japanese corporate research projects involved collaboration with other firms or government entities.[32]

A similar problem occurs in the area of worker training, as we discovered in Chapter 2. Employee skills have certain properties that make it irrational for firms unilaterally to provide sufficient training for their workers.[33] Again there is uncertainty; the returns to training are very difficult to estimate, much less to predict in advance. Perhaps more important, where labor markets are open—that is, where employees are free to switch firms fairly frequently—worker skills are no more appropriable for a company than are the products of its research. Companies face the threat that investments they make in training their workforce will go for naught, as other firms "poach" their skilled workers.

Again, cooperation can help, and trade associations can play an integral role in fostering cooperative behavior. One solution is to form a training consortium, whereby firms pool resources to sponsor training at an external institution. Alternatively, firms can collectively force themselves to invest in in-house training. This is the route taken by Germany, where industry associations require firms to participate in an apprenticeship system offering extensive job training to future and present employees.[34] A hybrid strategy is to levy a training tax. Under this scheme companies can either spend a percentage of their payroll on certain specified types of training for their workforce or contribute the equivalent amount to a public training fund. Germany, Japan, Sweden, and France all have such a "play-or-pay" system, with employers required to allocate 1 to 3 percent of payroll either to training or to the fund.[35]

In addition to standards, R&D, and training, trade associations and consortiums of competing firms can provide assistance with matters such as financing, technology diffusion, design, accounting, marketing, and export promotion. The pooling of resources to secure these sorts of benefits is particularly helpful for small firms and has been critical to the success of such firms in the "Third Italy," as well as various industries in Japan.[36]

Micro-Level Cooperation

Cooperation between labor and management. In the standard neoclassical model of the labor relationship, transactions between workers and employers occur through a spot market. Exchanges are discrete and relationships are temporary. As is the case with purchaser-supplier relations, this form of interaction has important drawbacks. Continuous searching by both parties is costly. Each is vulnerable to opportunism. And perhaps most significant, workers have little incentive to share valuable knowledge with their employer, to develop new skills, or to welcome the introduction of new technologies. Because employment is temporary, there is no guarantee that employees will benefit from any improvement in productivity. Indeed, new ideas and techniques may end up reducing the number of jobs at the firm.

With a few exceptions (such as migrant farm workers, some construction work, and professional temporary employees) the modern labor relationship consists not of spot market employment, but rather of hierarchical coordination. Workers are generally hired not for single projects, but on a continuous basis. Routinizing the employment relationship in this way reduces costs associated with search and monitoring and facilitates specialization of tasks and realization of scale economies. There are no doubt additional reasons why the modern firm developed historically,[37] but efficiency gains associated with cooperation are surely an important part of why it has persisted.[38] However, simple hierarchical coordination is only minimally cooperative. For although employment is somewhat routinized, workers still have no guarantee that the relationship will persist. Employers remain essentially free to fire at will. Workers, therefore, still have little incentive to upgrade productivity.

One strategy for inducing workers to cooperate in raising productivity is to increase pay. Employers can pay workers an "efficiency wage" above the market rate in exchange for greater effort.[39] Large, dominant U.S. firms in a variety of industries have used this strategy since the 1930s to secure motivation on the shop floor.[40] The degree of income equality within firms and/or nations may similarly affect the willingness of workers to cooperate with management in increasing productivity. In Chapter 3 we found evidence suggesting that across developed capitalist nations, greater income equality is associated with stronger productivity growth. Where employees perceive distributive arrangements to be relatively fair, they may be more willing to share information and less likely to resist the introduction of new technology.

Yet, reliance strictly on monetary incentives may have limited utility, for employees realize they may not be around to share in the future gains of enhanced productivity. A solution is for employers and workers to forge a long-term pact. Where workers have a guarantee of future employment, they are more likely to invest in skills training, more likely to share ideas with management, and less prone to resist new machines or work practices (including those critical to flexible and/or lean production, such as computer-controlled machines, total quality management, and rapid machine change-over techniques).[41] And contrary to conventional wisdom, recent studies suggest that these gains require little or no sacrifice of flexibility by firms.[42]

Many firms offer a de facto job guarantee for white-collar workers, but that misses a substantial portion of the workforce. In Japan, the typical large firm offers such a guarantee to blue-collar workers as well.[43] When a company faces a downturn, workers are reallocated, working time is reduced, and pay is cut (for management first) in an effort to avoid laying off employees. A number of large companies in nations such as Austria and Germany follow the same practice. A full employment commitment on the part of government can produce a similar effect. Rather than providing security in a particular job, Swedish companies work closely with public labor market boards to guarantee security of employment. Firms are not reluctant to let go of unneeded workers, but the displaced are quickly retrained and placed in new jobs.[44]

Cooperation among workers. The standard wage payment used by firms, in which employees are compensated according to the amount of time worked, offers limited inducement for workers to put forth an optimal degree of effort. Individual workers have an incentive to shirk, to free ride on the efforts of their co-workers, because it will have little effect on their reward as long as others work hard. The standard remedy for this problem is monitoring by a hierarchical authority.[45] But monitoring can be costly and of limited efficacy.[46]

An alternative mechanism for discouraging such free riding is teamwork combined with employee participation in decision making. Worker decision making fosters trust and encourages groups or teams to monitor individual performance. As David Levine and Laura Tyson have noted:

> Participation can support the cooperative strategy when there is group interaction and peer pressure.... By working together, team members recognize their mutual interests and observe how shirking by one can hurt the group. Shirking or free riding now imposes an observable cost directly on all co-workers, so that social sanctions may be rationally applied against workers who deviate from the cooperative work norm.[47]

The effect is to promote effort and cooperation among employees. Empirical studies have found that substantive employee participation in shop-floor decision making typically increases productivity.[48]

A more direct means of eliciting cooperative behavior among workers is collective pay (profit sharing or gain sharing), whereby part of employee compensation is determined by the group's productivity or the firm's profit.[49] Yet, structuring compensation to reward group performance directly may not suffice in and of itself, for collective pay arrangements are no less vulnerable to free riding than the standard wage payment. Here again, participation can help. Case studies have found that participatory processes improve the productivity of collective pay programs.[50] And the combination of widespread teamwork, employee participation, and bonus pay may help account for the high rate of productivity growth in large Japanese firms. About 20-25 percent of the typical Japanese worker's compensation is paid in the form of bonus payments, at least part of which corresponds directly to company performance; and Japanese firms feature substantial use of teams and employee decision making.[51]

Cooperation along the production chain within firms. I argued earlier that cooperation among firms can help promote beneficial levels of research and development. Cooperation is equally important in managing the link between R&D and production *within* firms. In competitive markets, success often hinges in part on the speed with which firms can turn innovations into products. During the post-World War II period, many large firms in the United States and other countries have elected to institutionalize a clear separation between the various functional stages along the production chain. Although such firms may be successful at generating new product innovations, functional specialization of this sort can render them slow and ineffective at moving from creation through design and development to production.[52] Richard Florida and Martin Kenney describe the result in a typical American corporation:

> Projects and products would simply be passed over the transom from R&D to product development, from product development to pilot production, and from

pilot production to manufacturing. Once a project was handed on, the receiving group was confronted with a fait accompli, their freedom of operation constrained by earlier decisions. Each group optimized according to its own situation and not on the basis of the entire product. Delays and redesign at each stage were common. It typically took a very long time to complete this process, and the complexity added by each stage often made the end products very difficult to manufacture.[53]

Achieving a quick, effective transition from innovation to production requires extensive coordination among the various stages of the process, which is a function of the organizational arrangements used by the firm and the degree of communication among those involved. Japanese automakers again offer a useful illustration of the benefits of cooperation.[54] Instead of relying on the individual contributions of atomized, fractionalized departments, Japanese car manufacturers organize the design and development process for a particular car model around a team of employees. Team members represent the various functional departments of the firm (market assessment, product planning, styling, engineering, factory operations, and so on). Although they retain ties to their individual departments, team members are under the direct control of a team leader. The team is assigned to the development project for the duration of its life, moving with it through its various stages. This continuity enables a much smoother and more rapid transition through the design, development, and production process. In a study of development projects between 1983 and 1987, Kim Clark and Takahiro Fujimoto of the Harvard Business School found that a new Japanese car required an average of 1.7 million hours of engineering effort and took 46 months to complete. For U.S. and European manufacturers, which relied predominantly on the standard mode of functional specialization, new cars of comparable complexity took an average of 3 million engineering hours and consumed 60 months.[55] Team-based cooperation along the production chain has served as a competitive advantage for large Japanese firms in an assortment of other industries as well.[56]

◈ Cooperative and Individualistic Economies

The foregoing discussion suggests that cooperation is a key component of economic success. I do not mean to imply that all cooperation is economically beneficial. But there is good reason to think that economies that complement competition with the types of cooperation outlined here should achieve better performance results, whereas those relying more heavily on individualistic, atomistic competition should fare worse.

To assess this thesis I have created a numerical index of the degree of economic cooperation in our 17 advanced industrialized democracies. The index is shown in Table 6.2. Each nation receives a score for each of the nine dimensions of cooperation discussed in the previous section. The scoring aims to capture the actual degree of cooperation obtaining; in almost all cases this is consistent with the prominence of cooperation-inducing institutions. The scores are 1 for highly cooperative, 0.5 for moderately cooperative, and 0 for individualistic. I hypothesize that each of the nine relationships is of roughly equal importance in contributing to economic success. The cooperation index is thus formed by summing the nine scores for each country.

This is plainly a somewhat crude measure, a reflection of the fact that patterns of cooperation are not always consistent across industries and firms within a particular country and that information for some nations in some areas is limited. As cross-national research on various types of cooperative behavior progresses, it will, I hope, become possible to generate more refined and precise measures. The rationale for the scoring is as follows.

Japan's economy features the most extensive cooperation.[57] The degree of cooperative behavior at the meso and micro levels in Japan exceeds that in any other industrialized nation. Japanese purchasers and suppliers in a variety of industries use voice-based relationships, in which the purchaser commits to a long-term relation and the parties engage in close and constant communication. Japanese investors and producers—especially companies and banks linked through cross-ownership—are typically committed to a long-term partnership and communicate directly with each other when problems or dissatisfactions arise. Competing firms in most sectors are organized in strong industry trade associations, which have helped forge rapid agreement on standards and serve as an important source of information flow among companies. R&D collaboration among firms occurs frequently, in some cases via an industry-wide consortium.

The standard labor-management relationship in large Japanese companies features permanent employment for workers, a substantial amount of team-based employee decision making on the shop floor, and bonus pay. These firms have proved extremely successful at encouraging employee skill development and in eliciting the sharing of useful knowledge; and labor tends to accommodate new technologies. A relatively egalitarian income distribution further contributes to employee motivation. Japan is to my knowledge the only developed nation that has made widespread use of design teams to coordinate the transition from R&D through production within firms.

Cooperation is also high at the macro level. Japanese business is organized on a national basis. The central employer federation, the Keidenran, helps

Table 6.2 Index of Economic Cooperation

	Cooperation Index	Macro Level			Meso Level			Micro Level		
		Industries	Unions	Government-Interest Groups	Purchasers-Suppliers	Investors-Producers	Competing Firms	Labor-Management	Workers	Production Chain
Japan	8.5	1	0.5	1	1	1	1	1	1	1
Austria	7[a]	1	1	1	0.5	1	0.5	1	0.5	0
Germany	6.5	1	1	1	0.5	1	1	0.5	0.5	0
Norway	6.5	1	1	1	0.5	1	0.5	1	0.5	0
Sweden	6.5	1	1	1	0.5	1	0.5	1	0.5	0
Finland	6.5	1	1	1	0.5	1	0.5	1	0.5	0
Denmark	5.5	0.5	1	1	0.5	1	0.5	0.5	0.5	0
Belgium	5	0.5	0.5	1	0.5	1	0.5	0.5	0.5	0
Italy	5	0.5	0.5	0	1	1	1	0.5	0.5	0
Netherlands	3	0.5	0.5	1	0	0	0	0.5	0.5	0
Switzerland	3	0.5	0.5	0	0.5	1	0.5	0.5	0.5	0
France	2	0	0	1	0	1	0	0	0	0
Australia	0.5	0	0.5	0	0	0	0	0	0	0
New Zealand	0.5	0	0.5	0	0	0	0	0	0	0
Canada	0	0	0	0	0	0	0	0	0	0
United States	0	0	0	0	0	0	0	0	0	0
United Kingdom	0	0	0	0	0	0	0	0	0	0

a. Includes an additional 0.5 for macro-level cooperation (see p. 172).

171

moderate rent-seeking by firms and industries. Unions in Japan are fragmented in an organizational sense; but wage setting for most industries occurs at the same time each spring, and powerful employer associations work closely together, generally with union cooperation, to assure coordination in the bargaining process. Finally, government policy has contributed to and supported Japanese economic success, aided by a high degree of coordination within the state and a strongly cooperative relationship between government and business.

Austria is the next most cooperative economy.[58] Austrian-style cooperation centers around a highly centralized process of negotiation between societal interest groups and the state. Labor and business are each represented by a single national federation that guides and coordinates wage setting. Of equal importance, business, labor, and agricultural producers are each organized in a national "chamber." Membership is compulsory, so that practically every working Austrian is a voting member of one of the chambers. Approximately once a month representatives of the government, the central trade union federation, and the three chambers meet in the so-called Parity Commission. This quintessentially corporatist body has no statutory authority, but it reviews and advises on proposed economic legislation, approves wage and price increases, and is instrumental in shaping national economic policy. Austria's "social partnership" is the most well-developed mechanism among industrialized nations for ensuring that economic policy favors the general community rather than special interests. Because of its exceptionally high degree of business and labor encompassingness and its extremely centralized process of negotiation between interest groups and the state, I add an additional 0.5 to Austria's score for macro-level cooperation.

Economic relationships at the meso and micro levels are also characterized by cooperative behavior. The state-owned sector accounts for about a quarter of output and employment, including many of Austria's largest firms in industries ranging from chemicals to finance. Nationalized firms have exhibited a strong tendency to guarantee employment to their workforce during turbulent periods, and government has helped maintain very low unemployment levels through active countercyclical demand management. By encouraging training and knowledge sharing and by discouraging opposition to new technology, employment security has contributed to the country's strong productivity growth rates. Underdevelopment of Austria's capital market has fostered close relationships between firms and large investors. The resulting long time horizons on the part of management have contributed to Austria having one of the highest investment rates among developed nations. Industry associations encourage a variety of cooperative efforts among competing firms, and relationships between purchasers and suppliers are often voice-based. Neither of the latter two phenomena, however, is as common or extensive as in Japan.

Germany is also one of the world's more cooperative economies, exhibiting relatively extensive cooperation at each of the three levels.[59] The country's bank-led system of industrial finance is perhaps its most striking attribute. Large banks typically hold not only loan portfolios, but also substantial equity ownership, in companies. The banks therefore have an incentive to be concerned chiefly with long-term results, and they use their leverage to steer corporate decision making in this direction. German business is organized in powerful trade associations that encourage various types of cooperative activity, from joint R&D ventures to the highly successful apprenticeship program that provides on-the-job training to a large share of the German workforce. Purchaser and supplier firms frequently collaborate in long-term partnerships. In all firms with more than five employees, firings and plant closings require advance consent by the company's works council. If mass layoffs are required, management must secure works council approval of a plan providing either alternative employment in the firm, retraining, or severance pay. In many large German firms, workers therefore have a de facto job guarantee. This encourages a harmonious relationship between labor and management, with attendant benefits.

The Federation of German Industry, of which more than 80 percent of German firms are members, moderates rent-seeking activity on the part of sectoral associations and individual firms. Although wage setting occurs primarily at the industry level, a high degree of union concentration, combined with wage leadership by the powerful metalworkers union, ensures substantial coordination in the bargaining process. Germany's national government is relatively unified and its relationship with business and labor tends to be cooperative. Although the state has not taken a strong hand in directing economic development, government policy has contributed to Germany's success through its consistency and its encouragement of cooperation among private actors.

The six small northern European countries—Norway, Sweden, Finland, Denmark, the Netherlands, and Belgium—all feature a rather extensive amount of cooperation.[60] Each has a fairly high degree of interest group centralization. National business and labor federations moderate special interest lobbying by industry coalitions and conduct centralized wage negotiations. Nowhere is the degree of coordination as great as in Austria, but it is nevertheless relatively high. As Peter Katzenstein has stressed, macro-level cooperative behavior in these countries is partly a response to their small domestic market size and consequent dependence on exports.[61] Vulnerable to shifting market trends and foreign policy currents, these nations can succeed only by being extremely adaptable. Hence, cooperation is a must. The Netherlands and Belgium are given an intermediate score for macro-level industry and union cooperation, as is Denmark for the former, because of their somewhat lesser degree of interest group centralization and coordination.

Unions and/or works councils in each of these countries have strong participatory rights vis-à-vis management in issues concerning firing and layoffs. As a result, job security is comparatively strong and labor-management cooperation is extensive. Government commitment to low unemployment supports this pattern, although that commitment subsided in Denmark, Belgium, and the Netherlands (as in Germany) during the 1980s. Egalitarian distributive arrangements further encourage worker motivation. With relatively underdeveloped capital markets, these nations rely disproportionately on large investors, often banks or financial groups, which frequently engage in close, long-term relationships with firms and thereby foster extended time horizons. The Netherlands is an exception in this regard; its investor-producer relationships tend to be short-term and arm's length. Business is generally well-organized at the sectoral level, and industry associations foster a variety of cooperative activities among competing firms. Long-term ties between buyer and supplier firms are relatively common. These latter two types of cooperation are less extensive than in Japan, however, and in the Netherlands they are quite rare.

Italy is a mixed case. In several respects it is relatively individualistic.[62] Ties within and among interest groups alternate between centralization and extreme fragmentation. Labor-management relations in large firms tend to be conflictual; Italy's strike rate during the past several decades has been by far the highest among developed countries. Despite periodic attempts, there has been little sustained coordination of wage setting since the mid 1960s. This has contributed to militant bargaining by unions and an extremely high rate of wage increases. Coalitions take advantage of political factionalism to enhance their particularistic interests, especially via Italy's extensive state-run sector.

Within particular regions, industries, and firms, however, Italy features a wide range of cooperative practices, especially at the meso level.[63] Local districts in regions such as Emilia-Romagna and Tuscany in northeastern and central Italy exhibit dense ties between firms, workers, and government actors. Suppliers and purchasers of products such as apparel, ceramic tiles, machinery, and engineering components are closely linked through an assortment of obligational subcontracting networks. Firms join together to conduct research on new products and production techniques, pool information on foreign markets, and sponsor training programs for the local labor force. Personalized banking and finance cooperatives organized by local investors foster a long-term outlook on the part of firms. Highly skilled workers participate extensively in shop-floor decision making and encourage the use of advanced technologies. Cooperative efforts by firms, labor unions, and local governments ensure a relatively high degree of de facto employment security by providing retraining and job placement services for unemployed workers.

Switzerland faces pressures similar to those of the other small, open European economies, but its economic institutions are quite different in several respects.[64] The Swiss labor movement is weak and decentralized, although communication among employer associations achieves a moderate level of wage coordination. Unlike their northern European counterparts, Swiss workers enjoy little in the way of employment protection or participation in company decision making. At the meso level, by contrast, a relatively high degree of cooperation obtains. Relations between purchasers and suppliers in key industries are close and long-term. "Widespread share ownership by banks and other institutions with a low proclivity for trading results in a governance structure in which investors have historically worked with management to renew companies rather than sell them or shut them down."[65] Business organization is strong at the sectoral level. Industry associations facilitate cooperation among competing firms in setting standards and in the operation of an apprenticeship system similar to Germany's.

Compared to most other industrialized nations, France exhibits relatively little cooperation. Business and labor are organizationally fragmented. Relationships between purchasers and suppliers, among competing firms, and between labor and management tend to be individualistic and adversarial.[66] However, cooperative behavior does obtain in the relations between investors and producers and between the state and interest groups. Although banks generally do not hold equity stakes in industrial companies, many firms rely heavily on long-term credit provided by state agencies, nationalized banks, and two large investment groups. As a result, ties between providers and users of finance are frequently close and voice-based.[67] France also has featured a highly centralized and cohesive state economic apparatus. Led by the Planning Commission and the Finance Ministry, the French state has engaged in indicative planning, transmitting information on production and consumption trends among companies and trade associations, and it has intervened heavily in the allocation of capital among industries and firms.[68] Although French business is weakly organized, its relationship with the Planning Commission has generally been cooperative.

Australia, New Zealand, Canada, the United States, and the United Kingdom are the most individualistic among developed economies.[69] Interest groups in each of these nations are severely fragmented. Business organization is limited to the industry level; central federations typically exist, but have very little authority over their constituents. The labor movement tends to be decentralized. Government and interest groups approach one another in an adversarial manner; as a result, state intervention tends to be incoherent and directed toward the satisfaction of particularistic interests. The financial system is based heavily on capital markets, with relations among investors and producers predominantly arm's length and guided by the threat of exit. Relationships between purchasers and suppliers, and among competing firms, are conflictual. Labor-management relations are generally hostile, marked by a substantial degree of conflict. Cooperation, and its concomitant benefits, is sacrificed in favor of managerial control and flexibility.

There are, of course, exceptions to this general pattern. New Zealand has traditionally had a moderately centralized system of wage setting, and Australia moved in this direction during the 1980s. These two nations thus receive an intermediate score for union cooperation. One can point to a variety of cases of interfirm cooperation in these countries. Suppliers and purchasers in U.S. industries such as information technology and apparel sometimes work closely together in long-term partnerships, and competing firms form joint ventures to conduct research. Individual firms in each of these nations can be found in which cooperative, harmonious labor-management relations are the norm—and in which workers undertake extensive skills training, offer substantial input into shop-floor decision making, and welcome the introduction of productivity-enhancing technology. A number of specific instances can be cited in which government and industry in these five countries have overcome their structural fragmentation to produce state policy beneficial to the general interest. The point is not that these nations exhibit no cooperation, but rather that the occurrence of cooperative activity is far outweighed by that of individualistic, atomistic behavior. Compared to those in other industrialized nations, relations among economic actors in these countries tend to be antagonistic and adversarial.

◈ Cooperation and Economic Success

This section offers an empirical assessment of the thesis that cooperation is an integral component of economic success in industrialized market economies. I use comparative data for our 17 OECD countries during the period 1960-1990. As in previous chapters, definitions and data sources for all variables are listed in Appendix A.

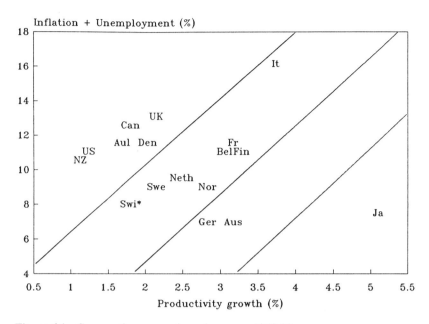

Figure 6.1 Comparative economic performance, 1960-90

NOTE: For data sources see Appendix A.
* Swiss unemployment rate is estimated.

The plausibility of the thesis is immediately apparent from Figure 6.1, which offers a simple, useful means of evaluating comparative economic success during the period 1960-1990. On the horizontal axis of the chart is productivity growth, the best available indicator of dynamic performance. On the vertical axis is an additive index of inflation and unemployment, commonly referred to as the misery index or Okun index. The slope of the lines in the figure is 4; this permits countries 4 percentage points of inflation and/or unemployment for every percentage point of productivity growth.[70] The countries fall into four groups (numbers in parentheses are cooperation scores):

Outstanding	Japan (8.5)
Strong	Austria (7), Germany (6.5)
Moderate	Norway (6.5), Sweden (6.5), Finland (6.5), Belgium (5), Italy (5), Netherlands (3), Switzerland (3), France (2)
Poor	Denmark (5.5), Australia (0.5), New Zealand (0.5), Canada (0), United States (0), United Kingdom (0)

Japan has by far the best record, with the highest rate of productivity increase and nearly the lowest misery index level. After Japan, the best performers have been Austria and Germany, both of which feature fairly strong productivity growth along with extremely low misery index levels. Following these two nations is a group consisting of Norway, Sweden, Finland, Belgium, Italy, the Netherlands, and France. Most of these countries score moderately on both measures. Italy is the exception, having the highest rate of productivity growth aside from Japan but by far the worst misery index level. Switzerland probably also falls into this group, although that is not certain because reliable figures on Swiss unemployment are not available. (For the purposes of this chart I have used the average unemployment rate for the other 16 countries, 4.2 percent, for Switzerland.) The weakest performers during the past three decades have been Denmark, Australia, New Zealand, Canada, the United States, and the United Kingdom.

The correspondence between cooperation and economic success is rather striking. For the most part, the performance records of these countries are predicted quite accurately by their degrees of cooperation. Of course, no monocausal explanation can hope to fully explain the performance of all developed nations. Hence it is not surprising to find a few countries that do not correspond to the predictions. France, for instance, exhibits little coopera-tion but has had moderately strong performance. Denmark, on the other hand, is a fairly cooperative economy but has suffered relatively poor economic results. There is also unexplained performance variation among countries whose overall results are similar. Sweden and Finland, for example, each score 6.5 on the cooperation index and have moderately strong overall economic records; but Sweden has had better misery index results than Finland, whereas the reverse is true for productivity growth. Accounting for these types of differences would necessitate incorporating specific policy strategies and choices, among other factors, into the analysis.[71] On the whole, however, this measure of performance success—a combination of high pro-ductivity growth and a low misery index—appears strongly correlated with the degree of cooperative activity existing in these 17 countries.

More sophisticated statistical tests tell a similar story. I estimate a series of regression equations using cooperation and/or several alternative causal variables to predict various performance indicators—productivity growth and misery index levels, plus productivity levels and trade balances. As in prior chapters, several control variables are used: a catch-up variable for productivity growth, unem-ployment for productivity levels, and economic openness for trade balances.[72]

Table 6.3 shows the regression results for the cooperation variable. With the catch-up effect controlled for, the coefficient for the cooperation index as

Table 6.3 Regression Results for Cooperation

	Productivity Growth		Misery Index		Productivity Level		Trade Balance	
	A	B	C	D	E	F	G	H
1960-90								
Cooperation	.41**		−.46**				.38*	
w/o Japan		.39**		−.38*				.27
Catch-up	−.55***	−.56***						
Economic								
openness							.16	.24
Adjusted R^2	.69	.63	.15	.08			.08	.05
1974-90								
Cooperation	.40**		−.61***		−.12		.41**	
w/o Japan		.34*		−.52**		−.10		.29
Catch-up	−.52***	−.54***						
Unemployment					.60**	.57**		
Economic								
openness							.35*	.42*
Adjusted R^2	.57	.47	.32	.22	.36	.28	.26	.26
N	17	16	16	15	16	15	17	16

NOTE: Standardized coefficients. Switzerland is missing from the misery index and productivity level equations due to lack of data on unemployment. For variable definitions and data sources, see Appendix A.
* Significant at the 10% level; ** 5% level; *** 1% level.

a predictor of productivity growth for 1960-1990 is positive, as expected, and statistically significant at the 5 percent level. For misery index levels, the coefficient is negative, again as expected, and also significant at the 5 percent level. If we look just at the post-oil shock period, 1974-1990, the cooperation coefficient in the misery index equation is larger and the significance level suggests even greater confidence in its reliability.

As equation E in Table 6.3 shows, the coefficient for cooperation as a predictor of productivity levels has the wrong sign. The coefficient is very small, however, and is nowhere near statistical significance, which suggests that there is probably no relationship between the two variables. This is somewhat disappointing. But it may have largely to do with the fact that some of the most cooperative nations, such as Japan, Austria, and Germany, suffered extensive economic damage during World War II and thus have had a long way to go to catch up. If recent trends in productivity growth continue, we will likely find a positive association between cooperation and productivity levels a decade or two from now.

Cooperation proves to be a reasonably good predictor of trade performance. The regression coefficient for the 1960-1990 period is positive, as expected, and statistically significant. With international trade having accelerated during the past 20 years, the period since 1973 should provide a better test. For these years the cooperation coefficient is even larger.

Once again, Japan is a potential outlier. Japan rates highest among our 17 countries in its degree of cooperation, and its performance results have been by far the strongest. As Table 6.3 makes clear, however, omitting Japan has relatively little impact on the regression results. The coefficients for the cooperation variable in the productivity growth and misery index equations retain their signs and remain significant at the 10 percent level or better. (The same is also true with any of the other 16 countries omitted.) In the trade balance equations the cooperation coefficients fall just short of significance when Japan is not included.

On the whole, then, the comparative record seems at first glance quite supportive of the thesis that cooperation is a key determinant of national economic success. How does an account focusing on cooperation fare against rival explanations of performance variation? Among the various contending theories, by far the most influential is the market liberal view, which suggests that economic success is achieved through free markets and the force of competition. Most comparative empirical research on the market liberal thesis has focused on the relationship between levels of government spending (aggregate and/or transfer expenditures) and performance outcomes, the hypothesis being that high spending levels interfere with market processes and thereby undermine efficiency. As noted in Chapter 4, a number of studies have indeed found an inverse relationship between state expenditures and growth rates among industrialized market economies.[73]

However, there are several critical flaws in this research. First, spending levels are at best a very partial, and at worst a highly misleading, proxy for the degree of government intervention in economic affairs—which is itself a flawed indicator of the degree of market restriction. Governments intervene in a myriad of ways—fiscal policy, monetary policy, welfare policy, labor market policy, industrial policy, regulation, and so on—which may or may not involve high levels of expenditure. Japan, for instance, is characterized by heavy state activism, yet it has the lowest level of government spending (as a share of gross domestic product [GDP]) among advanced capitalist economies. This is particularly important because the finding of an inverse relationship between state expenditures and economic growth is due largely to Japan's influence. With Japan omitted from the data, there is little or no association between the two variables, as we discovered in Chapter 4. The same holds for productivity growth. As equation A in Table 6.4 suggests, there appears to be a moderately strong inverse relationship between government expenditures and productivity growth. With Japan excluded (equation B), however, the coefficient is quite small and very far from statistical significance. And when it is entered together with the cooperation variable (equation E), the government spending variable has a positive coefficient.

A second important weakness of this line of research is that it has examined only growth rates. If we turn to other performance indicators, government spending fares poorly as an explanatory variable. There is no apparent association between state expenditures and misery index levels, as equations G and I in Table 6.4 indicate. The same holds for productivity levels (equations J and L). And spending is, if anything, positively related to trade performance (equations M and O). Similar results, not shown here, are obtained using government transfers as the causal variable.

An additional, or alternative, way to operationalize the market liberal view might be via labor movement strength. As Chapter 5 discussed, proponents of market liberalism generally contend that labor organizations, like government activism, impede efficiency—for example, by blocking technological innovation, demanding wage increases that exceed the growth of productivity, reducing labor mobility, and generally interfering with the market for labor. The measure I use here is a composite index representing four dimensions of labor strength: union density, union concentration/centralization,[74] works councils, and codetermination. Scores for these four items were standardized, summed, and then standardized again to form the index.[75]

The regression coefficient for this variable as a predictor of productivity growth, shown in equation C of Table 6.4, is negative; but it is small and not statistically significant. When the cooperation index and the government spending variable are added (equation E), however, the labor strength coefficient is quite large and significant. Still, the cooperation variable is stronger, if only marginally so for the post-oil shock years. (This judgment is made by comparing the size of the standardized regression coefficients for the two variables when entered in the same equation.) Omitting Japan (equation F) has little effect here.

This result for the labor strength variable is consistent with the market liberal thesis. So are those for productivity levels (equation L) and trade balances (equation O), although less convincingly. Equations H and I, however, reveal that labor organization does not have the purported detrimental

Table 6.4 Regression Results for the Market Liberal Thesis

	Productivity Growth						Misery Index		
	A	B	C	D	E	F	G	H	I
1960-90									
Government spending	−.26**				.13*		−.04		.30
w/o Japan		−.04				.16			
Labor strength			−.10		−.72***			−.41*	−.47
w/o Japan				.09		−.96***			
Cooperation					.85***	1.10***			−.22
Catch-up	−.90***	−.86***	−.80***	−.72***	−.42***	−.53***			
Adjusted R^2	.74	.67	.57	.51	.95	.89	−.08	.11	.09
1974-90									
Government spending	−.22				.12		.01		.40
w/o Japan		−.07				.09			
Labor strength			−.12		−.66***			−.44**	−.44
w/o Japan				.02		−1.06***			
Cooperation					.70***	1.10***			−.42*
Catch-up	−.83***	−.77***	−.73***	−.66***	−.54***	−.65***			
Adjusted R^2	.57	.48	.43	.35	.79	.77	−.08	.14	.29
N	16	15	17	16	16	15	16	16	15

	Productivity Level			Trade Balance		
	J	K	L	M	N	O
1960-90						
Government spending				.25		.55*
Labor strength					.07	−.69**
Cooperation						.63**
Economic openness				.11	.20	.15
Adjusted R^2				−.03	−.07	.10
1974-90						
Government spending	−.01		.29	.08		.20
Labor strength		−.11	−.35		.15	−.33
Cooperation			−.17			.47*
Unemployment	.64***	.62***	.33			
Economic openness				.43*	.36*	.42
Adjusted R^2	.31	.36	.25	.12	.10	.14
N	15	16	15	16	17	16

NOTE: Standardized coefficients. Data are not available for unemployment in Switzerland and state expenditures in New Zealand; the former is thus missing from the misery index and productivity level equations, and the latter from equations in which the government spending variable is included. For variable definitions and data sources, see Appendix A.
* 10% level; ** 5% level; *** 1% level.

effect on misery index performance. Indeed, larger and stronger labor movements appear to contribute to better outcomes in this area.

There is, then, some empirical support for the market liberal view. Although government intervention has received the bulk of attention in the literature, the labor variable is the source of this support. Labor strength seems to have an adverse effect on productivity growth, and possibly also on productivity levels and trade balances. Offsetting this, however, is the fact that labor strength is strongly associated with lower misery index levels. Furthermore, for productivity growth the cooperation variable appears to have a greater impact in accounting for cross-national variation. On the whole, therefore, the market liberal thesis is less consistently and strongly supported by the comparative data than an explanation centered around cooperation.

A second prominent theory is Mancur Olson's institutional sclerosis argument.[76] Olson contends that narrow interest groups—labor unions, professional associations, farm organizations, trade associations, lobbies, cartels, and so on—that struggle for redistributive gains create institutional sclerosis in capitalist democracies. They do so by diverting resources away from efficient uses and blocking or delaying beneficial adjustments by economic actors. Nations in which there are relatively few such groups, or where interest group organizations are encompassing in character, are expected to achieve superior performance results. As noted earlier, encompassing groups have limited incentive to seek income gains via redistribution, because they would be taking largely from themselves.

Like the market liberal thesis, Olson's theory is difficult to operationalize. The few empirical tests conducted have used indicators such as the number of years countries have experienced stable democratic rule. Several analyses have found support for the Olson thesis,[77] whereas others suggest that the effect of institutional sclerosis may be minor once the catch-up process is taken into account.[78] In any event, this type of indicator is unsatisfactory, for two reasons. First, it is predicated upon an additional component of Olson's theory—an assertion that stability permits narrow interest groups to form and provides them the opportunity to successfully engage in rent-seeking behavior. Political or economic disruptions that break up such distributional coalitions are thereby viewed as beneficial. This part of Olson's argument is unconvincing. There is little or no empirical basis for the assumption that rent-seeking interest groups are less numerous and powerful in nations suffering disruptions than in those characterized by long periods of stability.[79] Second, this measure ignores Olson's point about the differing incentives facing narrow, localized versus encompassing organizations, which is the most insightful and important aspect of his theory.[80] Instead, it implicitly assumes that all interest groups have detrimental effects on economic performance.

If we take Olson's argument regarding the effects of organizational size and structure seriously, his theory becomes quite similar in practice to a third influential explanation of economic performance success—the corporatism thesis. There are two related but analytically distinct strands within the corporatism literature. All proponents agree that corporatism involves institutionalized bargaining between peak organizations representing business, labor, and/or the state. But the mechanism through which corporatism's benefits are said to be generated varies according to different theorists. One group of scholars stresses the payoffs of coordinated wage bargaining.[81] As we discovered in Chapter 5, wage restraint in developed economies can be achieved either by keeping unemployment relatively high or via coordinated wage negotiations (or both). Given a particular unemployment context, coordinated wage setting tends to produce greater wage moderation, and therefore lower inflation, than fragmented bargaining arrangements. As a result, nations with coordinated wage bargaining enjoy lower misery index levels.

A second strand in the corporatist literature emphasizes the benefits of generalized (i.e., extending beyond the issue of wages) negotiation between government and the major economic interest groups—what Peter Katzenstein refers to as "the voluntary, cooperative regulation of conflicts over economic and social issues through highly structured and interpenetrating political relationships between business, trade unions, and the state."[82] Corporatism in this broader sense is thought to enable nations to adjust quickly and effectively to changing conditions in the world market. Most of the qualitative evidence adduced in the literature supports the assertion that corporatist economies are comparatively flexible and adaptive. In addition, government policy tends to be more coherent and attentive to the general interest.

The corporatism thesis is not a competing explanation of economic performance variation, for it is subsumed within the cooperation argument. Corporatism in the narrow sense consists of cooperation among unions in the realm of wage bargaining, whereas in its broader version it is a form of cooperation between government and interest groups. The weakness of the corporatist explanation is that it focuses exclusively on economic relationships at the macro level, ignoring the potential benefits of cooperation among actors at the meso and micro levels.

Table 6.5 shows regression results for corporatism as a predictor of economic performance. The measure of corporatism I use, created by Marcus Crepaz and Arend Lijphart, is based on 12 indexes and rankings from the literature, which were standardized, summed, then standardized again.[83] Other commonly used measures—such as those of Michael Bruno and Jeffrey Sachs and of David Cameron[84]—yield similar results. As equations C and D in the

Table 6.5 Regression Results for the Corporatism Thesis

	Productivity Growth		Misery Index		Productivity Level		Trade Balance	
	A	B	C	D	E	F	G	H
1960-90								
Corporatism	.06	−.47**	−.60***	−.60*			.32	−.12
Cooperation		.82***		.01				.46
Catch-up	−.77***	−.45***						
Economic openness							.06	.21
Adjusted R^2	.56	.77	.32	.25			.00	.02
1974-90								
Corporatism	.09	−.48**	−.67***	−.50*	−.01	.14	.44*	.17
Cooperation		.81***		−.21		−.22		.29
Catch-up	−.68***	−.43**						
Unemployment					.66***	.62**		
Economic openness							.20	.28
Adjusted R^2	.43	.64	.42	.38	.35	.32	.24	.21
N	17	17	16	16	16	16	17	17

NOTE: Standardized coefficients. Switzerland is missing from the misery index and productivity level equations due to lack of data on unemployment. For variable definitions and data sources, see Appendix A.
* 10% level; ** 5% level; *** 1% level.

table indicate, corporatism is a very good predictor of low misery index levels. Equation D, in which the corporatism variable is entered together with the cooperation index, suggests that cooperation has little effect on misery index performance once corporatism is controlled for. In other words, cooperation's benefits in this area appear to be largely a function of corporatist-style cooperation at the macro level.

For productivity growth, the data suggest exactly the opposite. As equations A indicates, corporatism explains none of the variation in productivity growth rates across our 17 countries. Indeed, when the variable is entered together with the cooperation index (equation B), corporatism appears to have a detrimental impact on productivity growth. This suggests that cooperation at the meso and/or micro levels is the key to increasing productivity. As it happens, most of the strongly corporatist economies also feature a substantial

Table 6.6   Regression Results for Macro-, Meso-, and Micro-Level Cooperation

	Productivity Growth	Misery Index
1960-90		
Macro-level cooperation	−.47**	−.71*
Meso-level cooperation	.44**	.86**
Micro-level cooperation	.56***	−.58*
Catch-up	−.48***	
Adjusted R^2	.81	.34
1974-90		
Macro-level cooperation	−.41*	−.62*
Meso-level cooperation	.63**	.76**
Micro-level cooperation	.22	−.74**
Catch-up	−.58***	
Adjusted R^2	.66	.50
N	17	16

NOTE: Standardized coefficients. Switzerland is missing from the misery index equations due to lack of data on unemployment. For variable definitions and data sources, see Appendix A.
* 10% level; ** 5% level; *** 1% level.

degree of meso- and micro-level cooperation. But a focus on the macro level greatly understates the degree of cooperation in, for example, Japan and Italy, both of which have achieved relatively high rates of productivity growth during the past several decades.

The results shown in Table 6.6 bear out these conclusions about the effects of economic cooperation at different levels. Here the cooperation index is separated into its three component parts, each of which is entered as a variable in regression equations for productivity growth and misery index levels. Macro-level cooperation appears to have adverse effects on the growth of productivity, but it is a very good predictor of low misery index levels. Meso-level cooperation has exactly the opposite effects, whereas micro-level cooperation seems to have a beneficial impact in both areas.

Returning to Table 6.5, we see that corporatism does not have any discernable impact on productivity levels or trade balances. On the whole, then, the evidence suggests that corporatism is an important form of macro-level economic cooperation that enables countries to achieve lower inflation-unemployment combinations. Rapid productivity growth, however, appears to depend upon cooperation at the meso and micro levels.

A number of other factors have been prominent in recent comparative analyses of economic performance. A host of observers credit state intervention as a, if not the, key to national economic success.[85] Coherent, proactive industrial policies in Japan and France are said to be responsible for these countries' high growth rates and international competitiveness, whereas active labor market policies are believed to be the source of Sweden's highly trained workforce and consistently low unemployment rates. Another theory focuses on relations between the state, business, and labor, suggesting that a balance of power and close, coherent linkages tend to be more effective at promoting technological development and diffusion than dominance by one or another of these economic actors.[86] A third school stresses the advantages of flexible specialization—production of highly varied, high-quality goods in small batches—in the post-fordist era of microelectronics and volatile consumer demand. Analysts have attributed the success of Italy and Japan, in particular, to widespread use of flexible production.[87] Meso-level relationships have also been identified as critical by a number of researchers. Some focus on the structure of financial systems, whereas others stress the importance of governance relations between firms.[88] Germany, Japan, and Italy are among the countries commonly deemed most successful in these areas. Also seen as key by some analysts are labor relations institutions that promote high effort levels and continuous improvement in process and product technology.[89] Here, too, Japan and Germany have been the focus of attention. Finally, several recent studies posit that a culture or ideology of collectivism and/or consensus is a key to strong economic performance.[90] Thus, the cultural beliefs and practices of Japan, and to a lesser degree of European nations, are asserted to be more economically productive than those of the Anglo-American countries.

Each of these perspectives has merit, and I have drawn on several of their insights. I have argued, however, that the advantages associated with particular types of state-society relationships, financial systems, interfirm governance structures, and labor-management relations are best understood as stemming from the fact that they promote cooperation, and that each is merely one among many forms of beneficial cooperative behavior. The chief drawback of these explanations is that, like the corporatism literature, they focus on only a single type of economic relationship—at either the macro, meso, or micro level—implicitly or explicitly suggesting that particular relationship to be of primary importance in accounting for macroeconomic performance outcomes. It is more plausible, I contend, to suppose that relationships at all three levels matter. Research supporting these theories has been based on individual case studies and comparisons of very small groups of countries. Extending the assessment to a broader set of nations reveals the limitations of such theories. Government activism, for instance, cannot account for the success of Germany or Italy or various other countries. Nor is it plausible to attribute the strong performance results of Austria, Norway, and others to flexible specialization or the nature of their financial systems. And can it be persuasively argued that Japan's success is due solely or even primarily to any single one of these factors?

A final influential explanation of national performance success is offered in Michael Porter's recent book, *The Competitive Advantage of Nations*. Porter examines the performance of specific industries in 10 industrialized nations during the past several decades. Although he rightly emphasizes the role of domestic competition among firms in spurring innovation and improvement, Porter is also attentive to the importance of several types of cooperative behavior, particularly at the meso level. He notes, for example, the advantages of voice-based, long-term relationships between purchaser and supplier firms and among investors and producers, as well as the role of industry associations in promoting worker training.[91] Porter pays virtually no attention, however, to the potential benefits of cooperation at the macro and micro levels. This is surely a product of his focus on industry performance, but it is a crucial flaw in his account. The theoretical considerations outlined earlier along with inspection of the comparative record strongly suggest that cooperative behavior at all three levels contributes to national economic success.

Overall, then, a theory emphasizing cooperation in macro-, meso-, and micro-level relationships appears quite successful as an explanation of cross-national variation in economic performance. The results of my empirical examination are, of course, not definitive. But given the numerous ways in which cooperative behavior can be expected to produce superior outcomes, there is strong reason to suspect that the apparent association between cooperation and national economic success is genuine. The theory fares well against rival explanations of performance outcomes. Compared with the few perspectives that can be examined across the full set of developed capitalist economies, such as the market liberal and corporatist theses, an explanation centered around cooperation appears superior. At the very least, these findings suggest that the theory warrants further exploration.

As in earlier chapters, I have focused here on the period from 1960 to 1990. In this case, that is not due simply to data limitations. Many of the forms of cooperation I have highlighted emerged only in the post-World War II years. Although I would conjecture that cooperation—in the form of long-term relationships among investors and producers, cooperation between government and interest groups, and hierarchy in the labor process and in purchaser-supplier relations—was also a key to economic success in earlier periods, providing justification for such a claim is beyond the scope of this book.

◙ A U.S. Resurgence?

During the past several years headlines in the American media have suggested that, rather than being in a state of comparative decline, the U.S. economy is once again on the verge of becoming, or already is, the most competitive in the world.[92] For Japan, by contrast, the forecast is decidedly less optimistic. Current wisdom holds that the long era of continuous growth in Japan is over. The crash of the Japanese stock market in 1992-1993 and the accompanying recession are said to signal a thorough downslide in the Japanese economy, the result of which will have to be deep changes in its structure and behavior.[93] Europe is thought to be in even worse shape. Despite moves toward integration, the continent remains mired in a job crisis from which few believe its nations will emerge at any point in the near future. Even in Sweden, one of the last bastions of full employment, the unemployment rate reached 8 percent in 1993.

The signs of American economic resurgence are varied. After losing market share to the Japanese through the 1980s, U.S. firms in industries such as autos, computers, semiconductors, and banking have expanded their share of world sales. The *New York Times* notes that "After more than a decade of painful change and dislocation, many American industries are leaner and nimbler, and others have seized the leadership of sophisticated technologies that are ushering in the information age."[94] After hitting a postwar low in 1987, the U.S. share of world exports grew by a fifth (from 10.6 to 12.8 percent) by 1993.[95]

Productivity is said to be climbing at rates approaching historical highs. According to one observer: "Thanks to corporate America's restructurings and high-tech investment, the long-term trend of productivity growth is on a path not seen since the 1960s."[96] A key component of the restructuring effort by U.S. companies has been lowering labor costs. Relative unit labor costs in manufacturing fell by more than one third between 1985 and 1993, while nearly doubling for Japan during that period.[97] The United States is now viewed as the "low-cost provider of many sophisticated products and services from plastics to software to financial services."[98]

Job creation is the area in which the U.S. economic model is thought to be most spectacularly successful. While much of Europe has been mired in a job creation crisis for two decades, the U.S. economy has generated nearly 40 million new

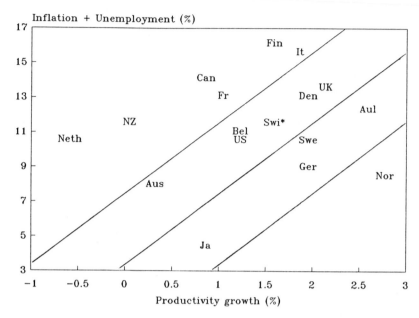

Figure 6.2 Comparative economic performance, 1991-93

NOTE: For data sources see Appendix A.
* Swiss unemployment rate is estimated.

jobs since 1970. Not even Japan can match that record. And the gap between the United States and Europe on this score has continued to widen since 1990. This is said to account for the fact that, whereas in the 1960s and 1970s Europe enjoyed lower unemployment rates than the United States, since the early 1980s the reverse has been true.

Do recent events signal a shift in patterns of comparative economic performance? Do they verify the wisdom of the market liberal model of economic success? There is good reason to think not.

First, consider overall performance trends in the years 1991-1993. These are depicted in Figure 6.2. Once again the lines in the chart are drawn with a slope of 4, allowing countries 4 percentage points of inflation and/or unemployment for every percentage point of productivity growth. The pattern here differs from what we saw in Figure 6.1. Japan and Austria have slid a bit, and Norway is the best overall performer. Australia, Denmark, the United States, and the United Kingdom have improved their relative positions, while the Netherlands has had the worst record.

However, the fact that this pattern looks quite different from that in Figure 6.1 should not surprise us. The results here are for a three-year period, whereas the earlier figure showed average performance results for a period of three decades. Moreover, 1991-1993 was a period of recession for developed nations. Were we to look at earlier recession years, such as 1974-1975 or 1981-1983, we would observe a similar scrambling of economic results.

More important in terms of the results for specific countries, the recent recession has been less synchronized than previous downturns. As the OECD has noted:

> In the 1970s, the cyclical trough was reached in 1975 in each of Japan and the European and North American regions, and during 1982-1983 troughs were only slightly more spread out. In the latest cycle, the North American region reached a peak in 1989 and a trough in 1991, while Europe and Japan did not peak until 1990 and 1991, respectively, and are only projected to reach the cyclical trough in 1994.[99]

The U.S. downturn was effectively over by early 1992, so the country was in recession for only one of the three years covered in Figure 6.2. (The same is true of Australia and Canada.) Japan, by contrast, was in recession for two of the three years, and most of Europe for all three. This renders recent U.S. performance results (and those of Australia) a bit less impressive. If the United States were indeed climbing back on top, its relative position ought to have been at least somewhat higher.

More generally, expectations of renewed U.S. dominance and Japanese and European malaise are almost certainly mistaken. More reasonable reflections on the state of the Japanese economy suggest that its prospects are quite strong, and that its domestic institutional arrangements and government policy orientation will likely continue more or less intact.[100] There is some sign of movement toward greater cooperation in the United States at the meso and micro levels, particularly among competing firms. This may help explain the improved performance of certain industries. But so far the shift has been quite limited.[101] The Clinton administration came into office in 1993 with an assortment of policy plans geared toward promoting cooperation along various lines, but most of these efforts have been blocked or watered down by opposition from business and Congress. The job creation story, finally, is misleading if the focus is placed solely on quantity. A disproportionate share of the new jobs created in the United States in recent years have been low-wage service sector positions, resulting in stagnant real wages and increasing income polarization. This trend, apparent to many observers by the end of the 1980s, has continued through the mid 1990s.[102] Moreover, as noted in Chapter 4, labor market performance varies considerably across Europe. Focusing on aggregate figures for the continent masks the fact that some of its nations have performed much better than the United States in this area.

It is, of course, difficult to predict with any certainty what performance trends for the world's rich economies will look like in the near, much less the distant, future. The analysis in this book suggests, however, that nations that balance competition and cooperation will continue to enjoy greater success.

◈ The Origins of Cooperation

Cooperative behavior is largely a product of institutional structure. Cooperation is induced by economic institutions that provide appropriate information and incentives. Centralization of business and labor discourages particularistic rent-seeking and engenders wage moderation. Organizational coherence within government supports an orientation in favor of the collective interest. Long-term arrangements between purchasers and suppliers foster information sharing and investments in new equipment. Thick, binding ties between firms and their investors encourage direct communication and an orientation toward long-run results rather than quick profits. Strong organizational links among competing firms induce cooperation on matters such as research and employee training. Guaranteed employment, worker participation in decision making, collective pay, and egalitarian compensation structures encourage workers to share ideas, welcome the introduction of new technology, invest in skills training, and put forth a high level of effort. Design and development teams facilitate cooperation among functional departments along the production chain within firms.

Why do certain countries have more cooperative economic institutions than others? For the most part, cooperation-inducing institutions are the intended and unintended products of specific historical struggles and compromises.[103] The development of northern European-style cooperation, which is centered around highly organized interest groups, is illustrative. As noted in Chapter 5, organization of business and labor was in part a mutually reinforcing process, as centralization by one group prompted a similar move by the other. Institutionalized cooperation between the interest groups was fostered by a relative balance of power that prevented each from imposing its will upon the other. It was also encouraged by the state, as well as by national dependence on exports and the consequent need for continuous adjustment in the face of turbulent world markets. Interest group centralization and cooperation was also fostered by historical peculiarities, such as the Scandinavian nations' lack of participation in World War I, which prevented a split in the labor movement between Social Democratic and Communist unions, and the fascist legacy in Germany and Austria, which encouraged business and labor to cooperate as "social partners" in order to maintain domestic harmony. Finally, as corporatist bargaining produced social peace and wage moderation in countries such as Sweden, other nations followed suit in an attempt to replicate that success. Cooperation was thus spawned in part via cross-national imitation.

The encompassing nature of interest groups in northern Europe has contributed not only to corporatist-style negotiation between peak organizations, but to other types of cooperation as well. Labor strength has helped bring about employment security. And business organization engenders cooperation among competing firms in the form of training programs and joint research efforts.

Cooperative institutions in Japan are likewise a product of history. In organizational terms, the Japanese labor movement is fragmented and relatively weak. Yet the Japanese industrial relations system, which features lifetime job tenure and seniority-based wages in large firms along with coordinated wage negotiations each spring, grew out of a compromise solution to a series of bitter labor-management struggles following World War II. The high degree of cooperation among Japanese firms is a legacy of the prewar *zaibatsu* networks, a product of encouragement by the state, and a defensive reaction by business against active government intervention in the economy. Voice-based relationships between investors and producers in Japan, as elsewhere, emerged in response to underdeveloped capital markets, which forced companies to rely heavily on large investors and on bank loans. They are also a product of lenient financial regulations, in contrast to the United States, where laws strongly discourage financial institutions and firms from holding large equity stakes in other companies.

In central and northern Italy, the preponderance of small firms is in part the result of an attempt by firms and investors to escape rapidly increasing unionized labor costs in the late 1960s and early 1970s. Cooperation among these firms is in turn partly a response to the interdependence that is a consequence of their small size. It has also been facilitated by local and regional government support. The success of Italy's small firm networks, aided by the increasing fragmentation and volatility of consumer demand in the post-fordist era, encourages the continuation of these cooperative practices.

There does not seem to be a correlation between the ideological orientation of government and the development of cooperative economic institutions. Cooperation has blossomed under Social Democratic hegemony in Scandinavia, paternalistic conservatism in Japan, and alternation of left and right governments in Germany and Austria. On the other hand, political stability and policy coherence do seem important. Repeated cooperation requires shared expectations and predictable behavior, which are facilitated and encouraged by a stable environment. The latter has been a pronounced feature of countries such as Japan, Austria, and Sweden, whereas nations such as the United States, Britain, and Australia have been characterized by more frequent and exaggerated policy swings.

The emergence and persistence of cooperative institutions may also be facilitated by culture or ideology. Asian culture is communitarian, whereas Anglo-American culture is highly individualistic. Cultural norms in the bulk of Europe fall somewhere between these two poles.[104] If culture is a causal determinant, we would expect Japanese institutions to be highly cooperative, those of European countries to be moderately cooperative, and the institutional structure of Anglo nations (the United States, the United Kingdom, Canada, Australia, New Zealand) to be the most individualistic. And as we have observed, that is in fact the case. Culture's effects may impinge in both the creation and the maintenance of such institutions. The British and American emphasis on autonomy and independence has no doubt discouraged firms from sharing information and participating in joint ventures and dissuaded unions and companies from ceding decision-making authority to a central associational body. Similarly, the effective perpetuation of cooperative relationships over time depends to some degree on the existence of trust, which is in part a function of norms. Firms making long-term investments must trust their major investors not to bail out. Suppliers investing in new equipment and sharing design information with purchasers must trust the latter not to switch abruptly to a lower-cost competitor.[105] Workers who share valuable knowledge and encourage the use of new technology must trust their firm not to turn around and lay them off. Still, although culture may make it more difficult for certain nations to create and sustain cooperative institutions, it by no means makes it impossible.

If cooperation has beneficial effects, presumably it would be a good thing for countries that are now highly individualistic to create or expand economic institutions that foster cooperative behavior. How can this be done?

One way is via imitation by private actors. Firms, business associations, and unions that observe the success of certain types of institutions in other nations may attempt to copy them. During the past decade, for instance, the three American car manufacturers have begun to shift their relationships with suppliers and employees toward the type so successfully used by Japanese automakers.[106] Some supplier firms have been given long-term contracts, and exchange of information and direct supplier participation in the design process are now much more common. The manufacturers have also conducted a number of experiments with worker participation in decision making, backed in some cases by employment guarantees. To this point the changes have been partial and halting, and it is unclear whether the big three are committed to making a genuine shift. But whatever change does occur owes no small debt to the example set by the Japanese firms. Another example of imitation involves the Australian labor movement. Having observed the beneficial effects of union coordination in northern Europe, Australian unions agreed in the early 1980s to give up their bargaining autonomy in favor of centralized wage setting.[107]

Cooperative institutions can also be created or encouraged through government policy. For years, strong antitrust laws in the United States deterred R&D collaboration among competing firms. In 1984 Congress passed the National Cooperative Research Act, which substantially loosened restrictions on cooperative research. Since then, joint R&D ventures have occurred with greater frequency. The U.S. government offers tax incentives to firms that create employee shareholding programs. It could do the same to promote worker participation in decision making and/or collective pay. In the area of finance, a number of proposals have been advanced that aim to reduce investor myopia in the United States. These include changing corporate ownership laws to give investors more control over company decisions, revising regulatory laws to allow banks to own stakes in nonfinancial companies, altering the tax structure on capital gains so that investments held for longer periods receive favorable tax treatment, and imposing a transaction tax on the sale of shares held for less than a specified amount of time. Government can also encourage interest group centralization, by offering material benefits or granting business and labor formal input into the policy-making process in exchange for coordination of demands. A number of European governments have successfully pursued this strategy for wage bargaining and other policy issues.[108]

Whether, and to what extent, such imitation and/or government-induced transformation will be forthcoming in the more individualistic nations is unclear. Nor is it certain that shifts toward more cooperative behavior would yield immediate benefits for these economies. It is conceivable that such shifts may involve a "transition trough," whereby change produces a temporary decline in collective welfare. The comparative record suggests, however, that the long-run benefits of cooperative economic institutions are substantial.

◙ The End of an Illusion

A long habit of not thinking a thing wrong gives it the superficial appearance of being right.

—*Thomas Paine*

The argument I have advanced in this chapter consists of three propositions:

1. In a variety of important macro-, meso-, and micro-level relationships in market-based economies, the structure of incentives is frequently such as to discourage collectively beneficial cooperative behavior.
2. Cooperation can be induced via non- or extramarket institutions such as formal organization and long-term, guaranteed relationships.
3. Countries in which such institutions are more prevalent should be more successful at combining competition with cooperation and should thereby exhibit superior economic performance.

Chapter 1 described how during the long postwar boom, laissez-faire doctrine was challenged and replaced by a Keynesian-redistributive view. In the United States, the economic ideas that dominated the golden age actually represented only a limited departure from the orthodox market liberal perspective. The new view suggested merely that government could manipulate demand at the edges of the economy and that social justice—in the form of a welfare state, regulation of business, labor unions, and so on—could be tacked on to an economy guided predominantly by the invisible hand. The assumption that individualistic competition drives economic success was never really questioned. Hence, when the economy turned sour in the 1970s, the ensuing debate focused solely on whether or not government and unions were responsible for the malaise. Intellectually, the contest was, and still is, a stalemate; politically, the market liberal view won out, at least for a time.

All the while, through good times and bad, the experience of other developed nations has proved that competition does not guarantee economic prosperity. Japan and a number of European countries have shown that success is achieved by combining competition with cooperation. They have also demonstrated that there is little or no trade-off between economic efficiency and equality, or government intervention, or labor strength and influence, or (some) nonmarket constraints on freedom of choice. Indeed, their experience indicates that, in part by encouraging cooperative behavior, these institutional features can contribute to a healthy economy.

Were we to attempt to draw conclusions based on the experience of a single country, this message might be hard to detect. Looking at the matter from a comparative perspective, it is difficult to miss.

Appendix A:
Quantitative Variable
Definitions and Data Sources

Economic performance indicators

Inflation	Change in the consumer price index. From OECD 1992, table 8.11. See Table B.6.
Investment	Gross fixed capital formation as a share of GDP. From OECD 1992, table 6.8. See Table B.1.
Misery index	Inflation plus unemployment. From OECD 1992, tables 8.11 and 2.15.
Output growth	Growth of real GDP per capita. From OECD 1992, table 3.2. See Table B.4.
Productivity	Index of GDP per employed person. GDP levels from OECD 1991c, pp. 146-47, table 1. Employment levels from OECD 1991b, pp. 26-27, table 4.0. Used for 1974-1990 only. See Table B.2.
Productivity growth	Change in real GDP per employed person. From OECD 1992, table 3.7; supplemented by other OECD data. See Table B.3.
Trade balances	Exports minus imports as a share of GDP. From OECD 1992, table 6.14. See Table B.5.
Unemployment	As a share of the total labor force. From OECD 1992, table 2.15; supplemented by Maddison 1982, table C.6. Data are not available for Switzerland. Most Swiss workers are not eligible for unemployment insurance and therefore have no incentive to register as unemployed when out of work. In addition, Switzerland makes considerable use of immigrant labor on temporary work contracts. When jobless, these workers typically return to their country of origin and so are not counted

as unemployed. Because these institutional peculiarities produce an extreme bias in Swiss unemployment figures (see Blaas 1992), the OECD does not list these data. See Table B.7.

Unit labor cost changes — Change in nominal wages (manufacturing sector only) minus change in productivity. Wage change data for 1962-90 are from International Monetary Fund 1992, pp. 100-01, for 1960-61 from International Monetary Fund 1990, p. 112. Productivity change data are from OECD 1992, table 3.7.

Causal variables

Codetermination — Prominence of codetermination rights. From Cameron 1984, table 7.6; "Employee Board-Level Representation," 1981. See Table 5.1.

Cooperation — Sum of scores for the nine dimensions of cooperation discussed in Chapter 6. See Table 6.2.

Corporatism — Index based on 12 indexes and rankings from the literature, which were standardized, summed, then standardized again. From Crepaz 1992, table 1.

Female labor force participation — As a share of the female population age 16 to 64. From OECD 1992, table 2.5. See Table 3.4.

Female/male pay ratio — Pay ration of women to men for full-time workers, manufacturing sector. Average for the years 1965, 1975, and 1985. From International Labour Office 1967, table 19, 1976, table 19, 1986, table 17; OECD 1988, chart 5.12; U.S. Bureau of the Census 1990, table 26. See Table 3.4.

Government expenditures — Total outlays of government as a share of GDP. From OECD 1992, table 6.5. Data are not available for New Zealand. Change variable is calculated as final year level minus initial year level. See Table 4.1.

Government tax revenues — As a share of GDP. From OECD 1992, table 6.6. Data are not available for New Zealand. Change variable is calculated as final year level minus initial year level. See Table 4.1.

Government transfers — As a share of GDP. From OECD 1992, table 6.3. Data are not available for New Zealand. Change variable is calculated as final year level minus initial year level. See Table 4.4.

Income equality — Share of national income going to the poorest quintile of households divided by that accruing to the richest quintile. Data for all countries except Austria are from World Bank 1991, table 30; World Bank 1989, table 30. Data for Austria are from J. Freeman 1989, pp. 176, 182. See Table 3.1.

Labor index — Composite index of scores for union density, works councils, and codetermination. The scores for the three were standardized, summed, then standardized again. See Table 5.1.

Labor organization index — Index of union concentration/centralization. From Cameron 1984, table 7.6. See Table 5.3 and pp. 133-135.

Labor strength index — Composite index of scores for union density, union concentration/centralization, works councils, and codetermination. The scores for the four were standardized, summed, then standardized again. Used in Chapter 6.

Unemployment	See above p. 197.
Union density	Employed union membership as a share of the employed labor force; average of 1970, 1980, and 1990 levels. From OECD 1994, table 5.7. See Table 5.1.
Works councils	Prominence of works councils. From Cameron 1984, table 7.6; Rogers and Streeck 1994. See Table 5.1.

Control variables for regression analysis

Catch-up	Per capita GDP at the beginning of the time period in question. Data for 1960 are from OECD 1991c, p. 130, tables 19 and 21 (average). Data for 1974 are from OECD 1991c, p. 146, table 3. Used in equations for investment, productivity growth, and output growth.
Economic openness	Average of exports and imports as a share of GDP. From OECD 1992, tables 6.12, 6.13. Used in equations for trade performance.
Government partisanship	Average share of cabinet portfolios held by parties of the left, including social democratic, labor, socialist, communist, and smaller left-wing parties. Data provided by Duane Swank. For discussion see Swank 1992. Used for political model in Chapter 5.
Labor force participation	As a share of the population age 16 to 64. From OECD 1992, table 2.6. Used in equations for unemployment.
Real interest rate	Average yield on five-year or longer-term government bonds adjusted for inflation. From OECD 1992, table 10.10. Interest rate data for several countries are based partly on extrapolation. Used in equations for investment, productivity growth, output growth, and unemployment.
Unemployment	See above. Used in equations for productivity and inflation.
Change in money supply	Change in currency outside banks plus demand deposits other than those of the central government. Data for 1962-90 are from International Monetary Fund 1992, pp. 78-79. Data for 1960-61 are from International Monetary Fund 1990, p. 90. Used in equations for inflation.

Other variables

Labor conflict	Average annual working days lost due to work stoppages per 1,000 employees. From U.S. Bureau of Labor Statistics 1993. Data for France exclude the May-June 1968 general strike.
Nominal wage changes	Manufacturing sector only. Data for 1962-90 are from International Monetary Fund 1992, pp. 100-01. Data for 1960-61 are from International Monetary Fund 1990, p. 112.
Savings	Gross national savings as a share of GDP. From OECD 1992, table 6.17.
Wage dispersion	Interindustry coefficient of variation in hourly earnings (expressed as a percentage), adjusted for part-time workers. From Rowthorn 1992, table 4.1, column 1.

Appendix B:
Economic Performance Data

Table B.1 Investment (in percentages)

	1960-90	1960-73	1974-90
Australia	24.7	25.5	24.0
Austria	25.6	26.7	24.6
Belgium	20.2	21.6	19.1
Canada	22.3	22.4	22.2
Denmark	21.4	23.8	19.4
Finland	26.1	26.4	25.9
France	22.6	23.8	21.7
Germany	22.5	24.9	20.5
Italy	23.3	24.5	22.2
Japan	31.3	32.5	30.2
Netherlands	22.4	25.0	20.3
New Zealand	22.8	22.2	23.4
Norway	28.3	28.3	28.3
Sweden	21.0	22.9	19.5
Switzerland	25.8	28.0	24.0
United Kingdom	18.2	18.3	18.2
United States	18.1	18.2	18.0

NOTE: Gross fixed capital formation as a share of GDP. For data source see Appendix A.

Table B.2 Labor Productivity Index

	1974-90
Australia	78.3
Austria	79.6
Belgium	88.5
Canada	89.2
Denmark	71.0
Finland	64.8
France	90.7
Germany	88.1
Italy	86.8
Japan	67.2
Netherlands	92.0
New Zealand	71.4
Norway	68.6
Sweden	70.6
Switzerland	88.6
United Kingdom	72.4
United States	100.0

NOTE: Output (GDP) per employed person. For data sources see Appendix A.

Table B.3 Productivity Growth (in percentages)

	1960-90	*1960-73*	*1974-90*
Australia	1.7	2.5	1.0
Austria	3.1	5.0	1.6
Belgium	3.0	4.3	2.1
Canada	1.8	2.6	1.2
Denmark	2.0	3.0	1.1
Finland	3.3	4.6	2.2
France	3.2	4.7	2.1
Germany	2.8	4.1	1.9
Italy	3.7	5.8	2.2
Japan	5.1	8.1	2.9
Netherlands	2.4	4.0	1.2
New Zealand	1.1	1.7	0.6
Norway	2.8	3.4	2.2
Sweden	2.1	3.6	1.0
Switzerland	1.8	2.9	0.7
United Kingdom	2.1	2.9	1.5
United States	1.2	2.0	0.6

NOTE: Change in real GDP per employed person. For data source see Appendix A.

Table B.4 Growth (in percentages)

	1960-90	1960-73	1974-90
Australia	2.3	3.2	1.6
Austria	3.2	4.2	2.4
Belgium	3.1	4.4	2.1
Canada	2.9	3.8	2.2
Denmark	2.5	3.6	1.7
Finland	3.4	4.4	2.5
France	2.9	4.3	1.9
Germany	2.6	3.5	2.0
Italy	3.4	4.6	2.6
Japan	5.3	8.4	3.1
Netherlands	2.4	3.6	1.4
New Zealand	1.2	2.1	0.4
Norway	3.2	3.5	3.0
Sweden	2.4	3.4	1.6
Switzerland	1.9	3.0	1.1
United Kingdom	2.1	2.6	1.8
United States	2.0	2.7	1.5

NOTE: Change in real GDP per capita. For data source see Appendix A.

Table B.5 Trade Balance (in percentages)

	1960-90	1960-73	1974-90
Australia	−0.9	−0.3	−1.5
Austria	0.1	0.2	0.1
Belgium	0.8	0.5	1.0
Canada	0.9	0.6	1.1
Denmark	−0.7	−1.6	−0.1
Finland	−0.3	−0.7	0.0
France	0.3	0.7	0.1
Germany	2.7	2.1	3.1
Italy	0.0	0.2	−0.3
Japan	1.1	0.8	1.3
Netherlands	1.7	0.0	3.1
New Zealand	−1.2	0.1	−2.2
Norway	0.3	−1.0	1.3
Sweden	0.4	0.2	0.5
Switzerland	−0.3	−1.1	0.5
United Kingdom	−0.5	−0.4	−0.5
United States	−0.6	0.4	−1.5

NOTE: Exports minus imports as a share of GDP. For data source see Appendix A.

Table B.6 Inflation (in percentages)

	1960-90	*1960-73*	*1974-90*
Australia	6.9	3.4	9.6
Austria	4.5	4.1	4.7
Belgium	4.9	3.6	6.0
Canada	5.5	3.2	7.3
Denmark	7.2	6.2	8.0
Finland	7.6	5.7	9.2
France	6.6	4.5	8.2
Germany	3.5	3.4	3.6
Italy	9.1	4.6	12.5
Japan	5.6	6.2	5.2
Netherlands	4.6	4.8	4.5
New Zealand	8.9	5.5	12.1
Norway	6.8	5.0	8.2
Sweden	6.9	4.6	8.7
Switzerland	3.9	4.2	3.7
United Kingdom	8.0	5.0	10.4
United States	5.1	3.1	6.6

NOTE: Change in consumer prices. For data source see Appendix A.

Table B.7 Unemployment (in percentages)

	1960-90	*1960-73*	*1974-90*
Australia	4.5	1.9	6.6
Austria	2.3	1.7	2.7
Belgium	6.0	2.2	9.1
Canada	6.9	5.1	8.5
Denmark	4.4	1.3	7.0
Finland	3.4	2.0	4.6
France	4.9	2.0	7.4
Germany	3.4	0.8	5.5
Italy	7.2	5.2	8.8
Japan	1.8	1.3	2.3
Netherlands	4.8	1.0	7.9
New Zealand	1.9	0.2	3.4
Norway	2.0	1.3	2.6
Sweden	2.0	1.9	2.2
Switzerland	na	na	na
United Kingdom	4.9	1.9	7.4
United States	6.0	4.8	6.9

NOTE: As a percentage of the total labor force. For data source see Appendix A; na = not available.

Appendix C:
Significance Levels

The quantitative data analysis in this book has relied upon two commonly-used statistical metods for examining associations between variables: correlation and regression. These procedures are described briefly in Chapter 3 (pp. 44, 54-56). But any two sets of numbers, even ones chosen purely at random, are likely to show *some* degree of association. How do we know if a numerical association reflects a genuine relationshiop between two variables?

To avoid reaching false conclusions, social scientists typically require that there be no more than a 10 percent probability that an association between variables is due to chance. Those that satisfy this requirement are deemed "statistically significant." In statistical lingo, we say they are "significant at the 10 percent level." Correlation or regression coefficients which do not meet this 10 percent requirement may nevertheless be genuine; we merely have less confidence that they are.

All tests of statistical significance throughout the book are "one-tailed." A one-tailed test is used when theoretical considerations suggest a particular direction (either positive or negative) to the relationship.

Significance levels for correlation and regression coefficients are as follows:

$*$ = 10% level
$**$ = 5% level
$***$ = 1% level

◧　　　　　　　　　　　　　　　　　　　　　　　　　　　　◧

Notes

◧　Introduction

1. Paul Krugman (1994) has noted that "There are many economic puzzles, but there are only two really great mysteries" (p. 24). This is one. The other is why business cycles occur.

2. "Historical" refers not just to things that occurred in the distant past, but to anything that happened before this moment.

◧　Chapter 1

1. This usage follows that of, among others, Korpi 1985 and Boaz and Crane 1993.

2. The term *conservative* applies primarily in the U.S. context. *Liberal* is more apt for many other national contexts.

3. Okun 1975, p. 1.

4. That is not to deny that government played an interventionist and promotional role in economic affairs prior to that time. On the contrary, there is an activist policy tradition in this country dating back to the colonial era. (See Bourgin 1989; Schlesinger 1986, chap. 9). State activism was even more pronounced in nations such as Japan and Germany.

5. Data for 1948-59 are from Council of Economic Advisers 1991, 1992. Data for 1960-73 are from OECD 1992.

6. U.S. Bureau of the Census 1990, p. 17.

7. Council of Economic Advisers 1991, p. 336. These figures are for the private sector.

8. Lebergott 1976, pp. 248-98.

9. Unless otherwise noted, the terms "growth" and "output growth" here always refer to change in real GDP per capita.

10. Maddison 1989, p. 88.

11. Cited in Krugman 1990, p. 197.

12. Galbraith 1984, p. 2.

13. Cited in Silberman 1971, p. 73. © 1971, Time, Inc., reprinted with permission.

14. Levitt 1967, p. 114.

15. Other social and economic developments in the 1960s and early 1970s similarly reflected the assumptions of the "post-scarcity" generation living in a society of abundance. The U.S. government expressed a heightened concern for economic development in Third World nations. Economic aid to developing countries was increased, and volunteer efforts such as the Peace Corps were created. The counterculture of the late 1960s—particularly its antimaterialist component—was to a large extent a product of affluence. As a mass phenomenon, the counterculture was unique to the industrialized world; no parallel occurred in less developed nations. Finally, the early 1970s were marked by an attempt on the part of blue-collar workers to gain a greater say in workplace decision making. This represented an effort to improve the quality of work, to move beyond a narrow focus on the cash nexus.

16. A notable dissent is Bowles, Gordon, and Weisskopf 1990, which dates the onset of decline in the United States in the mid 1960s.

17. Council of Economic Advisers 1992, p. 330. These income figures are slightly deceiving, because the share of compensation accounted for by benefits grew during this period and average family size decreased. On the other hand, an increasing number of families during these years included multiple earners, and a substantial chunk of the rise in benefits was needed to keep pace with hyperinflated medical costs.

18. Council of Economic Advisers 1992, p. 346. Data are for the private sector. Again, these figures do not account for benefits, which increased as a share of total compensation during these years.

19. For useful overviews see Glyn et al. 1990; Maddison 1982; Boltho 1982. Other factors would, of course, come into play in explaining differences in national performance during the boom.

20. See M. Stewart 1983, chap. 5.

21. I do not mean to imply that a strong economy is a sufficient or even a necessary condition for the ascendance of progressive economic ideas and policies, nor that orthodox market liberal notions necessarily flourish in times of economic malaise. The depression period, which sparked the New Deal, is an obvious counterexample to any such simpleminded thesis. There is a clear correlation, however, between economic expectations and domestic policy sentiment in the United States during the 1960s and 1970s. See Durr 1993.

22. Cited in Matusow 1984, p. 135.

23. See Ferguson and Rogers 1986, chap. 3; Vogel 1989, chap. 8; Edsall 1984, chap. 3.

24. Lobbyist and PAC figures are from Judis 1992, p. 20. Spending figure is from Ferguson and Rogers 1986, p. 88.

25. Huntington 1981, p. 177. Based on Gallup surveys.

26. Huntington 1981, p. 216.

27. Kuttner 1980, p. 24; Vogel 1989, p. 173.

28. Lipset 1986, p. 301.

29. Ferguson and Rogers 1986, chap. 1; Ladd 1978; Lipset and Schneider 1987, pp. 346-351; Shapiro and Young 1989.

30. See Ferguson and Rogers 1986, chap. 4; Vogel 1989, chaps. 7 and 9; Edsall 1984, chap. 6.

31. On these developments see Alber 1987; Lipset 1990; Therborn 1986, chap. 3; Canova 1994; "Politics of Privatisation" 1988; Hagemann, Jones, and Montador 1988; Visser 1991.

⧫ Chapter 2

1. Streeck 1987, p. 457.
2. See, for example, Friedman 1962; Friedman and Friedman 1990; Hayek 1944, 1960; Nozick 1974.
3. A. Smith 1776, p. 423 (book 4, chap. 2).
4. See in particular Elster 1979; Schelling 1960, chap. 2.
5. As far as I am aware, the burgeoning field of economic sociology has not systematically addressed this issue. There is no reference to it in Richard Swedberg's recent comprehensive reviews of the field, nor in his interviews with economists and sociologists working in this area. See Swedberg 1987, 1990, 1991. Nor is it dealt with in various recent anthologies in economic sociology, including Swedberg 1993; Granovetter and Swedberg 1992; Etzioni and Lawrence 1991; Coughlin 1991; Friedland and Robertson 1990; Zukin and DiMaggio 1990; Martinelli and Smelser 1990. Two important exceptions are Wolfgang Streeck (1987, 1988, 1989, 1991) and Ronald Dore (1986, 1987). The issue is also discussed in Keohane (1984) with regard to economic relations between countries. I owe a profound debt to Wolfgang Streeck, whose writings and seminar comments inspired this chapter.
6. For most actors welfare is said to have both a material and a psychological component, and it is considered an open question as to which dominates in any particular instance. An important exception is firms acting in a competitive environment, which are assumed to strive solely for profit maximization. This is mandated by the fact that such an environment systematically selects on the basis of profitability.
7. Bourdieu 1988; Elster 1989a, chap. 3, 1989b; Hodgson 1989; Langlois 1986; Nelson and Winter 1982.
8. H. Simon 1976; March 1982.
9. Williamson 1981, 1985.
10. Tversky and Kahneman 1990; Frank 1990.
11. Etzioni 1988; Sen 1977; Hirschman 1985; Mansbridge 1990; Collard 1978.
12. Marx [1867] 1976, part 8.
13. "The gearing of markets into a self-regulating system of tremendous power was not the result of any inherent tendency of markets towards excrescence, but rather the effect of highly artificial stimulants administered to the body social. . . . Deliberate state action in the fifteenth and sixteenth centuries foisted the mercantile system on the fiercely protectionist towns and principalities. Mercantilism destroyed the outworn particulars of local and intermunicipal trading by breaking down the barriers separating these two types of noncompetitive commerce and thus clearing the way for a national market" (Polanyi [1944] 1957, pp. 57, 65).
14. Hodgson 1989, pp. 158-59. See also Arrow 1990; Durkheim [1893] 1984, chap. 7.
15. See Powell and DiMaggio 1991.
16. Abolafia and Biggart 1991; C. Smith 1993; Zelizer 1978, 1993; McGuire, Granovetter, and Schwartz 1993; H. White 1981, 1988, 1993; Burt 1993.
17. See, for example, Granovetter 1973, 1985, 1993; Dore 1987, chap. 9; J. Coleman 1988; Baron 1988. This theme is highlighted in many of the essays in the anthologies cited in note 5 above.
18. See especially Bowles and Gintis 1990, 1993.
19. Berger and Piore 1980; Bergmann 1986; Bielby and Baron 1986; Gordon, Edwards, and Reich 1982.
20. Perrow 1986b; Pfeffer and Salancik 1978; J. Thompson 1967.
21. As Robert Sugden (1986) has aptly noted:

Most modern economic theory describes a world presided over by government. . . . The government is supposed to have the responsibility, the will and the power to restructure society in whatever way maximizes social welfare; like the US Cavalry in a good Western, the government stands ready to rush to the rescue whenever the market "fails," and the economist's job is to advise it on when and how to do so. Private individuals, in contrast, are credited with little or no ability to solve collective problems among themselves. (p. 3)

22. Buchanan 1975, chap. 9, 1988; Hayek 1979, chap. 12; Shepsle and Weingast 1984.

23. See Chapter 4.

24. Weber [1905] 1958, pp. 54-55.

25. Weber [1905] 1958, p. 60. See also J. Scott 1976; E. P. Thompson 1967.

26. Weber [1905] 1958, p. 172.

27. Weber readily admitted that Protestantism was not the only possible route to the emergence of the capitalist spirit. Indeed, capitalist business organization had existed in isolated areas long before the Reformation. Nevertheless, he maintained that without the influence of Calvinism, the same results might not have been achieved so rapidly or spread so widely.

28. Polanyi [1944] 1957, p. 73.

29. Froot, Perold, and Stein 1990, cited in Jacobs 1991, pp. 35-36.

30. Hirschman 1970.

31. Zysman and Tyson 1983; Johnson, Tyson, and Zysman 1989; Komiya, Okuno, and Suzumura 1988.

32. Marston 1990; Yamamoto 1989/90.

33. Ellsworth 1985; Knetter 1989; Magaziner and Patinkin 1989, chap. 4.

34. Even American management itself appears to view short time horizons as a problem. A 1987 survey of 400 chief executives found 70 percent agreeing that U.S. firms concentrate too heavily on tomorrow's stock price and next quarter's earnings. See "Business Week" 1987. In a 1990 study of 2,000 top corporate financial officers by the Financial Executives Institute, the two factors most frequently blamed for America's competitiveness difficulties were shortsighted investors and shortsighted corporate managers. Cited in M. Jacobs 1991, p. 8.

35. Porter 1992, pp. 25-26.

36. Dertouzos et al. 1989, chap. 4; Zysman and Tyson 1983.

37. Ellsworth 1985; Porter 1992; Office of Technology Assessment 1990a, chap. 3; M. Jacobs 1991; Wellons 1985.

38. In addition to those cited in note 37, see Dyson 1986; Zysman 1983, pp. 251-65.

39. According to Lester Thurow (1992, p. 34), of the 100 largest public firms in Germany, these banks own 10 to 25 percent of the shares in 48, 25 to 50 percent in 43, and over 50 percent in the other 9.

40. M. Jacobs 1991, p. 70. See also "A Survey" 1994, p. S8.

41. In addition to those cited in note 37, see Gerlach 1992; Abegglen and Stalk 1985, chap. 7; Dore 1987, chap. 6; Aoki 1988, chap. 4; Blinder 1992.

42. Blinder 1992, p. 55.

43. In addition to those cited in note 37, see Lowenstein 1988.

44. Stock turnover figure is from the New York Stock Exchange. Other figures are from Porter 1992, pp. 26, 42.

45. Another feature of the German and Japanese financial systems that has encouraged lengthy time horizons on the part of firms is the underdeveloped nature of these countries' capital markets. By necessity, German and Japanese companies have tended to secure a comparatively large share of their financing via bank loans—particularly long-term loans. (See Berglof 1990; Ellsworth

1985; Hodder 1988.) This reliance on debt rather than equity reinforces German and Japanese firms' emphasis on long-term performance for two reasons. First, it lessens the influence of shareholder pressure for short-term results. Second, interest payments typically are tax-deductible, whereas dividend payments are not. Firms that rely more heavily on debt thereby enjoy a lower cost of capital. Less expensive capital lowers the rate of return a firm must achieve to succeed financially, thus permitting greater allocation of funds toward investment.

46. Streeck 1989, 1991; Lynch 1994.

47. Becker 1964, p. 12.

48. Commission on the Skills of the American Workforce 1990.

49. Streeck 1989, p. 98.

50. Office of Technology Assessment 1990b, p. 132. See also Lynch 1994, pp. 85-86.

51. Dore 1987, chap. 2; Koike 1987; Tung 1984, chap. 2.

52. According to Lester Thurow (1992, p. 139), the employee turnover rate in Japan is 3.5 percent per year, compared to 4 percent per month in the United States.

53. Streeck 1987; Office of Technology Assessment 1990b, chap. 5; Wiggenhorn 1990.

54. Streeck 1989; Streeck et al. 1987; Kazis 1990.

55. Figure for spending on training is from Office of Technology Assessment 1990b, p. 15. Figure for number of companies is from Commission on the Skills of the American Workforce 1990, p. 49. Figure for percent of workforce is from Perry 1991, p. 71. Managers and professionals figure is from Commission on the Skills of the American Workforce 1990, p. 49. Figure for apprenticeship programs is from Office of Technology Assessment 1990b, p. 19.

56. Office of Technology Assessment 1990b, p. 3. See also Commission on the Skills of the American Workforce 1990; Lynch 1994; Kazis 1990.

57. Porter 1980, p. 124.

58. Helper 1991a.

59. Helper 1991c; Macaulay 1974; Womack, Jones, and Roos 1990, chap. 6. General Motors, Ford, and Chrysler have each been shifting away from this strategy since the early 1980s, but in a very tentative, halting fashion. See Helper 1991b; Womack, Jones, and Roos 1990, chap. 6; Hoffman and Kaplinsky 1988, chap. 6.

60. Womack, Jones, and Roos 1990, chap. 6; Helper 1991a, 1991c.

61. Womack, Jones, and Roos 1990, chap. 6; Smitka 1991; Cusumano and Takeishi 1991; Asanuma 1985.

62. Womack 1990; Womack, Jones, and Roos 1990; Cusumano 1985.

63. See Williamson 1981, 1985.

64. Scherrer 1991; L. White 1971, chap. 6.

65. On the drawbacks of vertical integration in the auto industry, see Moskal 1988.

66. Womack, Jones, and Roos 1990, fig. 6.1, p. 157.

67. Womack, Jones, and Roos 1990, pp. 167-68.

68. Axelrod 1984; Granovetter 1985; Gambetta 1988, pp. 225-29.

69. Dore 1987, chap. 9; Sako 1992, 1994; Helper 1991a; Smitka 1991; McMillan 1990. The point is also stressed in Porter 1990 (e.g., pp. 152-53).

70. Powell 1990; Pyke, Becattini, and Sengenberger 1990; Sabel 1989; Sabel et al. 1989.

71. Nove 1977, chap. 4.

◧ Chapter 3

1. Thurow 1981, p. 138.

2. Indeed, although my interest here is in income equality, there is substantial disagreement among egalitarians over precisely what it is that should be equalized. See, for example, Rawls 1971; Dworkin 1981; Arneson 1989; Cohen 1989; Le Grand 1991a; Sen 1992.

3. In the words of libertarian Friedrich Hayek (1960):

From the fact that people are very different it follows that, if we treat them equally, the result must be inequality in their actual position, and that the only way to place them in an equal position would be to treat them differently. Equality before the law and material equality are therefore not only different but are in conflict with each other; and we can achieve either the one or the other, but not both at the same time. The equality before the law which freedom requires leads to material inequality. . . . The desire of making people more alike in their condition cannot be accepted in a free society as a justification for further and discriminatory coercion. (p. 87)

4. Locke [1690] 1980; Nozick 1974.

5. Friedman and Friedman 1990, ch. 5; Hayek 1960; Flew 1983. Foreshadowing this line of argument, David Hume proffered the following observation as long ago as 1751:

Render possessions ever so equal, men's different degrees of art, care, and industry will immediately break that equality. . . . The most rigorous inquisition . . . is requisite to watch every inequality on its first appearance; and the most severe jurisdiction, to punish and redress it. . . . So much authority must soon degenerate into tyranny. ([1751] 1983, p. 28)

6. Cohen 1981; Roemer 1988; Tawney [1931] 1961, chaps. 5, 7.

7. Norman 1982; Tawney [1931] 1961, chaps. 3, 7; Lukes 1991; Preston 1984. As R. H. Tawney put it:

A society is free insofar, and only insofar, as, within the limits set by nature, knowledge, and resources, its institutions and policies are such as to enable all its members to grow to their fullest stature. . . . Insofar as the opportunity to lead a life worthy of human beings is needlessly confined to a minority, not a few of the conditions applauded as freedom would more properly be denounced as privilege. Action which causes such opportunities to be more widely shared is, therefore, twice blessed. It not only subtracts from inequality, but adds to freedom. (p. 268)

8. These are not the only such objections of this nature, merely the most influential. For others see Rae et al. 1981; Elster 1989a, pp. 228-29.

9. Bronfenbrenner 1971.

10. Rawls (1971) writes:

The existing distribution of income and wealth . . . is the cumulative effect of prior distributions of natural assets—that is, natural talents and abilities—as these have been developed or left unrealized, and their use favored or disfavored over time by social circumstances and such chance contingencies as accident and good fortune. Intuitively, the most obvious injustice of the system . . . is that it permits distributive shares to be improperly influenced by these factors so arbitrary from a moral standpoint. (p. 72)

See also Barry 1988; Dworkin 1985, p. 207.

11. For this reason, egalitarianism is sometimes said to be motivated by envy, rather than by true considerations of justice.

12. Among those who would not disagree is Karl Marx, who believed that in a pre-abundant society, income should ideally be proportional to each worker's labor contribution. Once abundance is reached, the social product would be distributed according to need. See Marx [1875] 1978; A. Wood 1986. Another is R. H. Tawney ([1931] 1961), who argued that "Nobody thinks it inequitable that, when a reasonable provision has been made for all, exceptional responsibilities should be compensated by exceptional rewards, as a recognition of the service performed" (p. 118).

13. Okun 1975, p. 48.

14. Okun 1975, p. 47.

15. Alfred Marshall (1907) offered a similar formulation of the dilemma:

Taking it for granted that a more equal distribution of wealth is to be desired, how far would this justify changes in the institutions of property or limitations of free enterprise even when they would be likely to diminish the aggregate wealth? (p. 41)

16. See, for example, Arrow 1979; Browning 1976; Browning and Johnson 1984; Friedman and Friedman 1990, chap. 5; Hayek 1960; Kristol 1978, pt. 3; Letwin 1983; Lindbeck 1986; Okun 1975.

17. Arrow 1979, p. 7.

18. Hume [1751] 1983, p. 28.

19. George Gilder (1981) has suggested, along these lines, that "In order to succeed, the poor need most of all the spur of their own poverty" (p. 118).

20. "At any given moment," opines Hayek (1960),

we could improve the position of the poorest by giving them what we took from the wealthy. But, while such an equalizing of the positions in the column of progress would temporarily quicken the closing-up of the ranks, it would, before long, slow down the movement of the whole and in the long run hold back those in the rear. (pp. 48-49)

21. This illustration is borrowed from Letwin 1983, p. 45. See also Baumol and Fischer (1979), who demonstrate formally that "under a set of reasonable assumptions, any attempt to guarantee absolute equality of incomes using . . . progressive income taxes and transfers for the purpose must, at least in theory, reduce society's output to zero" (p. 514).

22. As one bit of evidence bearing upon this issue, we might consider the attempts in Cuba and China in the late 1960s to rely predominantly on moral incentives for eliciting work effort. By most accounts these experiments were largely unsuccessful—although given the political and economic contexts in which they were undertaken, they certainly cannot be presumed to represent the final word on the matter. See Karl 1975; Mesa-Lago 1981, chap. 7; Walder 1986, chap. 7.

23. The following statement by Milton and Rose Friedman (1990) is representative:

Who can doubt the effect that the drive for equality has had on efficiency and productivity? Surely, that is one of the main reasons why economic growth in Britain has fallen so far behind its continental neighbors, the United States, Japan, and other nations over the past few decades. (p. 145)

24. The literature on this issue is extensive, but see especially Zukin and DiMaggio 1990; Granovetter 1985, 1990; Elster 1989b.

25. See Akerlof and Yellen 1990; Levine 1991; Solow 1990; Lazear 1989; Adams 1965; Kahneman, Knetsch, and Thaler 1991; Cook and Hegtvedt 1983; Deutsch 1985.

26. See Kelley and Evans 1993.

27. Reviewed in Burtless and Haveman 1987; Danziger, Haveman, and Plotnick 1981; Moffitt 1992.

28. See Chapter 4.

29. See Kuttner 1984; Thurow 1981; Bowles, Gordon, and Weisskopf 1990, chap. 14; J. Freeman 1989, chap. 6.

30. Persson and Tabellini 1994.

31. Members of the OECD are Australia, Austria, Belgium, Canada, Denmark, Finland, France, Germany, Greece, Iceland, Ireland, Italy, Japan, Luxembourg, the Netherlands, New Zealand, Norway, Portugal, Spain, Sweden, Switzerland, Turkey, the United Kingdom, and the United States.

32. No non-OECD countries meet the wealth criterion. OECD members Ireland, Greece, Portugal, Spain, and Turkey also fail to meet it; see OECD 1991c, p. 147, table 3. I exclude Iceland and Luxembourg because of their extremely small populations—less than 500,000 each.

33. It would be desirable to also examine the impact of changes in equality over time on performance outcomes, but data on income equality are neither comprehensive nor reliable enough to permit such analysis. See Mahler 1989, p. 27.

34. Correlation and regression measures, used later in the chapter, assume that the relationship between variables is linear.

35. In our case, there are two competing hypotheses—one contending that equality has a detrimental effect on economic performance and another positing that it has a favorable effect. A one-tailed test is therefore appropriate.

36. See Mahler 1989. A potentially more reliable source of data on income equality is the Luxembourg Income Study, but at this point data are available for only nine of our countries. See Smeeding 1991; Smeeding, O'Higgins, and Rainwater 1990.

37. A limitation of the World Bank data is that they are not adjusted for household size. If the size distribution of income varies significantly across countries, this could potentially bias comparative estimates of income equality. For instance, a nation might appear to be more egalitarian than it actually is simply because its poor households have more members than their counterparts in other countries, and thus more income. However, efforts to examine this issue have typically found that adjusting for household size has little effect on relative differences in national income distribution. See Mahler 1989, p. 21; Smeeding 1991, p. 45.

38. OECD 1993b; OECD 1992, table 6.3.

39. The measure most commonly used to represent income equality is the Gini index. The Gini coefficient for a country indicates the degree to which its income distribution departs from perfect equality. (It is thus a measure of *inequality*.) Unlike the quintile ratio measure, the Gini index takes into account income disparities within the middle three quintiles. Because data are not available for these middle quintiles for Austria, I am forced to use the poor/rich quintile ratio measure in order to include Austria in the analysis. In practice, the two measures tend to be very similar. The correlation for our 16 countries (excluding Austria) between the quintile ratio measure and the Gini index for 1980 is −.95.

40. See also van Arnhem, Corina, and Schotsman 1982.

41. Thus, for instance, Graef Crystal estimates the compensation of top-level corporate executives in Japan to be around 15 times that of an average production worker. In Germany, the corresponding figure is 20 times; in Britain, 25 times; and in the United States, 50 times. See Crystal 1991, chap. 13. Also see Byrne 1993.

42. The pattern is no different if net savings is used instead of gross.

43. Investment is measured here as gross fixed capital formation. This measure is less than ideal because it includes investment in housing, which does not directly contribute to future economic growth in the way that investment in machines or research does. But it is the only good comparative measure available, and there is little reason to suspect that excluding housing investment would substantially alter the results.

44. Burtless and Haveman 1987; Pencavel 1986; Saunders and Klau 1985, pp. 162-67; Brown 1980. For a contrary argument, see Hausman 1981.

45. Danziger, Haveman, and Plotnick 1981; Moffitt 1992; Sawhill 1988, pp. 1102-03.

46. Gross capital stock per employed person, excluding dwellings and government production. Capital stock data are from OECD 1991a. Purchasing power parities (rather than exchange rates) were used to convert capital stock figures into a common currency; these are from OECD 1991c, pp. 156-57, table 3. Data are not available for Austria, Denmark, Italy, the Netherlands, New Zealand, and Switzerland.

47. Tawney [1931] 1961, p. 211.

48. Productivity is measured here as real GDP per employed person. A better indicator is GDP per hour worked, but data based on this measure are not available for a number of our countries. Using the latter measure would alter the findings only slightly, if at all. Both the number of persons employed and average hours of work per employee have changed at roughly the same rate in most of our 17 countries since 1960, with the former figure increasing and the latter declining. The only exceptions are Canada, Japan, and the United States. Average hours in these three countries have declined more slowly than in other nations, and employment, particularly in Canada and the United States, has increased more rapidly. Hence, these nations' rates of productivity growth are somewhat overstated here relative to the other 14 countries. See Blyton 1989; OECD 1992, table 1.6.

49. See, for example, Magaziner and Patinkin 1989.

50. Due to lack of reliable unemployment data, Switzerland is not included here.

51. All regression equations throughout the book are estimated using ordinary least squares.

52. For a useful and highly readable introduction to regression analysis, see Lewis-Beck 1980.

53. With a small number of cases, including too many independent variables may diminish the reliability of regression parameter estimates.

54. The same will be true for the factors examined in Chapters 4, 5, and 6.

55. See, for example, Newell and Symons 1987.

56. See Dowrick and Nguyen 1989; Baumol 1986; Baumol, Blackman, and Wolff 1989, chap. 5; Abramovitz 1986.

57. See Katzenstein 1985.

58. See A. Phillips 1958.

59. See Friedman and Schwartz 1982. Also Friedman and Friedman 1990, chap. 9; Flemming 1978.

60. See Gordon 1975; Moore 1979; Lavoie 1984; Whitely 1987.

61. Willett et al. 1988.

62. Two additional factors that may influence inflation are central bank independence and government partisanship. (On the former see Alesina 1988; Suzuki 1993. On the latter see Hibbs 1977; Alesina and Roubini 1990; Suzuki 1993.) Both, however, are expected to have their effects

via changes in the money supply and/or in government spending. Hence, they are effectively controlled for in this analysis.

63. See Kuznets 1955.

64. The pattern is similar for other years.

65. Access to health care and housing are among a variety of other important components of genuine equality of opportunity. For useful comparative data on such issues, see Gorham 1986; A. Shapiro 1992.

66. Okun (1975, pp. 76-82) makes this point in his discussion of equality of opportunity.

67. Bowles, Gordon, and Weisskopf 1990, p. 221.

68. Of course, a substantial share of educational development is attributable to parental influence. But vigorous intervention in that area is outside the realm of acceptable government activity in a liberal society. Consequently, few believe this aspect of education can, or should, be significantly equalized. When we think of equal educational opportunity, therefore, we generally focus on schooling.

69. The problem of equalizing educational opportunity involves much more than equalizing funding. See Jencks 1988.

70. Kozol 1991.

71. Shapiro and Stiglitz 1984, p. 433.

72. Weisskopf 1987, p. 128. See also Bowles 1985; F. Green 1988.

73. Green and Weisskopf 1990; Oster 1980; Rebitzer 1987.

74. Esping-Andersen 1987, pp. 84-85.

75. Weisskopf 1987.

76. Weisskopf 1987, p. 150.

77. For an overview see Mankiw 1990.

78. On the logic of "political exchange" see Cameron 1984; Pizzorno 1978.

79. Gunderson 1989, pp. 51-52.

80. See, for example, Polachek 1981.

81. England 1982.

82. Bergmann 1986; Bielby and Baron 1986; Blau and Ferber 1987.

83. Greenstein and Barancik 1990.

84. Galbraith 1984, p. xxviii.

85. Here the units are families rather than households.

86. On the widening pay gap, see Freeman and Katz 1994; Card 1992; Harrison and Bluestone 1988, chap. 5; Levy and Murnane 1992; Ryscavage and Henle 1990. (This trend is not unique to the United States, but it is most pronounced here. See Freeman and Katz 1994; OECD 1993b; S. Davis 1993.) On part-time employment, see Blank 1990; Tilly 1990. On unemployment, see Burtless 1990. On income gains for the well-off, see K. Phillips 1990, chap. 6.

87. See the discussion on redistributive policy in Chapter 4.

88. For further evidence and discussion of heightened inequality, see Mishel and Bernstein 1993; Krugman 1992; K. Phillips 1990; Shapiro and Greenstein 1991; Burtless 1987; Braun 1991, chap. 5.

89. The literature is now voluminous. But see especially Office of Technology Assessment 1990a; Dertouzos et al. 1989; Cuomo Commission 1988.

90. See Bergmann 1986, table 2.2.

◈ **Chapter 4**

1. Cited in Zinn 1980, p. 70.
2. Boaz and Crane 1993; "American renewal" 1981; Friedman and Friedman 1990; Gilder 1981; Haberler 1979; Krauss 1978; Kristol 1978; Reagan 1981a, 1981c; Simon 1978; Wanniski 1978; Weidenbaum 1979.
3. John A. Davenport. "The welfare state vs. the public welfare," *Fortune*, June 1976, p. 132. © 1976 Time Inc. All rights reserved. Used with permission.
4. OECD 1985, p. 14.
5. See Hirschman 1991.
6. Lindbeck 1983, p. 285. See also Eltis 1983.
7. Reagan 1981b.
8. Reagan 1981c, pp. 218, 220.
9. Friedman and Friedman 1990, p. 265.
10. Kornai 1986; Le Grand 1991b; Wolf 1988.
11. McKenzie 1987, p. 176. See also Buchanan 1975, chap. 9, 1988; Hayek 1979, chap. 12; Shepsle and Weingast 1984.
12. Government revenue consists mainly of direct and indirect taxes and Social Security contributions paid by employers and employees. Government spending includes final consumption expenditures, interest on the public debt, subsidies, transfer payments to households, gross capital formation, and purchases of land and intangible assets.
13. See Cameron 1978; Katzenstein 1985.
14. Cameron 1985; Lindbeck 1983 (quote is from p. 289). See also Peacock and Ricketts 1978.
15. See, for example, Barro 1991; Kormendi and Meguire 1985; Landau 1983; Levine and Renelt 1992; Ram 1986; Scully 1989.
16. Those in the first group include Cameron 1982; Grier and Tullock 1989; Hagemann, Jones, and Montador 1988; Landau 1985; Marlow 1986, 1988; Pfaller with Gough 1991. The second group includes Castles and Dowrick 1990; Garrison and Lee 1992; Katz, Mahler, and Franz 1983; Korpi 1985; McCallum and Blais 1987. Those finding mixed results are Gould 1983; P. J. Grossman 1988, 1990; Saunders 1985, 1986; Wolf 1988, chap. 7.
17. Saunders 1986. See also Castles and Dowrick 1990.
18. Okun 1975, chap. 4.
19. Kristol 1978, p. 243.
20. Esping-Andersen 1990, chap. 6 (quote is from p. 149).
21. The studies are, respectively, Marlow 1986; Weede 1986; Pfaller with Gough 1991; Landau 1985; McCallum and Blais 1987; Korpi 1985; Castles and Dowrick 1990. An additional study, Friedland and Sanders 1985, found a positive association between changes in transfer spending and short-run (1 to 3 years) growth rates.
22. McCallum and Blais 1987, p. 10. They believe the level to be 16 percent of GDP.
23. Blank 1991; Danziger and Gottschalk 1985; Danziger, Haveman, and Plotnick 1986; Ellwood and Summers 1986; Marmor, Mashaw, and Harvey 1990, chap. 4; Sawhill 1988; Wilson 1987.
24. Danziger and Gottschalk 1985, p. 34.
25. Ellwood and Summers 1986, p. 59.
26. These poverty rates take into account only cash income. If noncash transfers—such as Food Stamps and the value of health care benefits and housing subsidies—were included, the

poverty rate for each nation would decrease somewhat (see, e.g., Sawhill 1988, p. 1083). However, the difference between countries would probably not be altered. A comprehensive study of comparative poverty in the 1980s, sponsored by the Joint Center for Political and Economic Studies, arrived at the same conclusion regarding the efficacy of the U.S. welfare state. See McFate 1991, p. 22. Also see Ruggles 1991.

27. Milton and Rose Friedman (1990) write:

> The lure of getting someone else's money is strong. Many, including the bureaucrats administering the programs, will try to get it for themselves rather than have it go to someone else. . . . The attempt by people to divert government expenditures to themselves . . . explains why many programs tend to benefit middle- and upper-income groups rather than the poor for whom they are supposedly intended. The poor tend to lack not only the skills valued in the market, but also the skills required to be successful in the political scramble for funds. Indeed, their disadvantage in the political market is likely to be greater than in the economic. (p. 118)

See also Stigler 1970; Tullock 1971.

28. Howe and Longman 1992, p. 93.

29. See Kuttner 1984, chap. 6; Skocpol 1990.

30. Tocqueville, "Memoir on Pauperism" [1835], cited in Danziger and Gottschalk 1985, pp. 32-33.

31. Murray 1984. See also Anderson 1978, chap. 2; Butler and Kondratas 1987.

32. Murray 1984, p. 218.

33. For a concrete illustration of the financial incentives involved, see Ellwood 1989, table 2; Jencks and Edin 1990, p. 43.

34. See Smeeding 1992.

35. Cogent proposals for reform can be found in Garfinkel 1992; Jencks and Edin 1990; Kamerman 1991; Schwarz and Volgy 1992; R. Shapiro 1990; Skocpol 1990. Interestingly, several elements of the general strategy advanced in these works have received backing from prominent conservative welfare policy analysts. See Gilder 1987; Kristol 1978, chap. 27; Novak et al. 1987, chap. 7.

36. See, for instance, McKenzie 1987, chap. 8.

37. Ginsburg 1983, chap. 6; Ohman 1974; Rehn 1985. Swedish employment policy is part of an overall labor market strategy devised in the 1950s by a group of economists, led by Gosta Rehn and Rudolf Meidner, tied to the labor movement. The key idea behind the Rehn strategy is that wages should be set as high as the international market will permit and should be roughly the same, for comparable work, across all firms, regardless of size or profitability. The effect is to encourage firms to compete based on high productivity rather than low wages. Inefficient firms are driven out of business. The catch is that workers are frequently displaced as their companies go under. To compensate for this dislocation, Rehn and his colleagues argued that the government must engage in an active labor market policy of retraining and placing workers who have lost their jobs.

38. Osterman 1988, p. 127.

39. The labor market boards do not make decisions for employers about whom to hire and fire. Their function is to remedy the informational barriers that impede labor market adjustment.

40. OECD 1992, tables 2.6, 2.15.

41. The following discussion draws on Bawden and Skidmore 1989; Commission on the Skills of the American Workforce 1990; Donahue 1989; J. Jacobs 1989; Johnston 1984; Kazis 1989; Lerman and Pouncy 1990; Osterman 1988; Office of Technology Assessment 1990b.

42. Donahue 1989, pp. 15-16.
43. Donahue 1989, p. 30.
44. Osterman 1988, p. 25.
45. Osterman 1988, p. 153.
46. Osterman 1988, p. 132.
47. See OECD 1993a.
48. See also Dore, Bounine-Cabale, and Tapiola 1989.
49. Casey and Bruche 1985; Furaker, Johansson, and Lind 1990; Osterman 1988, chap. 6; Wilensky and Turner 1987. Austria's nationalized firms play an important role in securing employment; see J. Freeman 1989, pp. 184-85.
50. See, for example, "Labour Pains" 1994 and "O Brave" 1994.
51. These figures are from "Labour Pains" 1994 and "The Trouble" 1994.
52. See, for example, Mishel and Bernstein 1993, chaps. 3-4; Freeman and Katz 1994; Harrison and Bluestone 1988, chap. 5.
53. Figures in this paragraph are from "The Trouble" 1994, which draws on a study by Richard Freeman.
54. G. M. Grossman 1990; Itoh et al. 1988a, 1988b, 1991; Krugman 1986; Magaziner and Reich 1983; Porter 1990, chap. 12; B. Scott 1985; Stiglitz 1989.
55. See, for instance, Bhagwati 1988; Eads 1981; Gilder 1983; Krugman 1983; Lawrence 1984, chap. 5; Nivola 1991; Schultze 1983; Teece 1991.
56. Porter 1990, p. 639.
57. Shapira 1990; Office of Technology Assessment 1990a, pp. 158-67.
58. Boltho 1985; Johnson 1982; Johnson, Tyson, and Zysman 1989; Komiya, Okuno, and Suzumura 1988; Magaziner and Hout 1980; Okimoto 1989; Office of Technology Assessment 1991, chap. 6; Prestowitz 1988.
59. Sakoh 1984; Saxonhouse 1983; Trezise 1984.
60. Eccleston 1986; Zysman 1983, pp. 245-51.
61. Gerlach 1989, p. 153.
62. Patrick 1986, p. 18; Sekiguchi and Horiuchi 1985, p. 377.
63. Boltho 1985, pp. 195-96.
64. Friedman 1988, 1983.
65. Friedman 1988, p. 20.
66. On autos see Magaziner and Hout 1980; Mutoh 1988. On machine tools see Collis 1988; Sarathy 1989.
67. See for example Womack, Jones, and Roos 1990, p. 236.
68. Amsden 1989; S. Smith 1991; Wade 1990.
69. Cohen, Halimi, and Zysman 1986; Hall 1986, chaps. 6-8; Seibel 1979; Zysman 1983, chap. 3.
70. Cohen, Halimi, and Zysman 1986, p. 125.
71. Bluestone, Jordan, and Sullivan 1981, chap. 7; Borrus 1988, chap. 4; Flamm 1987; Hooks 1990; Nelson 1982.
72. Evenson 1982; Tweeten 1970, chaps. 4-5.
73. Indeed, a recent study by Kent Calder suggests that industrial policy in Japan has been less proactive and effective in those areas and sectors where administrative authority is less centralized. See Calder 1993.
74. As Michael Porter (1990) has suggested: "Government's proper role is as a pusher and a challenger. . . . Sound government policy seeks to provide the tools necessary to compete . . . while ensuring a certain discomfort and strong competitive pressure" (p. 681).

75. See, for example, Friedman and Friedman 1990, chap. 7; W. Simon 1978; Weidenbaum 1979.

76. W. Simon 1978, p. 186.

77. Reagan 1981a, p. 231.

78. Weidenbaum 1978.

79. Christiansen and Haveman 1982; Denison 1978; Litan and Nordhaus 1983, ch 2.

80. Hopkins 1992, p. 25. See also Niskanen 1993.

81. Stigler 1971; Weidenbaum 1979.

82. Friedman and Friedman 1990, chap. 7; Weidenbaum et al. 1980.

83. Kahn 1988, p. 23.

84. Kahan 1992, p. 47.

85. Dempsey 1990, pp. 28-30.

86. Henwood 1989, p. 3.

87. Dempsey 1990, p. 13.

88. See Dempsey 1990; Kahan 1992; Kahn 1988.

89. See "Symposium" 1987; Chernow 1991.

90. Detailed accounts are provided in L. Davis 1990; Glassman 1990; Sherrill 1990.

91. See Benston et al. 1989; Haraf 1988.

92. Other deregulatory initiatives include investment banking in 1975, trucking and railroads in 1980, oil and radio in 1981, buses in 1982, and telecommunications and cable television in 1984.

93. For further, useful discussion see Ayres and Braithwaite 1992.

94. Vogel 1989.

95. Badaracco 1985; Kelman 1981; Vogel 1986.

96. Porter 1990, pp. 647-49.

97. Schultze 1977, p. 13.

98. See Ackerman and Stewart 1988; Blinder 1987, chap. 5; Schultze 1977; Stewart 1988; Sunstein 1990.

99. Reich 1987, p. 227.

100. See Ackerman and Stewart 1988.

101. Bagnara, Misiti, and Wintersberger 1985; "The Rights" 1989.

102. Garland 1990, p. 57.

103. Emissions and auto safety figures are from Sunstein 1990, pp. 75-76. See also Schwarz 1988, pp. 56-59; Vogel 1986, pp. 22-23. Workplace safety figures are from Warner 1992, p. 18.

104. NIOSH estimates are from Bureau of National Affairs 1989, p. 428. See also Noble 1986, chap. 7. Toxic regulation figure is from Sunstein 1990, p. 79.

105. Gallup poll is cited in "Environment Wins" 1992. New York Times/CBS poll is cited in Sagoff 1992, p. 39.

106. Stiglitz 1989, p. 37.

◈ Chapter 5

1. Gilbert Burck, "Union Power and the New Inflation," *Fortune* February 1971, p. 66. © 1971 Time Inc. All rights reserved. Used with permission.

2. Lipset 1986, pp. 301, 309-12. See also Medoff 1987.

3. See Burton 1978; Davenport 1971; Seligman 1982; Friedman and Friedman 1990, chap. 8; Haberler 1959; Hayek 1960, chap. 18; Hirsch 1992; Lindblom 1949; Simons 1948, chap. 6; Troy, Koeller, and Sheflin 1980.

4. A. Smith [1776] 1937, p. 128.

5. Keefe 1992, pp. 123-24. For an earlier review that reaches essentially the same conclusion, see Slichter, Healy, and Livernash 1960, chap. 12.

6. Eaton and Voos 1992, p. 184.

7. Bureau of National Affairs 1986, pp. 82-83.

8. Deiaco, Hornell, and Vickery 1990, p. 13; Flamm 1988, p. 276; Mowery 1988, p. 491.

9. Streeck 1987; Turner 1992; Womack, Jones, and Roos 1990, chap. 4.

10. Flanagan, Soskice, and Ulman 1983, pp. 365-66; Ulman 1968, p. 348.

11. For data on the United States, see Mishel and Bernstein 1993, table 3.34; Freeman and Medoff 1984, chap. 3.

12. The best available data on unionization levels come from Jelle Visser. See Visser 1991, table 4.1; OECD 1994a, table 5.7.

13. Rogers and Streeck 1994.

14. Addison and Hirsch 1989; Belman 1992. For a review of similar studies on British industry, see Metcalf 1990.

15. See Hirschman 1970.

16. Humphries 1990; Cameron 1984, table 7.7; Korpi and Shalev 1979.

17. Freeman and Medoff 1984, p. 14.

18. Freeman and Medoff 1984, chap. 6.

19. See R. Freeman 1992, pp. 148-49.

20. Freeman and Medoff 1984, p. 15. See also Freeman and Lazear 1993.

21. See Aoki 1990a; M. Jacobs 1991; Sabel 1992; Womack, Jones, and Roos 1990.

22. Addison and Hirsch 1989; Belman 1992.

23. Lindbeck 1990, p. 332.

24. Simons 1948, p. 122. For a recent argument along these lines see Lande and Zerbe 1985.

25. See Alvarez, Garrett, and Lange 1991; Bean, Layard, and Nickell 1986; Bruno and Sachs 1985, chap. 11; Calmfors and Driffill 1988; Cameron 1984; Castles 1987; Crepaz 1992; Crouch 1985, 1990; R. Freeman 1988; Golden 1993; Hicks 1988, 1994; Jackman 1990; Lange 1984; Lange and Garrett 1985; Lutz 1981; McCallum 1986; Moene and Wallerstein with Hoel 1993; Newell and Symons 1987; Paloheimo 1990; Schmidt 1982; Soskice 1990; Tarantelli 1986; Wallerstein 1990.

26. These models rely implicitly upon several assumptions. One is that the principal aim of worker organizations is to maximize the material welfare of their members, which consists of some stable combination of the (present and future) real wage rate and employment. A second is that unions face no formal constraints on their choice of wage-bargaining strategy. A third is that union demands are largely (if not entirely) determinative of wage bargaining outcomes. For some complications arising from relaxation of the third assumption, see Moene and Wallerstein with Hoel 1993.

27. See, for example, Flanagan, Soskice, and Ulman 1983, pp. 27-28; Crouch 1985, p. 107; Tarantelli 1986, pp. 2-3. Because most localized unions organize the bulk of the workforce within a company or plant, the reinvestment externality does not apply (see Olson 1982, p. 49). For craft unions, however, this is not the case. Craft unions, which are prominent in Britain but less so elsewhere, frequently organize only a small portion of a company's workforce. Because its members' skills are often in strong demand, a craft union has little stake in the survival of any particular firm, and hence has a strong incentive to seek redistributive gains from the company in the form of high wages.

Incentives related to unemployment are generally overlooked by proponents of the simple linear view, as discussed below.

28. According to Robert Flanagan (1990, p. 398), wage drift accounted for 30 to 60 percent of total wage increases in Denmark, Finland, Norway, and Sweden over the period 1970-85.

29. Calmfors 1990, p. 57; Elster 1989a, p. 179.

30. Calmfors and Driffill 1988. See also R. Freeman 1988; Pohjola 1992; Paloheimo 1990; Moene and Wallerstein with Hoel 1993.

31. This point is also made by Fritz Scharpf (1987, pp. 239, 253).

32. As Calmfors and Driffill (1988) note:

Each firm within the industry has the same incentive to raise its output price which, therefore, rises in the whole industry. Substitution now occurs only in relation to firms outside the industry, and no firm faces a fall in demand relative to other firms in the same industry. The consequence is that the elasticity of demand for labour with respect to the nominal wage becomes lower. (p. 33)

33. Calmfors and Driffill 1988, p. 34.

34. Lange and Garrett 1985, pp. 798-800. See also Alvarez, Garrett, and Lange 1991, p. 540; Lange 1984, pp. 110-11; Heady 1970, p. 435; Hicks 1988, p. 683.

35. Crouch 1985, p. 113.

36. Bruno and Sachs 1985, p. 231; Cameron 1984, pp. 171-74; Castles 1987, p. 383; Newell and Symons 1987, p. 579; Schmidt 1982, p. 241; Tarantelli 1986, p. 5. The notion of political exchange was developed originally in Pizzorno 1978.

37. Lange and Garrett 1985; Alvarez, Garrett, and Lange 1991.

38. Lange and Garrett 1985, p. 801.

39. Fritz Scharpf is, to my knowledge, alone in having noted this. He writes, for instance:

Job losses, unlike inflation, are primarily experienced not as a collective evil but as an individual risk whose avoidance is in the immediate self-interest of individual workers and hence not vulnerable to free-riding. As soon as unemployment is allowed to rise, there-fore, . . . there is no reason to assume that decentralized and fragmented union movements that are otherwise characterized by greater militancy should be any less "docile" than highly centralized and disciplined corporatist unions are said to be. (1987, p. 253)

40. See Calmfors 1993, pp. 167-68.

41. Golden 1993, p. 442; Soskice 1990, pp. 43-46; OECD 1994a; Streeck 1993; Visser 1990b, chap. 9.

42. Golden 1993, especially pp. 440-41.

43. Streeck 1993, p. 17.

44. Cameron 1984, table 7.6.

45. Cameron 1984, p. 164.

46. See Golden 1993.

47. In some cases other dimensions, such as the scope of collective bargaining or the presence of works councils, are added to or used instead of these three.

48. Streeck 1993; van Voorden 1984, p. 226.

49. See, for example, Visser 1990b, chap. 9.

50. Calmfors and Driffill 1988, table A1.

51. Lange, Wallerstein, and Golden forthcoming; Visser 1990b, chap. 7.

52. Lange, Wallerstein, and Golden forthcoming.

53. Soskice 1990, pp. 41-43.

54. For example, Calmfors and Driffill 1988, pp. 15, 33; Alvarez, Garrett, and Lange 1991, p. 541; Lange and Garrett 1985, p. 801.

55. Soskice has created an index of economy-wide wage bargaining coordination that he believes is analytically superior to models relying on indexes of union centralization and/or concentration. See Soskice 1990, table 1. But he provides scores for only 11 countries, without any claim that they constitute a random or even representative sample. This makes it impossible to conduct a fair test of his thesis.

56. Also, the particular industries included differ slightly from country to country.

57. For example, Alvarez, Garrett, and Lange 1991; Calmfors and Driffill 1988; Castles 1987; Crepaz 1992; Crouch 1985, 1990; Garrett and Lange 1986; Golden 1993; Hicks 1988; Lange and Garrett 1985; Lutz 1981; Paloheimo 1990; Schmidt 1982; Soskice 1990; Tarantelli 1986.

58. See, for example, Mitchell 1980; Rubin 1986.

59. See Mitchell 1993. Michael Smith (1992) is correct in emphasizing that wage pressures can only lead to inflation if accommodated by monetary authorities. I discuss this issue below.

60. See Lindberg and Maier 1985; Crouch and Pizzorno 1978.

61. Alvarez, Garrett, and Lange 1991; Bean, Layard, and Nickell 1986; Calmfors and Driffill 1988; Cameron 1984; Castles 1987; Crepaz 1992; McCallum 1986; Newell and Symons 1985; Paloheimo 1990; Schmidt 1982; Soskice 1990; Tarantelli 1986.

62. Therborn 1986, 1987; Korpi 1991; Kurzer 1987; Rowthorn and Glyn 1990, p. 254; Schmidt 1987; Boreham and Compston 1992.

63. In their 1991 article, Alvarez, Garrett, and Lange found favorable results for their model with (changes in) unemployment and inflation as dependent variables, but these were produced by a flawed methodology. See Beck et al. 1993.

64. For both unemployment and growth, similar results are obtained using real unit labor cost (or wage) changes.

65. See, for example, Crepaz 1992.

66. Government composition data were kindly provided to me by Duane Swank.

67. The notion that unemployment mediates the effect of labor organization on wage behavior suggests that perhaps a multiplicative interaction term for these two variables should be included in the regression equations. But that is not an appropriate strategy here. An interaction effect exists when the impact of one independent variable depends on the value of another independent variable (technically, when the slope of the relationship between an independent variable and the dependent variable varies according to the value of another independent variable). This is the case in the Lange-Garrett political model, in which encompassing unionism is said to be beneficial in a context of leftist government but detrimental where the right governs. In my model an interaction effect would obtain if, say, union encompassingness induced restraint in a high unemployment context but militancy in a low unemployment environment, or if the difference in wage behavior between encompassing versus localized unions was greater in a high unemployment context than in a low unemployment context.

But my model suggests no such effect. Differences in labor organization have the same type and degree of impact in both unemployment contexts. What the model posits is that encompassing union organization does not automatically produce greater wage moderation than localized unionism; that is true only within a given unemployment context. In other words, unemployment's effect on wage behavior may hide some of the effect that labor organization has. Thus, to assess the true impact of variation in labor organization, I need to control for unemployment.

68. Cameron 1984, table 7.6.

69. See Alvarez, Garrett, and Lange 1991, table A-1.

70. See Swank 1992.

71. See Alvarez, Garrett, and Lange 1991, p. 547.

72. Because there are so many tie scores in Cameron's union concentration index, it cannot be used as an alternative operationalization in testing the parabolic model.

73. Adjusted for degrees of freedom.

74. Crepaz 1992, table 1.

75. It is also worth noting that the models were much less successful in accounting for variation in wage and price changes using these two alternative labor organization indexes than when the union concentration index was used. This suggests that the latter is a more accurate indicator of differences in labor movement structure. See also Golden 1993.

76. Friedman 1977.

77. See Flanagan, Soskice, and Ulman 1983.

78. To check this, I reestimated the equations for the unemployment-mediated model over the two time periods. For each of the dependent variables the equation was estimated 15 times, each time with one of the 15 countries dropped (Japan was always omitted). (This follows the logic of the "jackknife" procedure; see Miller 1974.) The coefficients for the labor organization and unemployment variables as well as the R^2s were highly consistent.

79. Adjusted for degrees of freedom.

80. Soskice 1990.

81. Rogers and Streeck 1994, p. 148.

82. Engels 1991; Flanagan, Soskice, and Ulman 1983; Lash and Urry 1987; Offe 1985, chap. 6; Schmitter 1989; Streeck 1984; Windolf 1989.

83. Streeck 1984, p. 297.

84. The term is from Windolf 1989.

85. Ahlen 1989; Lash 1985; Martin 1987.

86. See Sabel 1989; Pyke, Becattini, and Sengenberger 1990.

87. See Streeck and Schmitter 1991.

88. See also Blanchflower and Freeman 1990.

89. On Belgium see Hancke 1991; Spineux 1990. On Denmark see Amoroso 1990; Dahl et al. 1989. On Germany see Streeck 1984; Windolf 1989. On the Netherlands see Visser 1990a; Wolinetz 1989. On Sweden see Ahlen 1989; Lash 1985; Martin 1987.

At the same time, wage bargaining in Australia became more centralized during the 1980s. See Archer 1992; Kyloh 1989; Niland 1987. The Australian labor movement evinced much greater restraint following the institutionalization of centralized wage setting in 1983. Hourly earnings increased at an annual rate of 13.0 percent between 1970 and 1982, but only 5.9 percent from 1983 to 1990. On the other hand, wage increases slowed in many nations after the 1982-83 recession. Hence it is difficult to estimate how much, if any, of the improvement in Australia is due to bargaining centralization.

90. See Lange, Wallerstein, and Golden forthcoming.

91. See Soskice 1990.

92. Fulcher 1988; Swenson 1991.

93. See Stephens 1991.

94. See Korpi 1983; Stephens 1979.

95. Wallerstein 1986. See also Katzenstein 1985.

96. Rogers 1990. Rogers also discusses the fact that in the United States, powerful legal barriers to increasing membership further direct unions' attention toward promoting the interests of present members.

97. See Streeck 1989. Also Kern and Sabel 1991; Kochan 1988; Miles 1989; Piore 1986.

98. Kelley and Harrison 1992; Levine and Tyson 1990.

99. Katz and Sabel 1985; Kern and Sabel 1991; Sabel 1987.
100. See Streeck 1987.

◪ Chapter 6

1. See, for example, North 1990.
2. An additional relationship, which I do not discuss here, is that among countries. See Keohane 1984; "Cooperation" 1985.
3. See Axelrod 1984; Taylor 1987; Hardin 1982, pp. 145-50.
4. See Olson 1965.
5. Olson 1982, especially pp. 41-47.
6. See Buchanan 1975, chap. 9, 1988; Hayek 1979, chap. 12.
7. This assumes that business is strong enough to influence government decisions. If it is not, fragmentation may have no detrimental effects.
8. On national variation in the degree of business association and centralization, see Coleman and Grant 1988; Windmuller and Gladstone 1984.
9. Olson 1982, p. 48.
10. See Chapter 5 above; Crouch 1985, p. 107; Flanagan, Soskice, and Ulman 1983, pp. 27-28; Tarantelli 1986, pp. 2-3; Calmfors and Driffill 1988, p. 34.
11. This point is stressed by Fritz Scharpf. See Scharpf 1987, pp. 239, 253.
12. As noted in Chapter 5, this moderation may be disrupted by wage drift—that is, by firm-level affiliates of an encompassing labor organization bargaining for wages in excess of centrally established levels. But encompassing unions should be expected to take this into account and to further restrain their own demands accordingly.
13. See Wilensky and Turner 1987; Shonfield 1965; Lodge 1990.
14. See, for example, Porter 1980, chap. 6.
15. As Oliver Williamson has stressed, purchasers are particularly vulnerable to opportunism when the purchasing arrangement involves asset-specific goods—that is, where the items exchanged are specialized. Where goods or services are easily interchangeable, buyers can more easily turn to other parties if a particular transaction proves unsatisfactory. See, for example, Williamson 1981, p. 555.
16. See Womack, Jones, and Roos 1990, chap. 6; Helper 1991a, 1991c.
17. Williamson 1981, 1985; Lazonick 1991.
18. Chandler 1977, 1980; Lazonick 1986; Piore and Sabel 1984, chap. 3. To say that hierarchy can be more efficient than markets is not to imply that greater efficiency was always and everywhere the reason for its use. Vertical integration may be motivated by a desire to erect barriers to entry or to reduce uncertainty. See DuBoff and Herman 1980; Perrow 1986b; Pfeffer and Salancik 1978.
19. See Womack, Jones, and Roos 1990, chap. 6; Smitka 1991; Cusumano and Takeishi 1991.
20. In a recent survey, Susan Helper (1991b, p. 24) found that a large share of U.S. automotive suppliers, most of which do not have long-term commitments from their customers, had not made such investments and consequently felt that just-in-time did nothing but "transfer responsibility for inventory from customers to suppliers."
21. Womack 1990; Womack, Jones, and Roos 1990; Cusumano 1985.
22. On the concepts of exit and voice see Hirschman 1970. Helper 1991a discusses their application to purchaser-supplier relations.

23. For an excellent overview see W. Powell 1990.

24. See M. Jacobs 1991, pp. 35-36.

25. See Porter 1992; Ellsworth 1985; M. Jacobs 1991; Office of Technology Assessment 1990a, chap. 3; Zysman 1983, pp. 251-65; Dore 1987, chap. 6; Wellons 1985.

26. Michael Porter (1990, p. 124) has found that privately owned companies, which rely heavily on internal financing, tend to focus more on long-term results than do publicly owned firms.

27. A recent survey of U.S. business firms in 130 industries found that patents were considered "highly effective" at preventing product duplication in only 5, and "moderately successful" in just 20 others. Even fewer respondents judged patents effective at preventing duplication of process innovations. Other mechanisms for protecting appropriability, such as secrecy, lead time, moving quickly down the learning curve, and sales efforts, were considered only slightly more effective. See Levin et al. 1987, pp. 794-96. Also see Mansfield 1986.

28. See Teece 1992; Jorde and Teece 1990; Ouchi and Bolton 1988; Congressional Budget Office 1990; Katz and Ordover 1990; Mowery and Rosenberg 1989, chap. 9. Elster 1983 offers a helpful overview of the logic(s) of noncooperative investment in innovation.

29. Hansen and Burton 1992.

30. Herrigel 1994.

31. Borrus, Millstein, and Zysman 1983, pp. 208-14; Ouchi 1984.

32. Cheney and Grimes 1991, p. 13.

33. See Streeck 1989, 1991; Lynch 1994.

34. See Kazis 1990; Streeck 1989.

35. Office of Technology Assessment 1990b, p. 94; Lynch 1993.

36. See Best 1990, chs. 7-8; Pyke, Becattini, and Sengenberger 1990; Dore 1986, pp. 179-81.

37. See Marglin 1974.

38. See Williamson 1985, chap. 9; Landes 1986. The advantages of hierarchical coordination do not, at least in theory, presuppose the typical capitalist firm, in which nonworker owners control decision making. Labor might just as efficiently hire capital as vice versa. See Putterman 1984.

39. Akerlof and Yellen 1986.

40. Lazonick 1990, pt. 2.

41. See Brown et al. 1993; Dore 1987, chap. 2; Koike 1987; Ouchi 1981, chap. 1; Streeck 1987.

42. See Abraham and Houseman 1994; Buechtemann 1993.

43. Dore, Bounine-Cabale, and Tapiola 1989; Koike 1987.

44. Ginsburg 1983.

45. The classic discussion is Alchian and Demsetz 1972.

46. See, for example, Leibenstein 1987.

47. Levine and Tyson 1990, p. 187.

48. The literature is reviewed in Levine and Tyson 1990. See also Lansbury, Sandkull, and Hammarstrom 1992.

49. A good exposition of the advantages of profit sharing is Weitzman 1984.

50. Weitzman and Kruse 1990, p. 114.

51. Freeman and Weitzman 1987; Hashimoto 1990; Kenney and Florida 1988, pp. 131-35; Levine and Tyson 1990, pp. 222-30.

52. Florida and Kenney 1990. Also see Womack, Jones, and Roos 1990, chap. 5; Best 1990, pp. 155-56; Reich 1987, chap. 10; Dore 1987, chap. 7.

53. Florida and Kenney 1990, pp. 22-23.

54. See Womack, Jones, and Roos 1990, chap. 5.

55. Cited in Womack, Jones, and Roos 1990, p. 111.

56. See Florida and Kenney 1990, chap. 8; Mowery and Rosenberg 1989, pp. 229-36.

57. See Dore 1986, 1987; Aoki 1988, 1990b; Gerlach 1992; Porter 1990, chap. 8; Johnson, Tyson, and Zysman 1989; Ozaki 1991; Soskice 1990, pp. 41-43.

58. See Katzenstein 1984, chap. 2; Marin 1985; J. Freeman 1989, chap. 7; Guger 1992; Kurzer 1993.

59. See Zysman 1983, pp. 251-65; Porter 1990, chap. 7; Streeck 1993; Soskice 1990, pp. 43-46; Fuerstenberg 1987; Katzenstein 1987; Hollingsworth, Schmitter, and Streeck 1994; Sabel et al. 1989; Hansen and Burton 1992.

60. See Katzenstein 1985; Baglioni and Crouch 1990; Wilensky and Turner 1987; Windmuller and Gladstone 1984; Kurzer 1993; Whitley 1992; Pekkarinen 1992; Visser 1990b; Marks 1986; Levine and Tyson 1990, pp. 230-35; Lindgren 1990.

61. Katzenstein 1985.

62. See Martinelli and Treu 1984; Negrelli and Santi 1990; Soskice 1990, pp. 47-48; J. Freeman 1989, chap. 8.

63. See Pyke, Becattini, and Sengenberger 1990; Brusco 1982; Brusco and Righi 1989; Best 1990, chs. 7-8; Porter 1990, chap. 8.

64. See Porter 1990, chap. 7; Katzenstein 1984, chap. 3; Blaas 1992; Danthine and Lambelet 1987; Soskice 1990, pp. 41-43.

65. Porter 1990, p. 326.

66. See Bunel and Saglio 1984; Goetschy and Rojot 1987; Hart 1992b, chap. 3.

67. See Zysman 1983, chap. 3; D. Green 1986. The 3 largest French commercial banks have been under state control since 1946; 36 others, along with the nation's 2 large investment groups, were nationalized in 1982.

68. Hall 1986, chs. 6-8; Cohen, Halimi, and Zysman 1986; Seibel 1979.

69. See Bamber and Lansbury 1987; Windmuller and Gladstone 1984; Wilensky and Turner 1987; Grant 1989; Office of Technology Assessment 1990a; Porter 1990, chap. 9; Hall 1986, chs. 2-3; Zysman 1983, chs. 3-4; M. Jacobs 1991; Campbell, Hollingsworth, and Lindberg 1991; Hollingsworth, Schmitter and Streeck 1994; Lodge 1990; Castles 1988; Archer 1992; Crocombe, Enright, and Porter 1991; Haworth 1990.

70. As it happens, this is also roughly equal to the average misery index level (10.4 percent) divided by the average productivity growth rate (2.5 percent).

71. See, for example, Scharpf 1991; Pekkarinen, Pohjola, and Rowthorn 1992.

72. An interest rate variable was used in the productivity growth equations in prior chapters. It is dropped here because of its lack of impact. Including it does not alter the results.

73. See, for example, Saunders 1986; Grier and Tullock 1989; Cameron 1982; Pfaller with Gough 1991; Landau 1985; Marlow 1986.

74. For discussion of the importance of union concentration relative to centralization, see Chapter 5; Golden 1993.

75. Various combinations of these four dimensions were tried, with little difference in the results.

76. See Olson 1982, 1983; Mueller 1983.

77. Choi 1983; Lane and Ersson 1987, 1990, chap. 8; Weede 1986.

78. Castles 1991; Abramovitz 1983.

79. See, for example, Cameron 1988, pp. 569-71; Lehner 1987, pp. 75-76. See also Olson's comments on Ireland in Olson 1991.

80. Olson (1983) notes, for instance, that:

The postwar growth rates of [Japan and Germany] werc likely enhanced not only by the absence of a dense accumulation of powerful special-interest groups but also by the encompassing character of many organizations that were created or reorganized after the war. (pp. 25-26)

81. See, for example, Bruno and Sachs 1985, chap. 11; Cameron 1984; Crouch 1985; Golden 1993; Soskice 1990; Tarantelli 1986. Others are cited in Chapter 5.

82. Katzenstein 1985, p. 32. See also Pekkarinen, Pohjola, and Rowthorn 1992; Wilensky and Turner 1987; Goldthorpe 1984; J. Freeman 1989; Lehmbruch and Schmitter 1982; Schmitter and Lehmbruch 1979.

83. Crepaz 1992, table 1.

84. Bruno and Sachs 1985, p. 226; Cameron 1984, p. 166.

85. See, for example, Shonfield 1965; Therborn 1986; Johnson 1982; Zysman and Tyson 1983; Magaziner and Reich 1983; B. Scott 1985.

86. Hart 1992a, 1992b.

87. On Italy see Piore and Sabel 1984. On Japan see D. Friedman 1983, 1988.

88. On financial systems see Zysman 1983; Wellons 1985; Ellsworth 1985; Porter 1992. On governance relations see Chandler 1990; Hollingsworth, Schmitter, and Streeck 1994; Harrison 1994; Schmitter 1990; Ferguson 1990; Pyke, Becattini, and Sengenberger 1990.

89. See Applebaum and Batt 1994; Blinder 1990; Dore 1989; Shimada 1983; Streeck 1987, 1991.

90. See Lodge and Vogel 1987; Kotkin 1992. Also see Dore 1990.

91. On the purchaser-supplier relationship see Porter 1990, pp. 152-53. On the investor-producer relationship see pp. 110-11. On industry associations and training see p. 594. See also the country studies in chs. 7-9.

92. See, for example, Kelly 1993; "Ready to Take" 1994; Cooper 1994; Cramer 1992; Levinson 1992.

93. Neff 1992, 1993a; "Losing Its Way" 1993; Levinson 1994; B. Powell 1993; Samuelson 1993; C. Wood 1992.

94. Sylvia Nasar. "The American Economy: Back on Top." February 27, 1994. Copyright © 1994 by the New York Times Company. Reprinted by permission.

95. OECD 1994b, Annex table 44.

96. James Cooper 1994, p. 62. © 1994 *Business Week*. Used with permission.

97. OECD 1994b, Annex table 41.

98. Nasar 1994.

99. OECD 1994b, p. 37.

100. Neff 1993b; "Japan in Recession" 1994; Fingleton 1993; "It's Hit" 1992.

101. See, for example, Applebaum and Batt 1994.

102. Bernstein 1994; Mishel and Bernstein 1993, chs. 3-4.

103. The following sketch draws on the sources cited above.

104. See Lodge and Vogel 1987.

105. See, for example, Lorenz 1988, p. 201.

106. See Woodruff 1992; "Detroit's New" 1992; Helper 1991b, 1991c; Turner 1988.

107. See Archer 1992; Niland 1987; Kyloh 1989.

108. See Berger 1981; Lehmbruch and Schmitter 1982; Schmitter and Lehmbruch 1979. This strategy is at the center of the recent proposal by Joshua Cohen and Joel Rogers (1992) for fostering "associative democracy."

References

Abegglen, J. C., and G. Stalk, Jr. 1985. *Kaisha, the Japanese corporation.* New York: Basic Books.

Abolafia, M. Y., and N. W. Biggart. 1991. Competition and markets: An institutional perspective. In *Socio-economics: Toward a new synthesis,* edited by A. Etzioni and P. R. Lawrence. Armonk, N.Y.: M. E. Sharpe.

Abraham, K. G., and S. N. Houseman. 1994. Does employment protection inhibit labor market flexibility? Lessons from Germany, France, and Belgium. In *Social protection versus economic flexibility: Is there a tradeoff?* edited by R. Blank. Chicago: University of Chicago Press.

Abramovitz, M. 1983. Notes on international differences in productivity growth rates. In *The political economy of growth,* edited by D. C. Mueller. New Haven, Conn.: Yale University Press.

———. 1986. Catching up, forging ahead, and falling behind. *Journal of Economic History* 46:385-406.

Ackerman, B. A., and R. B. Stewart. 1988. Reforming environmental law: The democratic case for market incentives. *Columbia Journal of Environmental Law* 13:171-99.

Adams, J. S. 1965. Inequity in social exchange. In *Advances in experimental social psychology.* Vol. 2, edited by L. Berkowitz. New York: Academic Press.

Addison, J. T., and B. T. Hirsch. 1989. Union effects on productivity, profits, and growth: Has the long run finally arrived? *Journal of Labor Economics* 7:72-105.

Ahlen, K. 1989. Swedish collective bargaining under pressure: Inter-union rivalry and incomes policies. *British Journal of Industrial Relations* 27:330-46.

Akerlof, G. A., and J. L. Yellen. 1990. The fair wage-effort hypothesis and unemployment. *Quarterly Journal of Economics* 55:255-83.

———, eds. 1986. *Efficiency wage models of the labor market.* Cambridge: Cambridge University Press.

Alber, J. 1987. Cross-national evidence on the crisis of the welfare state. Paper presented at the annual meeting of the American Sociological Association.

Alchian, A. A., and H. Demsetz. 1972. Production, information costs, and economic organization. *American Economic Review* 62:777-95.

Alesina, A. 1988. Macroeconomics and politics. In *NBER macroeconomics annual.* Cambridge, Mass.: National Bureau of Economic Research.

Alesina, A., and N. Roubini. 1990. Political cycles in OECD economies. Working Paper 3478, National Bureau of Economic Research, Cambridge, Mass.

Alvarez, R. M., G. Garrett, and P. Lange. 1991. Government partisanship, labor organization, and macroeconomic performance. *American Political Science Review* 85:539-56.

American renewal. 1981. *Fortune,* 9 March, 71-115.

Amoroso, B. 1990. Development and crisis of the Scandinavian model of labour relations in Denmark. In *European industrial relations,* edited by G. Baglioni and C. Crouch. London: Sage.

Amsden, A. 1989. *Asia's next giant: South Korea and late industrialization.* Oxford: Oxford University Press.

Anderson, M. 1978. *Welfare.* Stanford, Calif.: Hoover Institution.

Aoki, M. 1988. *Information, incentives, and bargaining in the Japanese economy.* Cambridge: Cambridge University Press.

———. 1990a. The participatory generation of information rents and the theory of the firm. In *The firm as a nexus of treaties,* edited by M. Aoki, B. Gustafsson, and O. E. Williamson. London: Sage.

———. 1990b. Toward an economic model of the Japanese firm. *Journal of Economic Literature* 28:1-27.

Applebaum, E., and R. Batt. 1994. *The new American workplace.* Ithaca, N.Y.: ILR Press.

Archer, R. 1992. The unexpected emergence of Australian corporatism. In *Social corporatism: A superior economic system?* edited by J. Pekkarinen, M. Pohjola, and B. Rowthorn. Oxford: Clarendon Press.

Arneson, R. 1989. Equality and equality of opportunity for welfare. *Philosophical Studies* 55:77-93.

Arrow, K. J. 1979. The trade-off between growth and equity. In *Theory for economic efficiency: Essays in honor of Abba P. Lerner,* edited by H. I. Greenfield, A. M. Levenson, W. Hamovitch, and E. Rotwein. Cambridge: MIT Press.

———. 1990. Interview with Richard Swedberg. In *Economics and sociology: Conversations with economists and sociologists.* Princeton, N.J.: Princeton University Press.

Asanuma, B. 1985. The organization of parts purchases in the Japanese automotive industry. *Japanese Economic Studies* 13(4): 32-53.

Axelrod, R. 1984. *The evolution of cooperation.* New York: Basic Books.

Ayres, I., and J. Braithwaite. 1992. *Responsive regulation.* New York: Oxford University Press.

Badaracco, J. L., Jr. 1985. *Loading the dice: A five-country study of vinyl chloride regulation.* Boston: Harvard Business School Press.

Baglioni, G., and C. Crouch, eds. 1990. *European industrial relations.* London: Sage.

Bagnara, S., R. Misiti, and H. Wintersberger, eds. 1985. *Work and health in the 1980s: Experiences of direct workers' participation in occupational health.* Berlin: Wissenschaftszentrum.

Bamber, G. J., and R. D. Lansbury, eds. 1987. *International and comparative industrial relations.* London: Allen & Unwin.

Baron, J. N. 1988. The employment relation as a social relation. *Journal of the Japanese and International Economies* 2:492-525.

Barro, R. J. 1991. Economic growth in a cross section of countries. *Quarterly Journal of Economics* 56:407-44.

Barry, B. 1988. Equal opportunity and moral arbitrariness. In *Equal opportunity,* edited by N. E. Bowie. Boulder, Colo.: Westview Press.

Baumol, W. J. 1986. Productivity growth, convergence, and welfare: What the long-run data show. *American Economic Review* 76:1072-85.

Baumol, W. J., S. A. B. Blackman, and E. N. Wolff. 1989. *Productivity and American leadership: The long view.* Cambridge: MIT Press.

Baumol, W. J., and D. Fischer. 1979. The output distribution frontier: Alternatives to income taxes and transfers for strong equality goals. *American Economic Review* 69:514-25.

Bawden, D. L., and F. Skidmore, eds. 1989. *Rethinking employment policy.* Washington, D.C.: Urban Institute Press.

Bean, C. R., P. R. G. Layard, and S. J. Nickell. 1986. The rise in unemployment: A multi-country study. *Economica* 53(supplement): S1-S22.

Beck, N., J. N. Katz, R. M. Alvarez, G. Garrett, and P. Lange. 1993. Government partisanship, labor organization and macroeconomic performance: A corrigendum. *American Political Science Review* 87:945-48.

Becker, G. S. 1964. *Human capital.* New York: National Bureau of Economic Research.

Belman, D. 1992. Unions, the quality of labor relations, and firm performance. In *Unions and economic competitiveness,* edited by L. Mishel and P. B. Voos. Armonk, N.Y.: M. E. Sharpe.

Benston, G. J., R. D. Brumbaugh, Jr., J. M. Guttentag, R. J. Herring, G. G. Kaufman, R. E. Litan, and K. E. Scott. 1989. *Restructuring America's financial institutions.* Washington, D.C.: Brookings Institution.

Berger, S. D., ed. 1981. *Organizing interests in Western Europe.* Cambridge: Cambridge University Press.

Berger, S., and M. Piore. 1980. *Dualism and discontinuity in industrial societies.* Cambridge: Cambridge University Press.

Berglof, E. 1990. Capital structure as a mechanism of control: A comparison of financial systems. In *The firm as a nexus of treaties,* edited by M. Aoki, B. Gustafsson, and O. E. Williamson. London: Sage.

Bergmann, B. R. 1986. *The economic emergence of women.* New York: Basic Books.

Bernstein, A. 1994. The U.S. is still cranking out lousy jobs. *Business Week,* 10 October, 122.

Best, M. H. 1990. *The new competition: Institutions of industrial restructuring.* Cambridge: Harvard University Press.

Bhagwati, J. 1988. *Protectionism.* Cambridge: MIT Press.

Bielby, W. T., and J. N. Baron. 1986. Men and women at work: Sex segregation and statistical discrimination. *American Journal of Sociology* 91:759-99.

Blaas, W. 1992. The Swiss model: Corporatism or liberal capitalism? In *Social corporatism: A superior economic system?* edited by J. Pekkarinen, M. Pohjola, and B. Rowthorn. Oxford: Clarendon Press.

Blanchflower, D. G., and R. B. Freeman. 1990. Going different ways: Unionism in the U.S. and other advanced OECD countries. Working Paper 3342, National Bureau of Economic Research, Cambridge, Mass.

Blank, R. M. 1990. Are part-time jobs bad jobs? In *A future of lousy jobs?* edited by G. Burtless. Washington, D.C.: Brookings Institution.

———. 1991. Why were poverty rates so high in the 1980s? Working Paper 3878, National Bureau of Economic Research, Cambridge, Mass.

Blau, F. D., and M. A. Ferber. 1987. Discrimination: Empirical evidence from the United States. *American Economic Review* 77(Papers and Proceedings): 316-20.

Blinder, A. S. 1987. *Hard heads, soft hearts: Tough-minded economics for a just society.* Reading, Mass.: Addison-Wesley.

―――. 1992. More like them? *The American Prospect* (winter): 51-62.

―――. 1990. *Paying for productivity.* Washington, D.C.: Brookings Institution.

Bluestone, B., P. Jordan, and M. Sullivan. 1981. *Aircraft industry dynamics.* Boston: Auburn House.

Blyton, P. 1989. Hours of work. In *International labour statistics,* edited by R. Bean. London: Routledge.

Boaz, D., & Crane, E. H., eds. 1993. *Market liberalism.* Washington, D.C.: Cato Institute.

Boltho, A. 1982. Growth. In *The European economy: Growth and crisis,* edited by A. Boltho. New York: Oxford University Press.

―――. 1985. Was Japan's industrial policy successful? *Cambridge Journal of Economics* 9:187-201.

Boreham, P., and H. Compston. 1992. Labour movement organization and political intervention: The politics of unemployment in the OECD countries, 1974-1986. *European Journal of Political Research* 22:143-70.

Borrus, M. 1988. *Competing for control: America's stakes in microelectronics.* Cambridge, Mass.: Ballinger.

Borrus, M., J. E. Millstein, and J. Zysman. 1983. Trade and development in the semiconductor industry: Japanese challenge and American response. In *American industry in international competition,* edited by J. Zysman and L. Tyson. Ithaca, N.Y.: Cornell University Press.

Bourdieu, P. 1988. Vive la crise! For heterodoxy in social science. *Theory and Society* 17:773-87.

Bourgin, F. 1989. *The great challenge: The myth of laissez-faire in the early Republic.* New York: Harper & Row.

Bowles, S. 1985. The production process in a competitive economy: Walrasian, neo-Hobbesian, and Marxian models. *American Economic Review* 75:16-36.

Bowles, S., and H. Gintis. 1990. Contested exchange: New microfoundations for the political economy of capitalism. *Politics and Society* 18:165-222.

―――. 1993. The revenge of homo economicus: Contested exchange and the revival of political economy. *Journal of Economic Perspectives* 7(1): 83-102.

Bowles, S., D. M. Gordon, and T. E. Weisskopf. 1990. *After the waste land.* Armonk, N.Y.: M. E. Sharpe.

Braun, D. 1991. *The rich get richer.* Chicago: Nelson-Hall.

Bronfenbrenner, M. 1971. *Income distribution theory.* Chicago: Aldine.

Brown, C. V. 1980. *Taxation and the incentive to work.* Oxford: Oxford University Press.

Brown, C., M. Reich, D. Stern, and L. Ulman. 1993. Conflict and cooperation in labor-management relations in Japan and the United States. Industrial Relations Research Association Series, Proceedings of the Forty-Fifth Annual Meeting, 426-36.

Browning, E. K. 1976. How much more equality can we afford? *The Public Interest* (spring): 90-110.

Browning, E. K., and W. R. Johnson. 1984. The trade-off between equality and efficiency. *Journal of Political Economy* 92:175-203.

Bruno, M., and J. D. Sachs. 1985. *Economics of worldwide stagflation.* Cambridge: Harvard University Press.

Brusco, S. 1982. The Emilian model: Productive decentralisation and social integration. *Cambridge Journal of Economics* 6:167-84.

Brusco, S., and E. Righi. 1989. Local government, industrial policy and social consensus: The case of Modena (Italy). *Economy and Society* 18:405-24.

Buchanan, J. M. 1975. *The limits of liberty: Between anarchy and leviathan.* Chicago: University of Chicago Press.

————. 1988. The economic theory of politics reborn. *Challenge,* March-April, 4-10.

Buechtemann, C. F., ed. 1993. *Employment security and labor market behavior.* Ithaca, N.Y.: ILR Press.

Bunel, J., and J. Saglio. 1984. Employers associations in France. In *Employers associations and industrial relations,* edited by J. P. Windmuller and A. Gladstone. Oxford: Clarendon Press.

Burck, G. 1971. Union power and the new inflation. *Fortune,* February, 65-69, 119-20.

Bureau of National Affairs. 1986. *Basic patterns in union contracts.* Washington, D.C.: Bureau of National Affairs.

————. 1989. *Labor Relations Week,* 3 May.

Burt, R. S. 1993. The social structure of competition. In *Explorations in economic sociology,* edited by R. Swedberg. New York: Russell Sage Foundation.

Burtless, G. 1987. Inequality in America: Where do we stand? *Brookings Review* (summer): 9-16.

————. 1990. Earnings inequality over the business and demographic cycles. In *A future of lousy jobs?* edited by G. Burtless. Washington, D.C.: Brookings Institution.

Burtless, G. T., and R. H. Haveman. 1987. Taxes and transfers: How much economic loss? *Challenge,* March-April, 45-51.

Burton, J. 1978. Are trade unions a public good/"bad"? In *Trade unions: Public goods or public "bads"?* London: Institute of Economic Affairs.

Business Week/Harris executive poll. 1987. *Business Week,* 23 October, 28.

Butler, S., and A. Kondratas. 1987. *Out of the poverty trap.* New York: Free Press.

Byrne, J. A. 1993. Executive pay: The party ain't over yet. *Business Week,* 26 April, 56-64.

Calder, K. E. 1993. *Strategic capitalism: Private business and public purpose in Japanese industrial finance.* Princeton, N.J.: Princeton University Press.

Calmfors, L. 1990. Wage formation and macroeconomic policy in the Nordic countries: A summary. In *Wage formation and macroeconomic policy in the Nordic countries,* edited by L. Calmfors. Oxford: Oxford University Press.

————. 1993. Centralisation of wage bargaining and macroeconomic performance: A survey. *OECD Economic Studies* no. 21:161-91.

Calmfors, L., and J. Driffill. 1988. Bargaining structure, corporatism and macroeconomic performance. *Economic Policy* no. 6:14-61.

Cameron, D. R. 1978. The expansion of the public economy: A comparative analysis. *American Political Science Review* 72:1243-61.

————. 1982. On the limits of the public economy. *Annals of the American Academy of Political and Social Science* 459:46-62.

————. 1984. Social democracy, corporatism, labour quiescence and the representation of economic interest in advanced capitalist society. In *Order and conflict in contemporary capitalism,* edited by J. H. Goldthorpe. Oxford: Clarendon Press.

————. 1985. Does government cause inflation? Taxes, spending, and deficits. In *The politics of inflation and economic stagnation,* edited by L. N. Lindberg and C. S. Maier. Washington, D.C.: Brookings Institution.

————. 1988. Distributional coalitions and other sources of economic stagnation: On Olson's *Rise and Decline of Nations. International Organization* 42:561-603.

Campbell, J. L., J. R. Hollingsworth, and L. N. Lindberg, eds. 1991. *The governance of the American economy.* Cambridge: Cambridge University Press.

Canova, T. A. 1994. The Swedish model betrayed. *Challenge,* May-June, 36-40.

Card, D. 1992. The effect of unions on the distribution of wages: Redistribution or relabelling? Working Paper 4195, National Bureau of Economic Research, Cambridge, Mass.

232   IN SEARCH OF NATIONAL ECONOMIC SUCCESS

Casey, B., and G. Bruche. 1985. Active labor market policy: An international overview. *Industrial Relations* 24:37-61.
Castles, F. G. 1987. Neocorporatism and the "happiness index," or what the trade unions get for their cooperation. *European Journal of Political Research* 15:381-93.
———. 1988. *Australian public policy and economic vulnerability.* Sydney: Allen & Unwin.
———. 1991. Democratic politics, war and catch-up: Olson's thesis and long-term economic growth in the English-speaking nations of advanced capitalism. *Journal of Theoretical Politics* 3:5-25.
Castles, F. G., and S. Dowrick. 1990. The impact of government spending levels on medium-term economic growth in the OECD, 1960-85. *Journal of Theoretical Politics* 2:173-204.
Chandler, A. D., Jr. 1977. *The visible hand.* Cambridge: Harvard University Press.
———. 1980. The United States: Seedbed of managerial capitalism. In *Managerial hierarchies,* edited by A. D. Chandler and H. Daems. Cambridge: Harvard University Press.
———. 1990. *Scale and scope.* Cambridge: Harvard University Press.
Cheney, D. W., and W. W. Grimes. 1991. *Japanese technology policy: What's the secret?* Washington, D.C.: Council on Competitiveness.
Chernow, R. 1991. Why save the banks? *The American Prospect* (summer):67-80.
Choi, K. 1983. A statistical test of Olson's model. In *The political economy of growth,* edited by D. C. Mueller. New Haven, Conn.: Yale University Press.
Christiansen, G. B., and R. H. Haveman. 1982. Government regulations and their impact on the economy. *Annals of the American Academy of Political and Social Science* 459:112-22.
Cohen, G. A. 1981. Freedom, justice and capitalism. *New Left Review* (no. 126): 3-16.
———. 1989. On the currency of egalitarian justice. *Ethics* 99:906-44.
Cohen, J., and J. Rogers. 1992. Secondary associations and democratic governance. *Politics and Society* 20:393-472.
Cohen, S., S. Halimi, and J. Zysman. 1986. Institutions, politics, and industrial policy in France. In *The politics of industrial policy,* edited by C. E. Barfield and W. A. Schambra. Washington, D.C.: American Enterprise Institute.
Coleman, J. S. 1988. Social capital in the creation of human capital. *American Journal of Sociology* 94(Supplement): S95-S120.
Coleman, W., and W. Grant. 1988. The organizational cohesion and political access of business: A study of comprehensive associations. *European Journal of Political Research* 16:467-87.
Collard, D. 1978. *Altruism and economy: A study in non-selfish economics.* Oxford: Martin Robertson.
Collis, D. J. 1988. The machine tool industry and industrial policy, 1955-82. In *International competitiveness,* edited by M. Spence and H. A. Hazard. Cambridge, Mass.: Ballinger.
Commission on the Skills of the American Workforce. 1990. *America's choice: High skills or low wages!* Rochester, N.Y.: National Center on Education and the Economy.
Congressional Budget Office (U.S. Congress). 1990. *Using R&D consortia for commercial innovation.* Washington, D.C.: GPO.
Cook, K., and K. Hegtvedt. 1983. Distributive justice, equity and equality. *Annual Review of Sociology* 9:217-41.
Cooper, J. C. 1994. The new golden age of productivity. *Business Week,* 26 September, 62.
Cooperation under anarchy [Special issue]. 1985. *World Politics* 38(1).
Coughlin, R. M., ed. 1991. *Morality, rationality, and efficiency: New perspectives on socio-economics.* Armonk, N.Y.: M. E. Sharpe.
Council of Economic Advisers. 1991. *Economic report of the President 1991.* Washington, D.C.: GPO.

————. 1992. *Economic report of the President 1992*. Washington, D.C.: GPO.

Cramer, J. J. 1992. Heavy metal: The revival of American manufacturing. *The New Republic,* 27 April, 23-27.

Crepaz, M. M. L. 1992. Corporatism in decline? An empirical analysis of the impact of corporatism on macroeconomic performance and industrial disputes in 18 industrialized countries. *Comparative Political Studies* 25:139-68.

Crocombe, G. T., M. J. Enright, and M. E. Porter. 1991. *Upgrading New Zealand's competitive advantage.* Oxford: Oxford University Press.

Crouch, C. 1985. Conditions for trade union wage restraint. In *The politics of inflation and economic stagnation,* edited by L. N. Lindberg and C. S. Maier. Washington, D.C.: Brookings Institution.

————. 1990. Trade unions in the exposed sector: Their influence on neo-corporatist behavior. In *Labour relations and economic performance,* edited by R. Brunetta and C. Dell'Aringa. New York: New York University Press.

Crouch, C., and A. Pizzorno, eds. 1978. *The resurgence of class conflict in Western Europe since 1968.* London: Macmillan.

Crystal, G. S. 1991. *In search of excess: The overcompensation of American executives.* New York: W. W. Norton.

Cuomo Commission on Trade and Competitiveness. 1988. *The Cuomo Commission report.* New York: Touchstone.

Cusumano, M. A. 1985. *The Japanese automobile industry.* Cambridge: Harvard University Press.

Cusumano, M. A., and A. Takeishi. 1991. Supplier relations and management: A survey of Japanese, Japanese-transplant, and U.S. auto plants. *Strategic Management Journal* 12:563-88.

Dahl, H. M., H. Marstrand, E. Edelberg, P. Jorning, E. H. Kristensen, and K. M. Sorensen. 1989. Collective bargaining in Denmark: Recent trends and problems. In *Current approaches to collective bargaining.* Geneva: International Labour Office.

Danthine, J.-P., and J.-C. Lambelet. 1987. The Swiss recipe: Conservative policies ain't enough! *Economic Policy* no. 5:149-79.

Danziger, S., and P. Gottschalk. 1985. The poverty of losing ground. *Challenge,* May-June, 32-38.

Danziger, S., R. Haveman, and R. Plotnick. 1981. How income transfer programs affect work, savings, and the income distribution: A critical review. *Journal of Economic Literature* 19:975-1028.

————. 1986. Antipoverty policy: Effects on the poor and the nonpoor. In *Fighting poverty: What works and what doesn't,* edited by S. H. Danziger and D. H. Weinberg. Cambridge: Harvard University Press.

Davenport, J. 1971. How to curb union power. *Fortune,* July, 52-56.

————. 1976. The welfare state vs. the public welfare. *Fortune,* June, 132-135, 198-206.

Davis, L. J. 1990. How deregulation begat the S&L scandal. *Harper's,* September, 50-66.

Davis, S. 1993. Cross-country patterns of change in relative wages. Working Paper 4085, National Bureau of Economic Research, Cambridge, Mass.

Deiaco, E., E. Hornell, and G. Vickery. 1990. Technology and investment: Crucial issues for the 1990s. In *Technology and investment,* edited by E. Deiaco, E. Hornell, and G. Vickery. London: Pinter.

Dempsey, P. S. 1990. *Flying blind: The failure of airline deregulation.* Washington, D.C.: Economic Policy Institute.

Denison, E. 1978. Effects of selected changes in the institutional and human environment upon output per unit input. *Survey of Current Business,* January, 21-44.

Dertouzos, M. L., R. K. Lester, R. M. Solow, and the MIT Commission on Industrial Productivity. 1989. *Made in America.* Cambridge: MIT Press.
Detroit's new strategy to beat back Japanese is to copy their ideas. 1992. *Wall Street Journal,* 1 October.
Deutsch, M. 1985. *Distributive justice: A social psychological perspective.* New Haven, Conn.: Yale University Press.
Donahue, J. D. 1989. *Shortchanging the workforce: The Job Training Partnership Act and the overselling of privatized training.* Washington, D.C.: Economic Policy Institute.
Dore, R. 1986. *Flexible rigidities.* Stanford, Calif.: Stanford University Press.
———. 1987. *Taking Japan seriously.* Stanford, Calif.: Stanford University Press.
———. 1989. Where we are now: Musings of an evolutionist. *Work, Employment and Society* 3:426-46.
———. 1990. Reflections on culture and social change. In *Manufacturing miracles: Paths of industrialization in Latin America and East Asia,* edited by G. Gereffi and D. L. Wyman. Princeton, N.J.: Princeton University Press.
Dore, R, J. Bounine-Cabale, and K. Tapiola. 1989. *Japan at work.* Paris: OECD.
Dowrick, S., and D.-T. Nguyen. 1989. OECD comparative economic growth 1950-85: Catch-up and convergence. *American Economic Review* 79:1010-30.
DuBoff, R. B., and E. S. Herman. 1980. Alfred Chandler's new business history: A review. *Politics and Society* 10:87-110.
Durkheim, E. [1893] 1984. *The division of labor in society.* Translated by W. D. Halls. New York: Free Press.
Durr, R. H. 1993. What moves policy sentiment? *American Political Science Review* 87:158-70.
Dworkin, R. 1981. What is equality? Part 2: Equality of resources. *Philosophy and Public Affairs* 10:283-345.
———. 1985. *A matter of principle.* Cambridge: Harvard University Press.
Dyson, K. 1986. The state, banks and industry: The West German case. In *State, finance and industry,* edited by A. Cox. London: Wheatsheaf.
Eads, G. C. 1981. The political experience in allocating investment: Lessons from the United States and elsewhere. In *Toward a new U.S. industrial policy?* edited by M. L. Wachter and S. M. Wachter. Philadelphia: University of Pennsylvania Press.
Eaton, A. E., and P. B. Voos. 1992. Unions and contemporary innovations in work organization, compensation, and employee participation. In *Unions and economic competitiveness,* edited by L. Mishel and P. B. Voos. Armonk, N.Y.: M. E. Sharpe.
Eccleston, B. 1986. The state, finance and industry in Japan. In *State, finance and industry,* edited by A. Cox. London: Wheatsheaf.
Edsall, T. B. 1984. *The new politics of inequality.* New York: W. W. Norton.
Ellsworth, R. R. 1985. Capital markets and competitive decline. *Harvard Business Review,* September-October, 171-83.
Ellwood, D. T. 1989. The origins of "dependency": Choices, confidence, or culture? *Focus* 12(1): 6-13.
Ellwood, D. T., and L. H. Summers. 1986. Is welfare really the problem? *The Public Interest* (spring): 57-78.
Elster, J. 1979. *Ulysses and the sirens.* Cambridge: Cambridge University Press.
———. 1983. *Explaining technical change.* Cambridge: Cambridge University Press.
———. 1989a. *The cement of society.* Cambridge: Cambridge University Press.
———. 1989b. Social norms and economic theory. *Journal of Economic Perspectives* 3(4): 99-117.

Eltis, W. 1983. The interconnection between public expenditure and inflation in Britain. *American Economic Review* 73(Papers and Proceedings): 291-96.

Employee board-level representation in eight countries. 1981. *European Industrial Relations Review,* January, 20-25.

Engels, C. 1991. A different role for trade unions? *Bulletin of Comparative Labour Relations* 22:33-56.

England, P. 1982. The failure of human capital theory to explain occupational sex segregation. *Journal of Human Resources* 17:358-70.

Environment wins over economy. 1992. *Wall Street Journal,* 6 May.

Esping-Andersen, G. 1987. Institutional accommodation to full employment: A comparison of policy regimes. In *Coping with the economic crisis,* edited by H. Keman, H. Paloheimo, and P. F. Whiteley. London: Sage.

———. 1990. *The three worlds of welfare capitalism.* Princeton, N.J.: Princeton University Press.

Etzioni, A. 1988. *The moral dimension: Toward a new economics.* New York: Free Press.

Etzioni, A., and P. R. Lawrence, eds. 1991. *Socio-economics: Toward a new synthesis.* Armonk, N.Y.: M. E. Sharpe.

Evenson, R. E. 1982. Agriculture. In *Government and technical progress,* edited by R. R. Nelson. New York: Pergamon Press.

Ferguson, C. H. 1990. Computers and the coming of the U.S. keiretsu. *Harvard Business Review* (July-August): 55-70.

Ferguson, T., and J. Rogers. 1986. *Right turn: The decline of the Democrats and the future of American politics.* New York: Hill & Wang.

Fingleton, E. 1993. Fine, thank you. *The Atlantic Monthly,* May, 39.

Flamm, K. 1987. *Targeting the computer.* Washington, D.C.: Brookings Institution.

———. 1988. The changing pattern of industrial robot use. In *The impact of technological change on employment and economic growth,* edited by R. M. Cyert and D. C. Mowery. Cambridge, Mass.: Ballinger.

Flanagan, R. J. 1990. Centralized and decentralized pay determination in Nordic countries. In *Wage formation and macroeconomic policy in the Nordic countries,* edited by L. Calmfors. Oxford: Oxford University Press.

Flanagan, R. J., D. W. Soskice, and L. Ulman. 1983. *Unionism, economic stabilization and incomes policies: European experience.* Washington, D.C.: Brookings Institution.

Flemming, J. S. 1978. The economic explanation of inflation. In *The political economy of inflation,* edited by F. Hirsch and J. H. Goldthorpe. Cambridge: Harvard University Press.

Flew, A. 1983. The procrustean ideal: Libertarians v. egalitarians. In *Against equality,* edited by W. Letwin. London: Macmillan.

Florida, R., and M. Kenney. 1990. *The breakthrough illusion: Corporate America's failure to move from innovation to mass production.* New York: Basic Books.

Frank, R. H. 1990. Rethinking rational choice. In *Beyond the marketplace,* edited by R. Friedland and A. F. Robertson. New York: Aldine de Gruyter.

Freeman, J. R. 1989. *Democracy and markets: The politics of mixed economies.* Ithaca, N.Y.: Cornell University Press.

Freeman, R. B. 1988. Labour market institutions and economic performance. *Economic Policy* (no. 6):63-80.

———. 1992. Is declining unionization of the U.S. good, bad, or irrelevant? In *Unions and economic competitiveness,* edited by L. Mishel and P. B. Voos. Armonk, N.Y.: M. E. Sharpe.

Freeman, R. B., and L. F. Katz. 1994. Rising wage inequality: The United States vs. other advanced countries. In *Working under different rules,* edited by R. B. Freeman. New York: Russell Sage Foundation.

Freeman, R. B., and E. P. Lazear. 1993. An economic analysis of works councils. Unpublished manuscript, Works Councils Project, Madison, Wis.

Freeman, R. B., and J. L. Medoff. 1984. *What do unions do?* New York: Basic Books.

Freeman, R. B., and M. L. Weitzman. 1987. Bonuses and employment in Japan. *Journal of the Japanese and International Economies* 1:168-94.

Friedland, R., and A. F. Robertson, eds. 1990. *Beyond the marketplace: Rethinking economy and society.* New York: Aldine de Gruyter.

Friedland, R., and J. Sanders. 1985. The public economy and economic growth in Western market economies. *American Sociological Review* 50:421-37.

Friedman, D. 1983. Beyond the age of Ford: The strategic bases of Japanese success in automobiles. In *American industry in international competition,* edited by J. Zysman and L. Tyson. Ithaca, N.Y.: Cornell University Press.

———. 1988. *The misunderstood miracle: Industrial development and political change in Japan.* Ithaca, N.Y.: Cornell University Press.

Friedman, M. 1962. *Capitalism and freedom.* Chicago: University of Chicago Press.

———. 1977. Inflation and unemployment. *Journal of Political Economy* 85:451-72.

Friedman, M., and R. Friedman. 1990. *Free to choose.* San Diego: Harcourt Brace Jovanovich, 1979. Reprint, Harcourt Brace Jovanovich.

Friedman, M., and A. Schwartz. 1982. *Monetary trends in the United States and the United Kingdom: Their relation to income, prices, and interest rates, 1867-1975.* Chicago: University of Chicago Press.

Froot, K., A. Perold, and J. Stein. 1990. Shareholder trading practices and corporate investment horizons. Paper prepared for the Time Horizons of American Management project, sponsored by the Council on Competitiveness and the Harvard Business School.

Fuerstenberg, F. 1987. Industrial relations in the Federal Republic of Germany. In *International and comparative industrial relations,* edited by G. J. Bamber and R. D. Lansbury. London: Allen & Unwin.

Fulcher, J. 1988. On the explanation of industrial relations diversity: Labour movements, employers and the state in Britain and Sweden. *British Journal of Industrial Relations* 26:246-74.

Furaker, B., L. Johannson, and J. Lind. 1990. Unemployment and labour market policies in the Scandinavian countries. *Acta Sociologica* 33·141-64.

Galbraith, J. K. 1984. *The affluent society.* 4th ed. New York: Houghton Mifflin. (Original work published 1958)

Gambetta, D. 1988. Can we trust trust? In *Trust: Making and breaking cooperative relations,* edited by D. Gambetta. New York: Basil Blackwell.

Garfinkel, I. 1992. Bringing fathers back in: The child support assurance strategy. *The American Prospect* (spring): 74-83.

Garland, S. B. 1990. A new chief has OSHA growling again. *Business Week,* 20 August, 57.

Garrison, C. B., and F.-Y. Lee. 1992. Taxation, aggregate activity and economic growth: Further cross-country evidence on some supply-side hypotheses. *Economic Inquiry* 30:172-76.

Gerlach, M. L. 1989. Keiretsu organization in the Japanese economy. In *Politics and productivity: The real story of why Japan works,* edited by C. Johnson, L. D'Andrea Tyson, and J. Zysman. Cambridge, Mass.: Ballinger.

———. 1992. *Alliance capitalism: The social organization of Japanese business.* Berkeley: University of California Press.

Gilder, G. 1981. *Wealth and poverty.* New York: Basic Books.

———. 1983. A supply-side economics of the left. *The Public Interest* (summer): 29-43.

———. 1987. Welfare's "new consensus." *The Public Interest* (fall): 20-25.

Ginsburg, H. 1983. *Full employment and public policy: The United States and Sweden.* Lexington, Mass.: D. C. Heath.

Glassman, J. K. 1990. The great banks robbery. *The New Republic,* 8 October, 16-21.

Glyn, A., A. Hughes, A. Lipietz, and A. Singh. 1990. The rise and fall of the golden age. In *The golden age of capitalism,* edited by S. A. Marglin and J. B. Schor. Oxford: Clarendon Press.

Goetschy, J., and J. Rojot. 1987. French industrial relations. In *International and comparative industrial relations,* edited by G. J. Bamber and R. D. Lansbury. London: Allen & Unwin.

Golden, M. 1993. The dynamics of trade unionism and national economic performance. *American Political Science Review* 87:439-54.

Goldthorpe, J. H., ed. 1984. *Order and conflict in contemporary capitalism.* Oxford: Clarendon Press.

Gordon, D. M., R. Edwards, and M. Reich. 1982. *Segmented work, divided workers.* Cambridge: Cambridge University Press.

Gordon, R. J. 1975. The demand for and supply of inflation. *Journal of Law and Economics* 18:807-36.

Gorham, L. 1986. *No longer leading: A scorecard on U.S. economic performance and the role of the public sector compared with Japan, West Germany and Sweden.* Washington, D.C.: Economic Policy Institute.

Gould, F. 1983. The development of public expenditures in Western, industrialised countries: A comparative analysis. *Public Finance* 38:38-69.

Granovetter, M. 1973. The strength of weak ties. *American Journal of Sociology* 78:1360-80.

———. 1985. Economic action and social structure: The problem of embeddedness. *American Journal of Sociology* 91:481-510.

———. 1990. The old and the new economic sociology: A history and an agenda. In *Beyond the marketplace,* edited by R. Friedland and A. F. Robertson. New York: Aldine de Gruyter.

———. 1993. The nature of economic relationships. In *Explorations in economic sociology,* edited by R. Swedberg. New York: Russell Sage Foundation.

Granovetter, M., and R. Swedberg, eds. 1992. *The sociology of economic life.* Boulder, Colo.: Westview Press.

Grant, W. 1989. *Government and industry: A comparative analysis of the US, Canada and the UK.* London: Edward Elgar.

Green, D. 1986. The state, finance and industry in France. In *State, finance and industry,* edited by A. Cox. London: Wheatsheaf.

Green, F. 1988. Neoclassical and Marxian conceptions of production. *Cambridge Journal of Economics* 12:299-312.

Green, F., and T. E. Weisskopf. 1990. The worker discipline effect: A disaggregative analysis. *Review of Economics and Statistics* 72:241-49.

Greenstein, R., and S. Barancik. 1990. *Drifting apart: New findings on the growing income disparities between the rich, the poor, and the middle class.* Washington, D.C.: Center on Budget and Policy Priorities.

Grier, K., and G. Tullock. 1989. An empirical analysis of cross-national economic growth, 1951-1980. *Journal of Monetary Economics* 24:259-76.

Grossman, G. M. 1990. Promoting new industrial activities: A survey of recent arguments and evidence. *OECD Economic Studies* (no. 14):87-125.

Grossman, P. J. 1988. Government and economic growth: A non-linear relationship. *Public Choice* 56:193-200.

———. 1990. Government and growth: Cross-sectional evidence. *Public Choice* 65:217-27.

238

238   IN SEARCH OF NATIONAL ECONOMIC SUCCESS

Guger, A. 1992. Corporatism: Success or failure? Austrian experiences. In *Social corporatism: A superior economic system?* edited by J. Pekkarinen, M. Pohjola, and B. Rowthorn. Oxford: Clarendon Press.

Gunderson, M. 1989. Male-female wage differentials and policy responses. *Journal of Economic Literature* 27:46-72.

Haberler, G. 1959. Wage policy and inflation. In *The public stake in union power,* edited by P. D. Bradley. Charlottesville: University of Virginia Press.

———. 1979. The present economic malaise. In *Contemporary economic problems,* edited by W. Fellner. Washington, D.C.: American Enterprise Institute.

Hagemann, R. P., B. R. Jones, and R. B. Montador. 1988. Tax reform in OECD countries: Motives, constraints, and practice. *OECD Economic Studies* (no. 10):185-226.

Hall, P. A. 1986. *Governing the economy.* New York: Oxford University Press.

Hancke, B. 1991. The crisis of national unions: Belgian labor in decline. *Politics and Society* 19:463-87.

Hansen, K. M., and D. F. Burton. 1992. *German technology policy: Incentive for industrial innovation.* Washington, D.C.: Council on Competitiveness.

Haraf, W. S. 1988. Bank and thrift regulation. *Regulation* (no. 3):50-56.

Hardin, R. 1982. *Collective action.* Baltimore: The Johns Hopkins University Press.

Harrison, B. 1994. *Lean and mean: The changing landscape of corporate power in the age of flexibility.* New York: Basic Books.

Harrison, B., and Barry Bluestone. 1988. *The great U-turn.* New York: Basic Books.

Hart, J. A. 1992a. The effects of state-societal arrangements on international competitiveness: Steel, motor vehicles and semiconductors in the United States, Japan and Western Europe. *British Journal of Political Science* 22:255-300.

———. 1992b. *Rival capitalists: International competitiveness in the United States, Japan, and Western Europe.* Ithaca, N.Y.: Cornell University Press.

Hashimoto, M. 1990. Employment and wage systems in Japan and their implications for productivity. In *Paying for productivity,* edited by A. S. Blinder. Washington, D.C.: Brookings Institution.

Hausman, J. A. 1981. Labor supply. In *How taxes affect economic behavior,* edited by H. J. Aaron and J. A. Pechman. Washington, D.C.: Brookings Institution.

Haworth, N. 1990. Industrial restructuring and industrial relations in New Zealand: Towards a new consensus? *Bulletin of Comparative Labour Relations* 20:167-90.

Hayek, F. A. 1944. *The road to serfdom.* Chicago: University of Chicago Press.

———. 1960. *The constitution of liberty.* Chicago: University of Chicago Press.

———. 1979. *Law, legislation, and liberty.* Vol. 3. London: Routledge & Kegan Paul.

Heady, B. W. 1970. Trade unions and national wage policies. *Journal of Politics* 32:407-39.

Helper, S. 1991a. An exit-voice analysis of supplier relations. In *Morality, rationality, and efficiency: New perspectives on socio-economics,* edited by R. M. Coughlin. Armonk, N.Y.: M. E. Sharpe.

———. 1991b. How much has really changed between U.S. automakers and their suppliers? *Sloan Management Review* 32(4): 15-28.

———. 1991c. Strategy and irreversibility in supplier relations: The case of the U.S. automobile industry. *Business History Review* 65:781-824.

Henwood, D. 1989. Deregulation's knife. *Left Business Observer,* September.

Herrigel, G. 1994. Industry as a form of order: A comparison of the historical development of the machine tool industries in the United States and Germany. In *Governing capitalist econo-*

mies: Performance and control of economic sectors, edited by J. R. Hollingsworth, P. C. Schmitter, and W. Streeck. New York: Oxford University Press.

Hibbs, D. 1977. Political parties and macroeconomic policy. *American Political Science Review* 71:1467-87.

Hicks, A. 1988. Social democratic corporatism and economic growth. *Journal of Politics* 50:677-704.

———. 1994. The social democratic corporatist model of economic performance in the short- and medium-run perspective. In *The comparative political economy of the welfare state,* edited by T. Janoski and A. M. Hicks. Cambridge: Cambridge University Press.

Hirsch, B. T. 1992. Firm investment behavior and collective bargaining strategy. In *Labor market institutions and the future role of unions,* edited by M. F. Bognanno and M. M. Kleiner. Oxford: Blackwell.

Hirschman, A. O. 1970. *Exit, voice, and loyalty.* Cambridge: Harvard University Press.

———. 1985. Against parsimony: Three easy ways of complicating some categories of economic discourse. *Economics and Philosophy* 1:7-21.

———. 1991. *The rhetoric of reaction.* Cambridge: Harvard University Press.

Hodder, J. E. 1988. Corporate capital structure in the United States and Japan: Financial intermediation and implications of financial deregulation. In *Government policy towards industry in the United States and Japan,* edited by J. B. Shoven. Cambridge: Cambridge University Press.

Hodgson, G. M. 1989. *Economics and institutions.* Philadelphia: University of Pennsylvania Press.

Hoffman, K., and R. Kaplinsky. 1988. *Driving force: The global restructuring of technology, labour, and investment in the automobile and components industries.* Boulder, Colo.: Westview Press.

Hollingsworth, J. R., P. C. Schmitter, and W. Streeck, eds. 1994. *Governing capitalist economies: Performance and control of economic sectors.* New York: Oxford University Press.

Hooks, G. 1990. The rise of the Pentagon and U.S. state-building: The defense program as industrial policy. *American Journal of Sociology* 96:358-404.

Hopkins, T. D. 1992. The costs of federal regulation. *Journal of Regulation and Social Costs* (March): 5-31.

Howe, N., and P. Longman. 1992. The next New Deal. *The Atlantic Monthly,* April, 88-99.

Hume, D. [1751] 1983. *An enquiry concerning the principles of morals.* Indianapolis: Hackett.

Humphries, C. 1990. Explaining cross-national variation in levels of strike activity. *Comparative Politics* 22:167-84.

Huntington, S. P. 1981. *American politics: The promise of disharmony.* Cambridge: Harvard University Press.

International Labour Office. *Yearbook of labour statistics.* [Various years.] Geneva: ILO.

International Monetary Fund. 1990, 1992. *International financial statistics yearbook.* Washington, D.C.: IMF.

Itoh, M., K. Kiyono, M. Okuno, and K. Suzumura. 1988a. Industrial policy as a corrective to market failures. In *Industrial policy of Japan,* edited by R. Komiya, M. Okuno, and K. Suzumura. Tokyo: Academic Press.

———. 1988b. Industry promotion and trade. In *Industrial policy of Japan,* edited by R. Komiya, M. Okuno, and K. Suzumura. Tokyo: Academic Press.

———. 1991. *Economic analysis of industrial policy.* San Diego: Academic Press.

It's hit a rough patch, but Japan's economy is still enviably robust. 1992. *Wall Street Journal,* 23 March.

Jackman, R. 1990. Wage formation in the Nordic countries viewed from an international perspective. In *Wage formation and macroeconomic policy in the Nordic countries,* edited by L. Calmfors. Oxford: Oxford University Press.

Jacobs, J. 1989. Training the workforce of the future. *Technology Review,* August-September, 66-72.

Jacobs, M. T. 1991. *Short-term America.* Boston: Harvard Business School Press.

Japan in recession: A conversation with Ronald Dore. 1994. *Dollars and Sense,* March-April, 20-21, 37-38.

Jencks, C. 1988. What must be equal for opportunity to be equal? In *Equal opportunity,* edited by N. E. Bowie. Boulder, Colo.: Westview Press.

Jencks, C., and K. Edin. 1990. The real welfare problem. *The American Prospect* (spring): 31-50.

Johnson, C. 1982. *MITI and the Japanese miracle.* Stanford, Calif.: Stanford University Press.

Johnson, C., L. D. Tyson, and J. Zysman, eds. 1989. *Politics and productivity: The real story of why Japan works.* Cambridge, Mass.: Ballinger.

Johnston, J. W. 1984. An overview of US federal employment and training programmes. In *Unemployment: Policy responses of Western democracies,* edited by J. Richardson and R. Henning. London: Sage.

Jorde, T. M., and D. J. Teece. 1990. Innovation and cooperation: Implications for competition and antitrust. *Journal of Economic Perspectives* 4(3): 75-96.

Judis, J. B. 1992. The pressure elite: Inside the narrow world of advocacy group politics. *The American Prospect* (spring): 15-29.

Kahan, M. S. 1992. Confessions of an airline deregulator. *The American Prospect* (winter): 38-50.

Kahn, A. E. 1988. I would do it again. *Regulation* no. 2:22-28.

Kahn, H. 1967. *The year 2000.* New York: Macmillan.

Kahneman, D., J. L. Knetsch, and R. H. Thaler. 1991. Fairness and the assumptions of economics. In *Quasi rational economics,* edited by R. H. Thaler. New York: Russell Sage Foundation.

Kamerman, S. B. 1991. Starting right: What we owe to children under three. *The American Prospect* (winter): 63-73.

Karl, T. 1975. Work incentives in Cuba. *Latin American Perspectives* 2(4)(supplement): 21-41.

Katz, C. J., V. A. Mahler, and M. G. Franz. 1983. The impact of taxes on growth and distribution in developed capitalist countries: A cross-national study. *American Political Science Review* 77:871-86.

Katz, H. C., and C. F. Sabel. 1985. Industrial relations and industrial organization in the car industry. *Industrial Relations* 24:295-315.

Katz, M. L., and J. A. Ordover. 1990. R&D cooperation and competition. *Brookings Papers on Economic Activity* (Microeconomics supplement): 137-203.

Katzenstein, P. J. 1984. *Corporatism and change: Austria, Switzerland, and the politics of industry.* Ithaca, N.Y.: Cornell University Press.

————. 1985. *Small states in world markets.* Ithaca, N.Y.: Cornell University Press.

————. 1987. *Policy and politics in West Germany.* Philadelphia: Temple University Press.

Kazis, R. 1989. Rags to riches? One industry's strategy for improving productivity. *Technology Review,* August-September, 42-53.

————. 1990. Education and training in the United States. In *Working Papers of the MIT Commission on Industrial Productivity.* Vol. 2. Cambridge: MIT Press.

Keefe, J. H. 1992. Do unions hinder technological change? In *Unions and economic competitiveness,* edited by L. Mishel and P. B. Voos. Armonk, N.Y.: M. E. Sharpe.

Kelley, J., and M. D. R. Evans. 1993. The legitimation of inequality: Occupational earnings in nine nations. *American Journal of Sociology* 99:75-125.

Kelley, M. R., and B. Harrison. 1992. Unions, technology, and labor-management cooperation. In *Unions and economic competitiveness,* edited by L. Mishel and P. B. Voos. Armonk, N.Y.: M. E. Sharpe.

Kelly, K. 1993. Besting Japan. *Business Week*, 7 June, 26-28.

Kelman, S. 1981. *Regulating America, regulating Sweden: A comparative study of occupational safety and health policy*. Cambridge: MIT Press.

Kenney, M., and R. Florida. 1988. Beyond mass production: Production and the labor process in Japan. *Politics and Society* 16:121-58.

Keohane, R. O. 1984. *After hegemony: Cooperation and discord in the world political economy*. Princeton, N.J.: Princeton University Press.

Kern, H., and C. F. Sabel. 1991. Trade unions and decentralized production: A sketch of strategic problems in the West German labor movement. *Politics and Society* 19:373-402.

Knetter, M. 1989. Price discrimination by US and German exporters. *American Economic Review* 79.

Kochan, T. A. 1988. The future of worker representation: An American perspective. *Labour and Society* 13:183-201.

Koike, K. 1987. Human resource development and labor-management relations. In *The political economy of Japan*. Vol. 1, edited by K. Yamamura and Y. Yasuba. Stanford, Calif.: Stanford University Press.

Komiya, R., M. Okuno, and K. Suzumura, eds. 1988. *Industrial policy of Japan*. Tokyo: Academic Press.

Kormendi, R., and P. Meguire. 1985. Macroeconomic determinants of growth: Cross-country evidence. *Journal of Monetary Economics* 16:141-63.

Kornai, J. 1986. "Hard" and "soft" budget constraint. In Kornai, *Contradictions and dilemmas: Studies on the socialist economy and society*. Budapest: Magveto, 1983. Reprint, Cambridge: MIT Press.

Korpi, W. 1983. *The democratic class struggle*. London: Routledge and Kegan Paul.

———. 1985. Economic growth and the welfare state: Leaky bucket or irrigation system? *European Sociological Review* 1:97-118.

———. 1991. Political and economic explanations for unemployment: A cross-national and long-term analysis. *British Journal of Political Science* 21:315-48.

Korpi, W., and M. Shalev. 1979. Strikes, industrial relations and class conflict in capitalist societies. *British Journal of Sociology* 30:164-87.

Kotkin, J. 1992. *Tribes: How race, religion and identity determine success in the new global economy*. New York: Random House.

Kozol, J. 1991. *Savage inequalities: Children in America's schools*. New York: Crown.

Krauss, M. B. 1978. *The new protectionism: The welfare state and international trade*. New York: New York University Press.

Kristol, I. 1978. *Two cheers for capitalism*. New York: Basic Books.

Krugman, P. R. 1983. Targeted industrial policies: Theory and evidence. In *Industrial change and public policy*. Kansas City: Federal Reserve Bank of Kansas City.

———. 1990. *The age of diminished expectations*. Cambridge: MIT Press.

———. 1992. The right, the rich, and the facts. *The American Prospect* (fall): 19-31.

———. 1994. *Peddling prosperity*. New York: W. W. Norton.

———, ed. 1986. *Strategic trade policy and the new international economics*. Cambridge: MIT Press.

Kurzer, P. 1987. The politics of central banks: Austerity and unemployment in Europe. *Journal of Public Policy* 7:21-48.

———. 1993. *Business and banking: Political change and economic integration in Western Europe*. Ithaca, N.Y.: Cornell University Press.

Kuttner, R. 1980. *The revolt of the haves*. New York: Simon & Schuster.

————. 1984. *The economic illusion: False choices between prosperity and social justice.* Philadelphia: University of Pennsylvania Press.

Kuznets, S. 1955. Economic growth and income equality. *American Economic Review* 45:1-28.

Kyloh, R. H. 1989. Flexibility and structural adjustment through consensus: Some lessons from Australia. *Labour and Society* 128:103-23.

Labour pains. 1994. *The Economist,* 12 February, 74-75

Ladd, E. C. 1978. What the voters really want. *Fortune,* 18 December, 40-48.

Landau, D. 1983. Government expenditure and economic growth: A cross-country study. *Southern Economic Journal* 49:783-92.

————. 1985. Government expenditure and economic growth in the developed countries: 1952-76. *Public Choice* 47:459-77.

Lande, R. H., and R. O. Zerbe, Jr. 1985. Reducing unions' monopoly power: Costs and benefits. *Journal of Law and Economics* 28:297-310.

Landes, D. S. 1986. What do bosses really do? *Journal of Economic History* 46:585-623.

Lane, J.-E. and S. Ersson. 1987. Politics and economic growth. *Scandinavian Political Studies* 10:1-14.

————. 1990. *Comparative political economy.* London: Pinter.

Lange, P. 1984. Unions, workers and wage regulation: The rational bases of consent. In *Order and conflict in contemporary capitalism,* edited by J. H. Goldthorpe. Oxford: Clarendon Press.

Lange, P., and G. Garrett. 1985. The politics of growth: Strategic interaction and economic performance in the advanced industrial democracies, 1974-1980. *Journal of Politics* 47:792-827.

Lange, P., M. Wallerstein, and M. Golden. Forthcoming. The end of corporatism? Wage setting in the Nordic and Germanic countries. In *Work and society: Global perspectives,* edited by S. Jacoby. New York: Oxford University Press.

Langlois, R. N., ed. 1986. *Economics as a process: Essays in the new institutional economics.* Cambridge: Cambridge University Press.

Lansbury, R. D., B. Sandkull, and O. Hammarstrom. 1992. Industrial relations and productivity: Evidence from Sweden and Australia. *Economic and Industrial Democracy* 13:295-329.

Lash, S. 1985. The end of neo-corporatism? The breakdown of centralised bargaining in Sweden. *British Journal of Industrial Relations* 23:215-39.

Lash, S., and J. Urry. 1987. *The end of organized capitalism.* Madison: University of Wisconsin Press.

Lavoie, M. 1984. The endogenous flow of credit and the post Keynesian theory of money. *Journal of Economic Issues* 18:771-97.

Lawrence, R. Z. 1984. *Can America compete?* Washington, D.C.: Brookings Institution.

Lazear, E. P. 1989. Pay equality and industrial politics. *Journal of Political Economy* 97:561-80.

Lazonick, W. 1986. Organizations, markets, and productivity. Paper presented at the Economic History Association meetings, Hartford, Conn.

————. 1990. *Competitive advantage on the shop floor.* Cambridge: Harvard University Press.

————. 1991. *Business organization and the myth of the market economy.* Cambridge: Cambridge University Press.

Lebergott, S. 1976. *The American economy.* Princeton, N.J.: Princeton University Press.

Le Grand, J. 1991a. *Equity and choice.* London: HarperCollins.

————. 1991b. The theory of government failure. *British Journal of Political Science* 21:423-42.

Lehmbruch, G., and P. C. Schmitter, eds. 1982. *Patterns of corporatist policy-making.* London: Sage.

Lehner, F. 1987. Interest intermediation, institutional structures, and public policy. In *Coping with the economic crisis,* edited by H. Keman, H. Paloheimo, and P. F. Whiteley. London: Sage.

Leibenstein, H. 1987. *Inside the firm: The inefficiencies of hierarchy.* Cambridge: Harvard University Press.

Lerman, R. I., and H. Pouncy. 1990. Why America should develop a youth apprenticeship system. Policy Report 6, Progressive Policy Institute, Washington, D.C.

Letwin, W. 1983. The case against equality. In *Against equality,* edited by W. Letwin. London: Macmillan.

Levin, R. C., A. K. Klevorick, R. R. Nelson, and S. G. Winter. 1987. Appropriating the returns from industrial research and development. *Brookings Papers on Economic Activity* 3:783-820.

Levine, D. I. 1991. Cohesiveness, productivity, and wage dispersion. *Journal of Economic Behavior and Organization* 15:237-55.

Levine, D. I., and L. D. Tyson. 1990. Participation, productivity and the firm's environment. In *Paying for productivity,* edited by A. S. Blinder. Washington, D.C.: Brookings Institution.

Levine, R., and D. Renelt. 1992. A sensitivity analysis of cross-country growth regressions. *American Economic Review* 82:942-63.

Levinson, M. 1992. America's edge. *Newsweek,* 8 June, 40-43.

———. 1994. Running low on gas. *Newsweek,* 29 August, 38-39.

Levitt, T. 1967. The Johnson treatment. *Harvard Business Review,* January-February, 114-128.

Levy, F., and R. J. Murnane. 1992. U.S. earnings levels and earnings inequality: A review of recent trends and proposed explanations. *Journal of Economic Literature* 30:1333-81.

Lewis-Beck, M. S. 1980. *Applied regression: An introduction.* Beverly Hills, Calif.: Sage.

Lindbeck, A. 1983. Budget expansion and cost inflation. *American Economic Review* 73(Papers and Proceedings): 285-90.

———. 1986. Limits to the welfare state. *Challenge,* January-February, 31-36.

———. 1990. Comment. In *Wage formation and macroeconomic policy in the Nordic countries,* edited by L. Calmfors. Oxford: Oxford University Press.

Lindberg, L. N., and C. S. Maier, eds. 1985. *The politics of inflation and economic stagnation.* Washington, D.C.: Brookings Institution.

Lindblom, C. E. 1949. *Unions and capitalism.* New Haven, Conn.: Yale University Press.

Lindgren, H. 1990. Long-term contracts in financial markets: Bank-industry connections in Sweden. In *The firm as a nexus of treaties,* edited by M. Aoki, B. Gustafsson, and O. E. Williamson. London: Sage.

Lipset, S. M. 1986. Labor unions in the public mind. In *Unions in transition,* edited by S. M. Lipset. San Francisco: Institute for Contemporary Studies.

———. 1990. *Political renewal on the left: A comparative perspective.* Washington, D.C.: Progressive Policy Institute.

Lipset, S. M., & Schneider, W. 1987. *The confidence gap.* Baltimore: The Johns Hopkins University Press.

Litan, R., and W. Nordhaus. 1983. *Reforming federal regulation.* New Haven, Conn.: Yale University Press.

Locke, J. [1690] 1980. *Second treatise of government.* Indianapolis: Hackett.

Lodge, G. C. 1990. *Perestroika for America.* Boston: Harvard Business School Press.

Lodge, G. C., and E. F. Vogel, eds. 1987. *Ideology and national competitiveness.* Boston: Harvard Business School Press.

Lorenz, E. H. 1988. Neither friends nor strangers: Informal networks of subcontracting in French industry. In *Trust: Making and breaking cooperative relations,* edited by D. Gambetta. New York: Basil Blackwell.

Losing its way. 1993. *The Economist,* 18 September, 78-79.

Lowenstein, L. 1988. *What's wrong with Wall Street.* Reading, Mass.: Addison-Wesley.

Lukes, S. 1991. Equality and liberty: Must they conflict? In *Political theory today,* edited by D. Held. Oxford: Polity Press.

Lutz, M. A. 1981. Stagflation as an institutional problem. *Journal of Economic Issues* 15:745-68.

Lynch, L. M. 1993. *Strategies for workplace training: Lessons from abroad.* Washington, D.C.: Economic Policy Institute.

———. 1994. Payoffs to alternative training strategies at work. In *Working under different rules,* edited by R. B. Freeman. New York: Russell Sage Foundation.

Macaulay, S. 1974. The standardized contracts of United States automobile manufacturers. In *International encyclopedia of comparative law,* edited by R. David et al. Tubingen: J. C. B. Mohr.

Maddison, A. 1982. *Phases of capitalist development.* New York: Oxford University Press.

———. 1989. *The world economy in the 20th century.* Paris: OECD.

Magaziner, I. C., and T. M. Hout. 1980. *Japanese industrial policy.* Berkeley, Calif.: Institute for International Studies.

Magaziner, I. C., and M. Patinkin. 1989. *The silent war: Inside the global business battles shaping America's future.* New York: Vintage.

Magaziner, I. C., and R. B. Reich. 1983. *Minding America's business.* New York: Vintage.

Mahler, V. A. 1989. Income distribution within nations: Problems of cross-national comparison. *Comparative Political Studies* 22:3-32.

Mankiw, N. G. 1990. A quick refresher course in macroeconomics. *Journal of Economic Literature* 28:1645-60.

Mansbridge, J. J., ed. 1990. *Beyond self-interest.* Chicago: University of Chicago Press.

Mansfield, E. 1986. Patents and innovation: An empirical study. *Management Science* 32:173-81.

March, J. G. 1982. Theories of choice and making decisions. *Society,* November-December, 29-39.

Marglin, S. A. 1974. What do bosses do? The origins and functions of hierarchy in capitalist production. *Review of Radical Political Economics* 6(2): 33-60.

Marin, B. 1985. Austria—the paradigm case of liberal corporatism? In *The political economy of corporatism,* edited by W. Grant. London: Macmillan.

Marks, G. 1986. Neocorporatism and incomes policy in Western Europe and North America. *Comparative Politics* 18:253-77.

Marlow, M. L. 1986. Private sector shrinkage and the growth of industrialized economies. *Public Choice* 49:143-54.

———. 1988. Private sector shrinkage and the growth of industrialized economies: Reply. *Public Choice* 58:285-94.

Marmor, T. R., J. L. Mashaw, and P. L. Harvey. 1990. *America's misunderstood welfare state.* New York: Basic Books.

Marshall, A. 1907. *Principles of economics.* London: Macmillan.

Marston, R. C. 1990. Price behavior in Japanese and U.S. manufacturing. Working Paper 3364, National Bureau of Economic Research, Cambridge, Mass.

Martin, A. 1987. The end of the "Swedish model"? Recent developments in Swedish industrial relations. *Bulletin of Comparative Labor Relations* 16:93-128.

Martinelli, A., and N. J. Smelser, eds. 1990. *Economy and society: Overviews in economic sociology.* London: Sage.

Martinelli, A., and T. Treu. 1984. Employers assocations in Italy. In *Employers associations and industrial relations,* edited by J. P. Windmuller and A. Gladstone. Oxford: Clarendon Press.

Marx, K. [1867] 1976. *Capital.* Vol. 1, translated by Ben Fowkes. New York: Vintage.

————. [1875] 1978. Critique of the Gotha Program. In *The Marx-Engels reader.* 2d ed., edited by Robert C. Tucker. New York: W. W. Norton.

Matusow, A. J. 1984. *The unraveling of America: A history of liberalism in the 1960s.* New York: Harper & Row.

McCallum, J. 1986. Unemployment in OECD countries in the 1980s. *Economic Journal* 96:942-60.

McCallum, J., and A. Blais. 1987. Government, special interest groups, and economic growth. *Public Choice* 54:3-18.

McFate, K. 1991. *Poverty, inequality and the crisis of social policy: Summary of findings.* Washington, D.C.: Joint Center for Political and Economic Studies.

McGuire, P., M. Granovetter, and M. Schwartz. 1993. Thomas Edison and the social construction of the early electricity industry in America. In *Explorations in economic sociology,* edited by R. Swedberg. New York: Russell Sage Foundation.

McKenzie, R. B. 1987. *The fairness of markets.* Lexington, Mass.: D. C. Heath.

McMillan, J. 1990. Managing suppliers: Incentive systems in Japanese and U.S. industry. *California Management Review* (summer): 38-55.

Medoff, J. L. 1987. The public's image of labor and labor's response. *Detroit College of Law Review* 3:609-36.

Mesa-Lago, C. 1981. *The economy of socialist Cuba: A two-decade appraisal.* Albuquerque: University of New Mexico Press.

Metcalf, D. 1990. Trade unions and economic performance: The British evidence. In *Labour relations and economic performance,* edited by R. Brunetta and C. Dell'Aringa. New York: New York University Press.

Miles, R. 1989. Adapting to technology and competition: A new industrial relations system for the 21st century. *California Management Review* (winter): 9-28.

Miller, R. G. 1974. The jackknife: A review. *Biometrika* 61:1-15.

Mishel, L., and J. Bernstein. 1993. *The state of working America.* 1992-93 ed. Armonk, N.Y.: M. E. Sharpe.

Mitchell, D. J. B. 1980. *Unions, wages, and inflation.* Washington, D.C.: Brookings Institution.

————. 1993. Keynesian, old Keynesian, and new Keynesian wage nominalism. *Industrial Relations* 32:1-29.

Moene, K. O., and M. Wallerstein with M. Hoel. 1993. Bargaining structure and economic performance. In *Trade union behavior, pay bargaining, and economic performance,* edited by R. Flanagan, K. O. Moene, and M. Wallerstein. Oxford: Clarendon Press.

Moffitt, R. 1992. Incentive effects of the U.S. welfare system: A review. *Journal of Economic Literature* 30:1-61.

Moore, B. J. 1979. Monetary factors. In *A guide to post-Keynesian economics,* edited by A. S. Eichner. Armonk, N.Y.: M. E. Sharpe.

Moskal, B. S. 1988. Doing it all yourself . . . and ensuring worldclass "underperformance." *Industry Week,* 4 January, 47-54.

Mowery, D. C. 1988. The diffusion of new manufacturing technologies. In *The impact of technological change on employment and economic growth,* edited by R. M. Cyert and D. C. Mowery. Cambridge, Mass.: Ballinger.

Mowery, D. C., and N. Rosenberg. 1989. *Technology and the pursuit of economic growth.* Cambridge: Cambridge University Press.

Mueller, D. C., ed. 1983. *The political economy of growth.* New Haven, Conn.: Yale University Press.

Murray, C. 1984. *Losing ground: American social policy 1950-1980.* New York: Basic Books.

Mutoh, H. 1988. The automotive industry. In *Industrial policy of Japan,* edited by R. Komiya, M. Okuno, and K. Suzumura. Tokyo: Academic Press.

Nasar, Sylvia. 1994. "The American economy: Back on top." *New York Times,* 27 February.

Neff, R. 1992. Japan: Will it lose its competitive edge? *Business Week,* 27 April, 50-54.

———. 1993a. Fixing Japan. *Business Week,* 29 March, 68-74.

———. 1993b. Why Japan can still say no. *Business Week,* 5 July, 70-74.

Negrelli, S., and E. Santi. 1990. Industrial relations in Italy. In *European industrial relations,* edited by G. Baglioni and C. Crouch. London: Sage.

Nelson, R. R., ed. 1982. *Government and technical progress.* New York: Pergamon Press.

Nelson, R. R., and S. G. Winter. 1982. *An evolutionary theory of economic change.* Cambridge: Harvard University Press.

Newell, A., and J. S. V. Symons. 1987. Corporatism, laissez-faire and the rise in unemployment. *European Economic Review* 31:567-601.

Niland, J. 1987. Gaining against the tide: Australian trade unionism in the 1980s. *Bulletin of Comparative Labour Relations* 16:129-50.

Niskanen, W. A. 1993. Reduce federal regulation. In *Market liberalism,* edited by D. Boaz and E. H. Crane. Washington, D.C.: Cato Institute.

Nivola, P. S. 1991. More like them? The political feasibility of strategic trade policy. *Brookings Review* (spring): 14-21.

Noble, C. 1986. *Liberalism at work: The rise and fall of OSHA.* Philadelphia: Temple University Press.

Norman, R. 1982. Does equality destroy liberty? In *Contemporary political philosophy: Radical studies,* edited by K. Graham. Cambridge: Cambridge University Press.

North, D. C. 1990. *Institutions, institutional change, and economic performance.* Cambridge: Cambridge University Press.

Novak, M., J. Cogan, and the Working Seminar on Family and American Welfare Policy. 1987. *The new consensus on family and welfare.* Washington, D.C.: American Enterprise Institute.

Nove, A. 1977. *The Soviet economic system.* London: Allen & Unwin.

———. 1983. *The economics of feasible socialism.* London: George Allen & Unwin.

Nozick, R. 1974. *Anarchy, state, and utopia.* New York: Basic Books.

O brave new world. 1994. *The Economist,* 12 March, 19-26.

OCED (Organization for Economic Cooperation and Development). 1982. *Historical statistics 1960-1980.* Paris: OECD.

———. 1985. *Social expenditure 1960-1990: Problems of growth and control.* Paris: OECD.

———. 1988. Women's activity, employment and earnings: A review of recent developments. In *Employment outlook: September 1988.* Paris: OECD.

———. 1991a. *Flows and stocks of fixed capital 1964-1989.* Paris: OECD.

———. 1991b. *Labour force statistics 1969-1989.* Paris: OECD.

———. 1991c. *National accounts 1960-1990: Main aggregates.* Vol. 1. Paris: OECD.

———. 1992. *Historical statistics 1960-1990.* Paris: OECD.

———. 1993a. Active labour market policies: Assessing macroeconomic and microeconomic effects. In *Employment outlook: July 1993.* Paris: OECD.

———. 1993b. Earnings inequality: Changes in the 1980s. In *Employment outlook: July 1993.* Paris: OECD.

———. 1994a. Collective bargaining: Levels and coverage. In *Employment outlook: July 1994.* Paris: OECD.

———. 1994b. *Economic outlook. No. 55.* Paris: OECD.

Offe, C. 1985. *Disorganized capitalism.* Cambridge: MIT Press.

Office of Technology Assessment (U.S. Congress). 1990a. *Making things better: Competing in manufacturing.* Washington, D.C.: GPO.

———. 1990b. *Worker training: Competing in the new international economy.* Washington, D.C.: GPO.

———. 1991. *Competing economies: America, Europe, and the Pacific Rim.* Washington, D.C.: GPO.

Ohman, B. 1974. *LO and labour market policy since the Second World War.* Stockholm: Bokforlaget Prisma.

Okimoto, D. I. 1989. *Between MITI and the market: Japanese industrial policy for high technology.* Stanford, Calif.: Stanford University Press.

Okun, A. M. 1975. *Equality and efficiency: The big tradeoff.* Washington, D.C.: Brookings Institution.

Olson, M. 1965. *The logic of collective action.* Cambridge: Harvard University Press.

———. 1982. *The rise and decline of nations.* New Haven, Conn.: Yale University Press.

———. 1983. The political economy of comparative growth rates. In *The political economy of growth,* edited by D. C. Mueller. New Haven, Conn.: Yale University Press.

———. 1991. Francis Castles' "Democratic Politics . . . " *Journal of Theoretical Politics* 3:27-33.

Oster, G. 1980. Labour relations and demand relations: A case study of the "unemployment effect." *Cambridge Journal of Economics* 4:337-48.

Osterman, P. 1988. *Employment futures.* New York: Oxford University Press.

Ouchi, W. G. 1981. *Theory Z.* Reading, Mass.: Addison-Wesley.

———. 1984. Political and economic teamwork: The development of the microelectronics industry of Japan. *California Management Review* (summer): 8-34.

Ouchi, W. G., and M. K. Bolton. 1988. The logic of joint research and development. *California Management Review* (spring): 9-33.

Ozaki, R. 1991. *Human capitalism.* New York: Penguin Books.

Paloheimo, H. 1990. Micro foundations and macro practice of centralized industrial relations. *European Journal of Political Research* 18:389-406.

Patrick, H. 1986. Japanese high technology industrial policy in comparative context. In *Japan's high technology industries,* edited by H. Patrick. Seattle: University of Washington Press.

Peacock, A. T., and M. Ricketts. 1978. The growth of the public sector and inflation. In *The political economy of inflation,* edited by F. Hirsch and J. H. Goldthorpe. Cambridge: Harvard University Press.

Pekkarinen, J. 1992. Corporatism and economic performance in Sweden, Norway, and Finland. In *Social corporatism: A superior economic system?* edited by J. Pekkarinen, M. Pohjola, and B. Rowthorn. Oxford: Clarendon Press.

Pekkarinen, J., M. Pohjola, and B. Rowthorn, eds. 1992. *Social corporatism: A superior economic system?* Oxford: Clarendon Press.

Pencavel, J. 1986. Labor supply of men. In *Handbook of labor economics.* Vol. 1, edited by O. Ashenfelter and R. Layard. Amsterdam: North-Holland.

Perrow, C. 1986a. *Complex organizations: A critical essay.* 3rd ed. New York: Random House.

———. 1986b. Economic theories of organization. *Theory and Society* 15:11-45.

Perry, N. J. 1991. The workers of the future. *Fortune,* special issue on "The new American century," 68-72.

Persson, T., and G. Tabellini. 1994. Is inequality harmful for growth? *American Economic Review* 84:600-21.

Pfaller, A., with I. Gough. 1991. The competitiveness of industrialised welfare states: A cross-country survey. In *Can the welfare state compete?* edited by A. Pfaller, I. Gough, and G. Therborn. London: Macmillan.

Pfeffer, J., and G. R. Salancik. 1978. *The external control of organizations: A resource dependence perspective.* New York: Harper & Row.

Phillips, A. W. 1958. The relation between unemployment and the rate of change of money wage rates in the United Kingdom, 1861-1957. *Economica* 25:283-99.

Phillips, K. 1990. *The politics of rich and poor.* New York: HarperCollins.

Piore, M. 1986. The decline of mass production and the challenge to union survival. *Industrial Relations Journal* 17:207-13.

Piore, M. J., and C. F. Sabel. 1984. *The second industrial divide.* New York: Basic Books.

Pizzorno, A. 1978. Political exchange and collective identity in industrial conflict. In *The resurgence of class conflict in Western Europe since 1968.* Vol. 2, edited by C. Crouch and A. Pizzorno. London: Macmillan.

Pohjola, M. 1992. Corporatism and wage bargaining. In *Social corporatism: A superior economic system?* edited by J. Pekkarinen, M. Pohjola, and B. Rowthorn. Oxford: Clarendon Press.

Polachek, S. W. 1981. Occupational self-selection: A human capital approach to sex differences in occupational structure. *Review of Economics and Statistics* 58:60-69.

Polanyi, K. [1944] 1957. *The great transformation.* Boston: Beacon Press.

The politics of privatisation in Western Europe [Special issue]. 1988. *West European Politics* 11(4).

Porter, M. 1980. *Competitive strategy.* New York: Free Press.

————. 1990. *The competitive advantage of nations.* New York: Free Press.

————. 1992. *Capital choices: Changing the way America invests in industry.* Washington, D.C.: Council on Competitiveness.

Powell, B. 1993. Japan Inc.: R.I.P. *Newsweek,* 13 December, 48-50.

Powell, W. W. 1990. Neither market nor hierarchy: Network forms of organization. *Research in Organizational Behavior* 12:295-336.

Powell, W. W., and P. J. DiMaggio, eds. 1991. *The new institutionalism in organizational analysis.* Chicago: University of Chicago Press.

Preston, L. M. 1984. Freedom, markets, and voluntary exchange. *American Political Science Review* 78:959-70.

Prestowitz, C. V., Jr. 1988. *Trading places.* New York: Basic Books.

Putterman, L. 1984. On some recent explanations of why capital hires labor. *Economic Inquiry* 22:171-87.

Pyke, F., G. Becattini, and W. Sengenberger, eds. 1990. *Industrial districts and inter-firm cooperation in Italy.* Geneva: International Institute for Labor Studies.

Rae, D., D. Yates, J. Hochschild, J. Morone, and C. Fessler. 1981. *Equalities.* Cambridge: Harvard University Press.

Ram, R. 1986. Government size and economic growth: A new framework and some evidence from cross-section and time-series data. *American Economic Review* 76:191-203.

Rawls, J. 1971. *A theory of justice.* Cambridge: Harvard University Press.

Ready to take on the world. 1994. *The Economist,* 15 January, 65-66.

Reagan, R. 1981a. Address to joint session of Congress, 18 February 1981. In *A tide of discontent,* edited by E. Sandoz and C. V. Crabb, Jr. Washington, D.C.: Congressional Quarterly Press.

————. 1981b. Inaugural address, 20 January 1981. In *A tide of discontent,* edited by E. Sandoz and C. V. Crabb, Jr. Washington, D.C.: Congressional Quarterly Press.

———. 1981c. Report to the nation on the economy, 5 February 1981. In *A tide of discontent,* edited by E. Sandoz and C. V. Crabb, Jr. Washington, D.C.: Congressional Quarterly Press.

Rebitzer, J. B. 1987. Unemployment, long-term employment relations, and productivity growth. *Review of Economics and Statistics* 69:627-35.

Rehn, G. 1985. Swedish active labor market policy: Retrospect and prospect. *Industrial Relations* 24:62-89.

Reich, R. B. 1987. *Tales of a new America.* New York: Vintage.

The rights of workers' representatives: Health and safety. 1989. *European Industrial Relations Review,* April, 14-21.

Roemer, J. 1988. *Free to lose.* Cambridge: Harvard University Press.

Rogers, J. 1990. Divide and conquer: Further "reflections on the distinctive character of American labor laws." *Wisconsin Law Review* 1990:1-147.

Rogers, J., and W. Streeck. 1994. Workplace representation overseas: The works councils story. In *Working and earning under different rules,* edited by R. B. Freeman. Chicago: NBER and University of Chicago Press.

Rowthorn, B. 1992. Corporatism and labour market performance. In *Social corporatism: A superior economic system?* edited by J. Pekkarinen, M. Pohjola, and B. Rowthorn. Oxford: Clarendon Press.

Rowthorn, B., and A. Glyn 1990. The diversity of unemployment experience since 1973. In *The golden age of capitalism,* edited by S. A. Marglin and J. B. Schor. Oxford: Clarendon Press.

Rubin, B. A. 1986. Class struggle American style: Unions, strikes and wages. *American Sociological Review* 51:618-31.

Ruggles, P. 1991. The impact of government tax and expenditure programs on the distribution of income in the United States. In *Economic inequality and poverty: International perspectives,* edited by L. Osberg. Armonk, N.Y.: M. E. Sharpe.

Ryscavage, P., and P. Henle. 1990. Earnings inequality accelerates in the 1980s. *Monthly Labor Review,* December, 3-16.

Sabel, C. F. 1987. A fighting chance: Structural change and new labor strategies. *International Journal of Political Economy* 17(3): 26-56.

———. 1989. Flexible specialisation and the re-emergence of regional economies. In *Reversing industrial decline?* edited by P. Hirst and J. Zeitlin. Oxford: Berg.

———. 1992. Studied trust: Building new forms of cooperation in a volatile economy. In *Explorations in economic sociology,* edited by R. Swedberg. New York: Russell Sage Foundation.

Sabel, C. F., G. B. Herrigel, R. Deeg, and R. Kazis. 1989. Regional prosperities compared: Massachusetts and Baden-Wurttemberg in the 1980s. *Economy and Society* 18:374-404.

Sagoff, M. 1992. The great environmental awakening. *The American Prospect* (spring): 39-47.

Sako, M. 1992. *Prices, quality and trust: Inter-firm relations in Britain and Japan.* Cambridge: Cambridge University Press.

———. 1994. Neither markets nor hierarchies: A comparative study of the printed circuit board industry in Britain and Japan. In *Governing capitalist economies: Performance and control of economic sectors,* edited by J. R. Hollingsworth, P. C. Schmitter, and W. Streeck. New York: Oxford University Press.

Sakoh, K. 1984. Japanese economic success: Industrial policy or free market? *Cato Journal* 4:521-43.

Samuelson, R. J. 1993. Japan as number two. *Newsweek,* 6 December, 44.

Sarathy, R. 1989. The interplay of industrial policy and international strategy: Japan's machine tool industry. *California Management Review* (spring): 132-60.

Saunders, P. 1985. Public expenditure and economic performance in OECD countries. *Journal of Public Policy* 5:1-21.

———. 1986. What can we learn from international comparisons of public sector size and economic performance? *European Sociological Review* 2:52-60.

Saunders, P., and F. Klau. 1985. The role of the public sector: Causes and consequences of the growth of government. *OECD Economic Studies* no. 4:1-239.

Sawhill, I. V. 1988. Poverty in the U.S.: Why is it so persistent? *Journal of Economic Literature* 26:1073-119.

Saxonhouse, G. R. 1983. What is all this about "industrial targeting" in Japan? *World Economy* 6:253-73.

Scharpf, F. 1987. A game-theoretical interpretation of inflation and unemployment in Western Europe. *Journal of Public Policy* 7:227-57.

———. 1991. *Crisis and choice in European social democracy.* Frankfurt: Campus, 1987. Reprint, Ithaca, N.Y.: Cornell University Press.

Schelling, T. C. 1960. *The strategy of conflict.* Cambridge: Harvard University Press.

Scherrer, C. 1991. Governance of the automobile industry: The transformation of labor and supplier relations. In *Governance of the American economy,* edited by J. L. Campbell, J. R. Hollingsworth, and L. N. Lindberg. Cambridge: Cambridge University Press.

Schlesinger, A. M., Jr. 1986. *The cycles of American history.* Boston: Houghton Mifflin.

Schmidt, M. G. 1982. Does corporatism matter? Economic crisis, politics and rates of unemployment in capitalist democracies in the 1970s. In *Patterns of corporatist policy-making,* edited by G. Lehmbruch and P. C. Schmitter. London: Sage.

———. 1987. The politics of full employment in Western democracies. *Annals of the American Academy of Political and Social Science* 492:171-81.

Schmitter, P. C. 1989. Corporatism is dead! Long live corporatism! *Government and Opposition* 24:54-73.

———. 1990. Sectors in modern capitalism: Modes of governance and variations in performance. In *Labour relations and economic performance,* edited by R. Brunetta and C. Dell'Aringa. New York: New York University Press.

Schmitter, P. C., and G. Lehmbruch, eds. 1979. *Trends toward corporatist intermediation.* London: Sage.

Schultze, C. L. 1977. *The public use of private interest.* Washington, D.C.: Brookings Institution.

———. 1983. Industrial policy: A dissent. *Brookings Review* (fall): 3-12.

Schumpeter, J. A. [1942] 1950. *Capitalism, socialism and democracy.* New York: Harper & Row.

Schwarz, J. E. 1988. *America's hidden success: A reassessment of public policy from Kennedy to Reagan.* New York: W. W. Norton.

Schwarz, J. E., and T. J. Volgy. 1992. Social support for self-reliance: The politics of making work pay. *The American Prospect* (spring): 67-73.

Scott, B. R. 1985. National strategies: Key to international competition. In *U.S. competitiveness in the world economy,* edited by B. R. Scott and G. C. Lodge. Boston: Harvard Business School Press.

Scott, J. C. 1976. *The moral economy of the peasant.* New Haven, Conn.: Yale University Press.

Scully, G. W. 1989. The size of the state, economic growth and the efficient utilization of national resources. *Public Choice* 63:149-64.

Seibel, C. 1979. Planning in France. In *Comparative economic systems.* 4th ed., edited by M. Bornstein. Homewood, Ill.: Richard D. Irwin.

Sekiguchi, S., and T. Horiuchi. 1985. Myth and reality of Japan's industrial policies. *World Economy* 8:373-91.

Seligman, D. 1982. Who needs unions? *Fortune*, 12 July, 54-66.

Sen, A. K. 1977. Rational fools: A critique of the behavioral foundations of economic theory. *Philosophy and Public Affairs* 6:317-44.

———. 1992. *Inequality reexamined.* Cambridge: Harvard University Press.

Shapira, P. 1990. *Modernizing manufacturing: New policies to build industrial extension services.* Washington, D.C.: Economic Policy Institute.

Shapiro, A. L. 1992. *We're number one!* New York: Vintage Books.

Shapiro, C., and J. E. Stiglitz. 1984. Equilibrium unemployment as a worker discipline device. *American Economic Review* 74:433-44.

Shapiro, I., and R. Greenstein. 1991. *Selective prosperity: Increasing income disparities since 1977.* Washington, D.C.: Center on Budget and Policy Priorities.

Shapiro, R. J. 1990. An American working wage: Ending poverty in working families. Policy Report 3, Progressive Policy Institute, Washington, D.C.

Shapiro, R. Y., & Young, J. T. 1989. Public opinion and the welfare state: The United States in comparative perspective. *Political Science Quarterly* 104:59-89.

Shepsle, K. A., and B. R. Weingast. 1984. Political solutions to market problems. *American Political Science Review* 78:417-34.

Sherrill, R. 1990. The looting decade. *The Nation,* 19 November, 589-624.

Shimada, H. 1983. Japan's success story: Looking behind the legend. *Technology Review,* May-June, 47-52.

Shonfield, A. 1965. *Modern capitalism.* London: Oxford University Press.

Silberman, C. E. 1971. The U.S. economy in an age of uncertainty. *Fortune*, January, 72-77, 142-143.

Simon, H. A. 1976. From substantive to procedural rationality. In *Method and appraisal in economics,* edited by S. J. Latsis. Cambridge: Cambridge University Press.

Simon, W. E. 1978. *A time for truth.* New York: Reader's Digest Press.

Simons, H. C. 1948. *Economic policy for a free society.* Chicago: University of Chicago Press.

Skocpol, T. 1990. Sustainable social policy: Fighting poverty without poverty programs. *The American Prospect* (summer): 58-70.

Slichter, S. H., J. J. Healy, and E. R. Livernash. 1960. *The impact of collective bargaining on management.* Washington, D.C.: Brookings Institution.

Smeeding, T. M. 1991. Cross-national comparisons of inequality and poverty position. In *Economic inequality and poverty: International perspectives,* edited by L. Osberg. Armonk, N.Y.: M. E. Sharpe.

———. 1992. Why the U.S. antipoverty system doesn't work very well. *Challenge,* January-February, 30-35.

Smeeding, T. M., M. O'Higgins, and L. Rainwater, eds. 1990. *Poverty, inequality and income distribution in comparative perspective: The Luxembourg Income Study.* New York: Wheatsheaf.

Smith, A. [1776] 1937. *The wealth of nations.* New York: Random House.

Smith, C. W. 1993. Auctions: From Walras to the real world. In *Explorations in economic sociology,* edited by R. Swedberg. New York: Russell Sage Foundation.

Smith, M. R. 1992. *Power, norms, and inflation.* New York: Aldine de Gruyter.

Smith, S. C. 1991. *Industrial policy in developing countries.* Washington, D.C.: Economic Policy Institute.

Smitka, M. J. 1991. *Competitive ties: Subcontracting in the Japanese automotive industry.* New York: Columbia University Press.

Solow, R. M. 1990. *The labor market as a social institution.* Cambridge: Basil Blackwell.

Soskice, D. 1990. Wage determination: The changing role of institutions in advanced industrial-
ized societies. *Oxford Review of Economic Policy* 6(4): 36-61.
Spineux, A. 1990. Trade unionism in Belgium: The difficulties of a major renovation. In *European
industrial relations,* edited by G. Baglioni and C. Crouch. London: Sage.
Stephens, J. D. 1979. *The transition from capitalism to socialism.* Urbana: University of Illinois
Press.
———. 1991. Industrial concentration, country size and union membership. *American Political
Science Review* 85:942-49.
Stewart, M. 1983. *The age of interdependence.* Cambridge: MIT Press.
Stewart, R. B. 1988. Controlling environmental risks through economic incentives. *Columbia
Journal of Environmental Law* 13:153-69.
Stigler, G. 1970. Director's law of public income redistribution. *Journal of Law and Economics*
13:1-10.
———. 1971. The theory of economic regulation. *Bell Journal of Economics and Management
Science* 2:137-46.
Stiglitz, J. E. 1989. On the economic role of the state. In *The economic role of the state,* edited by
A. Heertje. London: Basil Blackwell.
Streeck, W. 1984. Neo-corporatist industrial relations and the economic crisis in West Germany.
In *Order and conflict in contemporary capitalism,* edited by J. H. Goldthorpe. Oxford:
Clarendon Press.
———. 1987. Industrial relations and industrial change: The restructuring of the world automobile
industry in the 1970s and 1980s. *Economic and Industrial Democracy* 8:437-62.
———. 1988. Comment on Ronald Dore, "Rigidities in the labour market." *Government and
Opposition* 23:413-23.
———. 1989. Skills and the limits of neo-liberalism: The enterprise of the future as a place of
learning. *Work, Employment and Society* 3:89-104.
———. 1991. On the institutional conditions of diversified quality production. In *Beyond
Keynesianism: The socio-economics of production and full employment,* edited by E.
Matzner and W. Streeck. London: Edward Elgar.
———. 1993. Pay restraint without incomes policy: Institutionalized monetarism and industrial
unionism in Germany. Unpublished manuscript, Department of Sociology, University of
Wisconsin-Madison.
Streeck, W., J. Hilbert, K.-H. van Kevelaer, F. Maier, and H. Weber. 1987. *The role of the social
partners in vocational training and further training in the Federal Republic of Germany.*
Berlin: European Centre for the Development of Vocational Training.
Streeck, W., and P. C. Schmitter. 1991. From national corporatism to transnational pluralism:
Organized interests in the single European market. *Politics and Society* 19:133-64.
Sugden, R. 1986. *The economics of rights, co-operation and welfare.* Oxford: Basil Blackwell.
Sunstein, C. R. 1990. Remaking regulation. *The American Prospect* (fall): 73-82.
A survey of corporate governance. 1994. *The Economist,* 29 January, S1-S18.
Suzuki, M. 1993. Domestic political determinants of inflation. *European Journal of Political
Research* 23:245-59.
Swank, D. 1992. Politics and the structural dependence of the state in democratic capitalist nations.
American Political Science Review 86:38-54.
Swedberg, R. 1987. Economic sociology: Past and present. *Current Sociology* 35:1-215.
———. 1990. *Economics and sociology: Conversations with economists and sociologists.* Prince-
ton, N.J.: Princeton University Press.
———. 1991. Major traditions of economic sociology. *Annual Review of Sociology* 17:251-76.

————, ed. 1993. *Explorations in economic sociology.* New York: Russell Sage Foundation.

Swenson, P. 1991. Bringing capital back in, or social democracy reconsidered: Employer power, cross-class alliances, and centralization of industrial relations in Denmark and Sweden. *World Politics* 43:513-44.

Symposium on financial restructuring. 1987. *Challenge,* November-December, 4-43.

Tarantelli, E. 1986. The regulation of inflation and unemployment. *Industrial Relations* 25:1-15.

Tawney, R. H. [1931] 1961. *Equality.* New York: Capricorn Books.

Taylor, M. 1987. *The possibility of cooperation.* Cambridge: Cambridge University Press.

Teece, D. J. 1991. Support policies for strategic industries: Impact on home economies. In *Strategic industries in a global economy.* Paris: OECD.

————. 1992. Competition, cooperation, and innovation: Organizational arrangements for regimes of rapid technological progress. *Journal of Economic Behavior and Organization* 18: 1-25.

Therborn, G. 1986. *Why some peoples are more unemployed than others.* London: Verso.

————. 1987. Does corporatism really matter? The economic crisis and issues of political theory. *Journal of Public Policy* 7:259-84.

Thompson, E. P. 1967. Time, work-discipline, and industrial capitalism. *Past and Present* no. 38:56-97.

Thompson, J. D. 1967. *Organizations in action.* New York: McGraw-Hill.

Thurow, L. C. 1981. Equity, efficiency, social justice, and redistribution. In *The welfare state in crisis.* Paris: OECD.

————. 1992. *Head to head: The coming economic battle among Japan, Europe, and America.* New York: William Morrow.

Tilly, C. 1990. *Short hours, short shrift.* Washington, D.C.: Economic Policy Institute.

Trezise, P. 1984. Japanese miracles revisited. *Society,* November-December, 36-40.

The trouble with success. 1994. *The Economist,* 12 March, 78.

Troy, L., C. T. Koeller, and N. Sheflin. 1980. The three faces of unionism. *Policy Review* (fall): 95-109.

Tullock, G. 1971. The charity of the uncharitable. *Western Economic Journal* 9:379-92.

Tung, R. L. 1984. *Key to Japan's economic strength: Human power.* Lexington, Mass.: D. C. Heath.

Turner, L. 1988. Are labor-management partnerships for competitiveness possible in America? The U.S. auto industry examined. Working Paper 36, Berkeley Roundtable on the International Economy, Berkeley, Calif.

————. 1992. Industrial relations and the reorganization of work in West Germany: Lessons for the U.S. In *Unions and economic competitiveness,* edited by L. Mishel and P. B. Voos. Armonk, N.Y.: M. E. Sharpe.

Tversky, A., and D. Kahneman. 1990. Rational choice and the framing of decisions. In *The limits of rationality,* edited by K. S. Cook and M. Levi. Chicago: University of Chicago Press.

Tweeten, L. 1970. *Foundations of farm policy.* Lincoln: University of Nebraska Press.

Ulman, L. 1968. Collective bargaining and industrial efficiency. In *Britain's economic prospects.* Washington, D.C.: Brookings Institution.

U.S. Bureau of the Census. 1990. *Trends in income, by selected characteristics: 1947 to 1988.* Current Population Reports, Series P-60, No. 167. Washington, D.C.: GPO.

————. 1993a. *Money income of households, families, and persons in the United States: 1992.* Current Population Reports, Series P-60, no. 184. Washington, D.C.: GPO.

————. 1993b. *Poverty in the United States: 1992.* Current Population Reports, Series P-60, no. 185. Washington, D.C.: GPO.

U.S. Bureau of Labor Statistics. 1993. Industrial disputes, workers involved, and worktime lost, 15 countries, 1955-1991. Unpublished data.

van Arnhem, J., M. Corina, and G. J. Schotsman. 1982. Do parties affect the distribution of income? The case of advanced capitalist democracies. In *The impact of parties,* edited by F. G. Castles. Beverly Hills, Calif.: Sage.

van Voorden, W. 1984. Employers associations in the Netherlands. In *Employers associations and industrial relations,* edited by J. P. Windmuller and A. Gladstone. Oxford: Clarendon Press.

Visser, J. 1990a. Continuity and change in Dutch industrial relations. In *European industrial relations,* edited by G. Baglioni and C. Crouch. London: Sage.

———. 1990b. In search of inclusive unionism. *Bulletin of Comparative Labour Relations* 18:1-278.

———. 1991. Trends in trade union membership. In *OECD employment outlook: July 1991.* Paris: OECD.

Vogel, D. 1986. *National styles of regulation: Environmental policy in Great Britain and the United States.* Ithaca, N.Y.: Cornell University Press.

———. 1989. *Fluctuating fortunes: The political power of business in America.* New York: Basic Books.

Wade, R. 1990. *Governing the market: Economic theory and the role of government in East Asian industrialization.* Princeton, N.J.: Princeton University Press.

Walder, A. G. 1986. *Communist neo-traditionalism: Work and authority in Chinese industry.* Berkeley: University of California Press.

Wallerstein, M. 1986. The micro-foundations of solidarity: Protectionist policies, welfare policies, and union centralization. Unpublished manuscript, University of California, Los Angeles.

———. 1990. Centralized bargaining and wage restraint. *American Journal of Political Science* 34:982-1004.

Wanniski, J. 1978. *The way the world works.* New York: Basic Books.

Warner, D. 1992. Protecting OSHA from "reform." *Nation's Business,* February, 16-21.

Weber, M. [1905] 1958. *The Protestant ethic and the spirit of capitalism.* Translated by Talcott Parsons. New York: Charles Scribner's Sons.

Weede, E. 1986. Sectoral reallocation, distributional coalitions and the welfare state as determinants of economic growth rates in industrialized democracies. *European Journal of Political Research* 14:501-19.

Weidenbaum, M. L. 1978. On estimating regulatory costs. *Regulation,* May-June, 14-17.

———. 1979. *The future of business regulation.* New York: Amacom.

Weidenbaum, M. L., A. Scalia, R. W. Crandall, J.C. Miller III, W. A. Niskanen, R. B. Helms, M. H. Kosters, and T. G. Moore. 1980. On saving the kingdom. *Regulation,* November-December, 14-35.

Weisskopf, T. E. 1987. The effect of unemployment on labour productivity: An international comparative analysis. *International Review of Applied Economics* 1:127-51.

Weitzman, M. L. 1984. *The share economy.* Cambridge: Harvard University Press.

Weitzman, M. L., and D. L. Kruse. 1990. Profit sharing and productivity. In *Paying for productivity,* edited by A. S. Blinder. Washington, D.C.: Brookings Institution.

Wellons, P. A. 1985. Competitiveness in the world economy: The role of the U.S. financial system. In *U.S. competitiveness in the world economy,* edited by B. R. Scott and G. C. Lodge. Boston: Harvard Business School Press.

White, H. C. 1981. Where do markets come from? *American Journal of Sociology* 87:517-47.

———. 1988. Varieties of markets. In *Social structures: A network approach,* edited by B. Wellman and S. D. Berkowitz. Cambridge: Cambridge University Press.

———. 1993. Markets in production networks. In *Explorations in economic sociology,* edited by R. Swedberg. New York: Russell Sage Foundation.

White, L. J. 1971. *The automobile industry since 1945.* Cambridge: Harvard University Press.

Whitely, P. F. 1987. The monetarist experiments in the United States and the United Kingdom: Policy responses to stagflation. In *Coping with the economic crisis,* edited by H. Keman, H. Paloheimo, and P. F. Whitely. London: Sage.

Whitley, R., ed. 1992. *European business systems.* London: Sage.

Wiggenhorn, W. 1990. Motorola U: When training becomes an education. *Harvard Business Review,* July-August, 71-83.

Wilensky, H. L., and L. Turner. 1987. *Democratic corporatism and policy linkages.* Berkeley, Calif.: Institute of International Studies.

Willett, T. D., K. Bansian, L. O. Laney, M. Merzkani, and A. D. Warga. 1988. Inflation hypotheses and monetary accomodation: Postwar evidence from the industrial countries. In *Political business cycles,* edited by T. D. Willett. Durham, N.C.: Duke University Press.

Williamson, O. E. 1981. The economics of organization: The transaction cost approach. *American Journal of Sociology* 87:548-77.

———. 1985. *The economic institutions of capitalism.* New York: Free Press.

Wilson, W. J. 1987. *The truly disadvantaged.* Chicago: University of Chicago Press.

Windmuller, J. P., and A. Gladstone, eds. 1984. *Employers associations and industrial relations.* Oxford: Clarendon Press.

Windolf, P. 1989. Productivity coalitions and the future of European corporatism. *Industrial Relations* 28:1-20.

Wolf, C., Jr. 1988. *Markets or governments.* Cambridge: MIT Press.

Wolinetz, S. 1989. Socio-economic bargaining in the Netherlands: Redefining the postwar policy coalition. *West European Politics* 12:79-98.

Womack, J. P. 1990. The US automobile industry in an era of international competition: Performance and prospects. In *Working papers of the MIT Commission on Industrial Productivity.* Vol. 1. Cambridge: MIT Press.

Womack, J. P., D. T. Jones, and D. Roos. 1990. *The machine that changed the world.* New York: Rawson Associates.

Wood, A. 1986. Marx and equality. In *Analytical Marxism,* edited by J. Roemer. Cambridge: Cambridge University Press.

Wood, C. 1992. Kerplunk: Japan's coming crash. *The New Republic,* 23 November, 22-26.

Woodruff, D. 1992. Where employees are management. *Business Week,* special issue on "Reinventing America," 66.

World Bank. *World development report.* [Various years]. New York: Oxford University Press.

Yamamoto, S. 1989/90. Japan's trade lead: Blame profit-hungry American firms. *Brookings Review* (winter): 14-18.

Zelizer, V. A. 1978. Human values and the market: The case of life insurance and death in 19th-century America. *American Journal of Sociology* 84:591-610.

———. 1993. Making multiple monies. In *Explorations in economic sociology,* edited by R. Swedberg. New York: Russell Sage Foundation.

Zinn, H. 1980. *A people's history of the United States.* New York: HarperCollins.

Zukin, S., and P. DiMaggio, eds. 1990. *Structures of capital: The social organization of the economy.* Cambridge: Cambridge University Press.

Zysman, J. 1983. *Governments, markets, and growth.* Ithaca, N.Y.: Cornell University Press.

Zysman, J., and L. Tyson, eds. 1983. *American industry in international competition.* Ithaca, N.Y.: Cornell University Press.

Index

About the Author

Lane Kenworthy is Assistant Professor of Sociology at the Rochester Institute of Technology. His research and published work have examined differing economic institutional arrangements, policy choices, and performance patterns across industrialized nations. His current research explores the causes and consequences of various types of long-term economic relationships.